PLAN GRAPHICS

PLAN GRAPHICS

THEODORE D. WALKER
DAVID A. DAVIS

FOURTH EDITION

VAN NOSTRAND REINHOLD
New York

Copyright 1990 by Van Nostrand Reinhold

Library of Congress Catalog Card Number 90-41669
ISBN 0-442-23779-0

Printed in the United States of America

Van Nostrand Reinhold
115 Fifth Avenue
New York, New York 10003

Van Nostrand Reinhold International Company Limited
11 New Fetter Lane
London EC4P 4EE, England

Van Nostrand Reinhold
102 Dodds Street
South Melbourne, Victoria 3205, Australia

Nelson Canada
1120 Birchmount Road
Scarborough, Ontario M1K 5G4, Canada

16 15 14 13 12 11 10 9 8 7 6 5 4 3 2 1

Library of Congress Cataloging-in-Publication Data

Walker. Theodore D.
   Plan graphics / Theodore D. Walker, David A. Davis.—4th ed.
     p. cm.
   Includes index.
   ISBN 0-442-23779-0
   1. Architectural drawing. I. Davis, David A. II. Title.
NA2700.W34 1990
720'.28'4—dc20
                                      90-41669
                                       CIP

CONTENTS

ACKNOWLEDGMENTS

The authors gratefully acknowledge the assistance and generosity of many individuals and offices who contributed examples for this book. Where possible, each is listed below his/her work. In most cases these individuals and firms are landscape architects unless otherwise identified. Where the name of a firm is followed by the name of an individual, the latter prepared the drawing for that firm.

WARNING

Since the principal intent of this book is to serve as a reference for graphic techniques, no design should be copied. The rights to each illustration herein belong to the individual or firm who originally designed it. Any copying is a violation of copyright law.

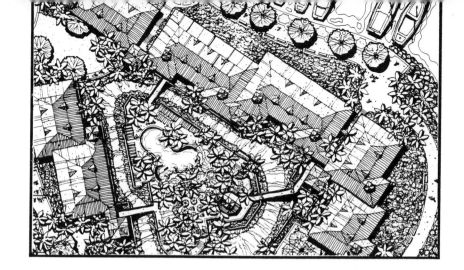

INTRODUCTION

During the entire design process, a designer must produce enough graphic information to effectively communicate his or her ideas. Along with perspective sketches, sections, and elevations, plan graphics are generally considered the most useful styles of graphic communication. In most cases plan graphics allow the viewer to see the entire project site in realistic context, and identify the order in which all the elements of the design are arranged.

High quality graphics are visually attractive. Simultaneously they communicate design intent more effectively than graphics that are not sharp, clean, or crisp. Good quality graphics also may be considered a work of art because composition, skill and talent are involved.

If this is your first encounter with this book, please do not be intimidated with what you see. Through some practice and effort, you also can acquire the skills to prepare graphics similar to what you see here. Patience and persistence are qualities to you will need as you pursue skill development.

In this introductory chapter a portion of some plans appearing throughout this book are presented at full size. This will help you to see the line weights as they were originally drawn before being photograpically reduced for reproduction in this book. These samples also will introduce you to the graphic variation of symbols used to present architectural features in plan view as well as vehicles, people, paving, turf and plants.

Lines

The width line you use on a plan is determined by the importance of what is being presented. The widest, darkest lines represent the most important item or object. For the preliminary subdivision plat presented on this page, it means the roads are the most important whereas the centerline from tee six to the green of the golf course is the least important and is the lightest line. On the next page it is the building that is the most important.

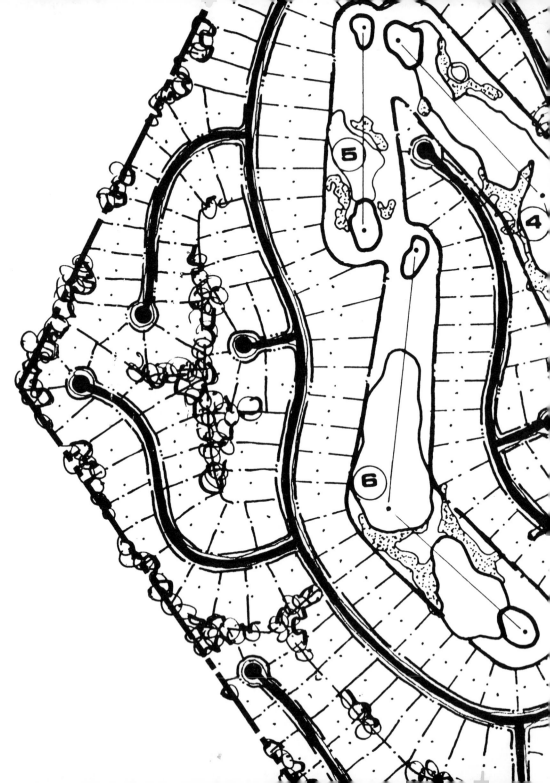

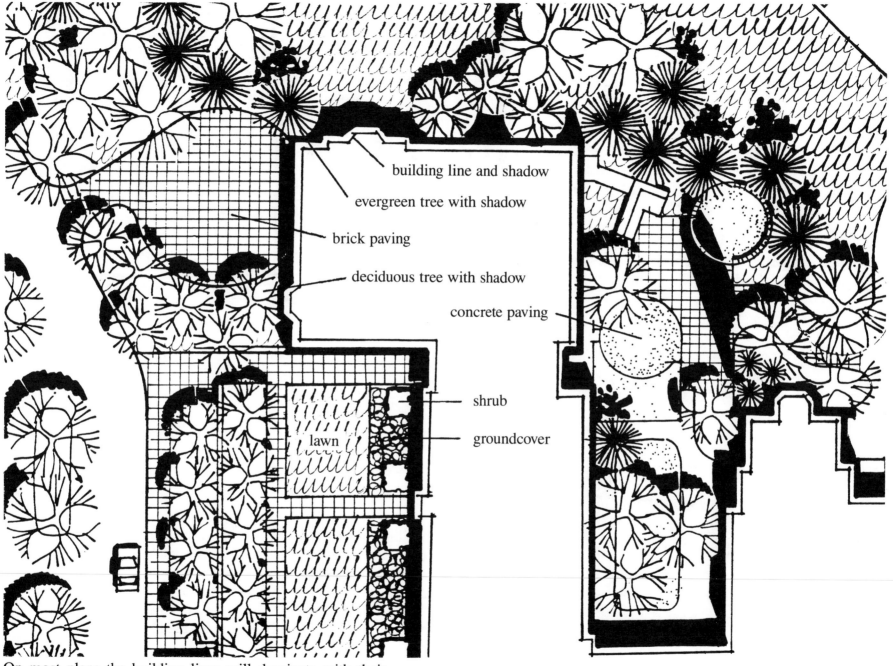

building line and shadow

evergreen tree with shadow

brick paving

deciduous tree with shadow

concrete paving

shrub

lawn

groundcover

On most plans the building lines will dominate with their boldness so they can be easily and quickly identified.

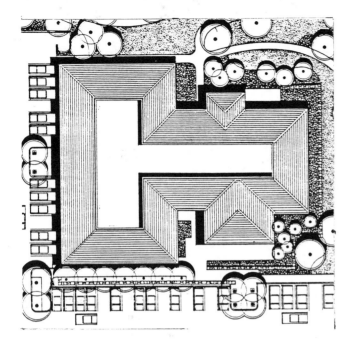

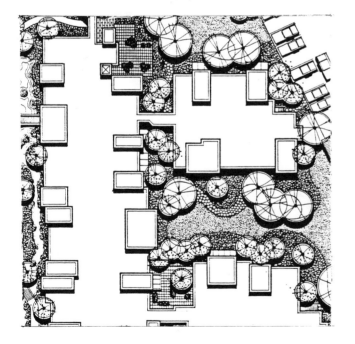

There are many different ways buildings may be identified. Some indicate only the ground space they occupy while others show a proposed roof pattern. Two examples here are drawn with a straight-edge while the third is drawn freehand. The level of detail used to represent roof patterns is determined by the amount and importance of the information available.

Another example of a freehand drawing. Note the loose
technique for brick paving in the circle drive.

Two examples of paving drawn freehand. The one on the right is more precise than the other.

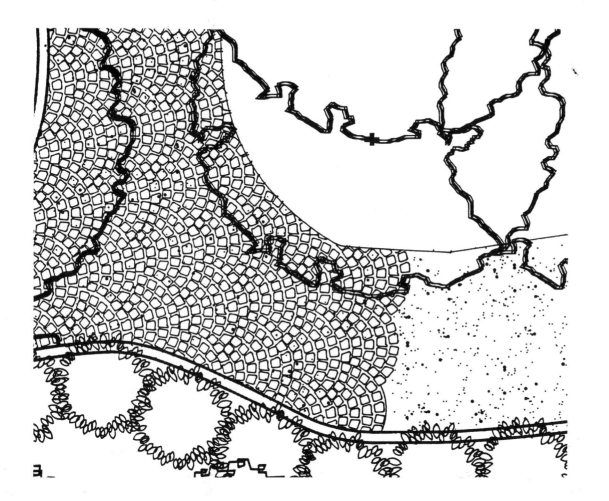
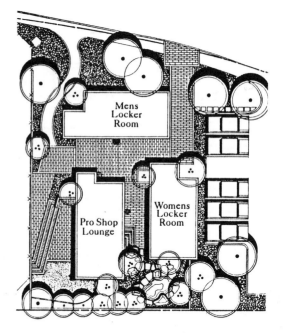

The sample computer generated plan on the left illustrates fish-scale paving and exposed aggregate concrete. The plan to the right features brick paving, reduced in size in comparison to the plan to the left.

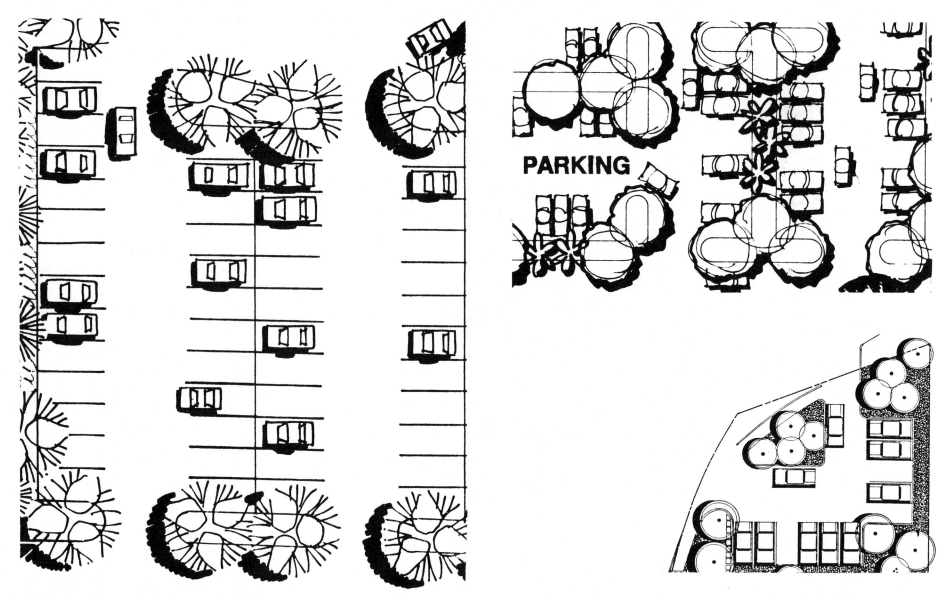

On this page, and the next page, five different styles for illustrating cars in parking situations are shown.

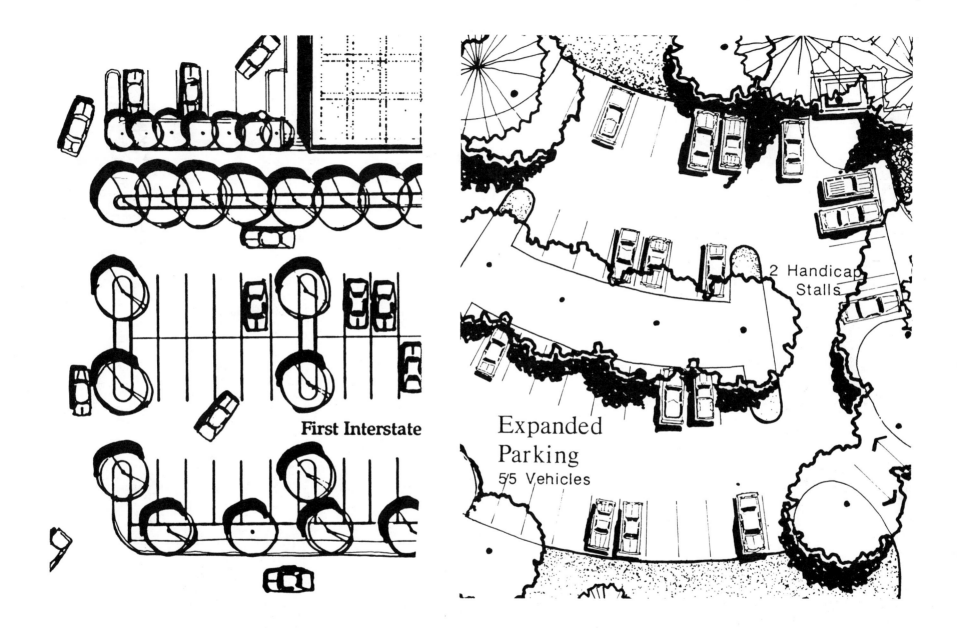

First Interstate

Expanded
Parking
55 Vehicles

2 Handicap
Stalls

9

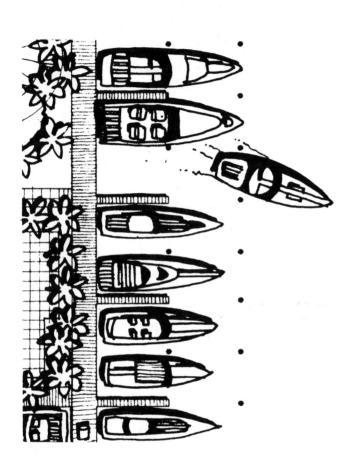

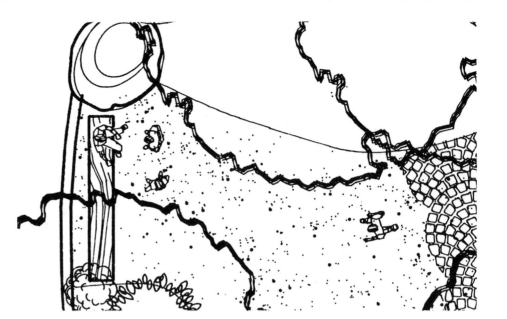

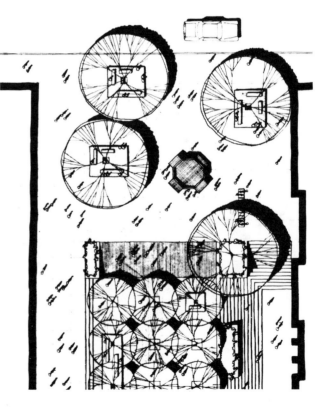

Boats and people are the plan graphics featured on these pages. The amount of detail shown for these depends upon the scale.

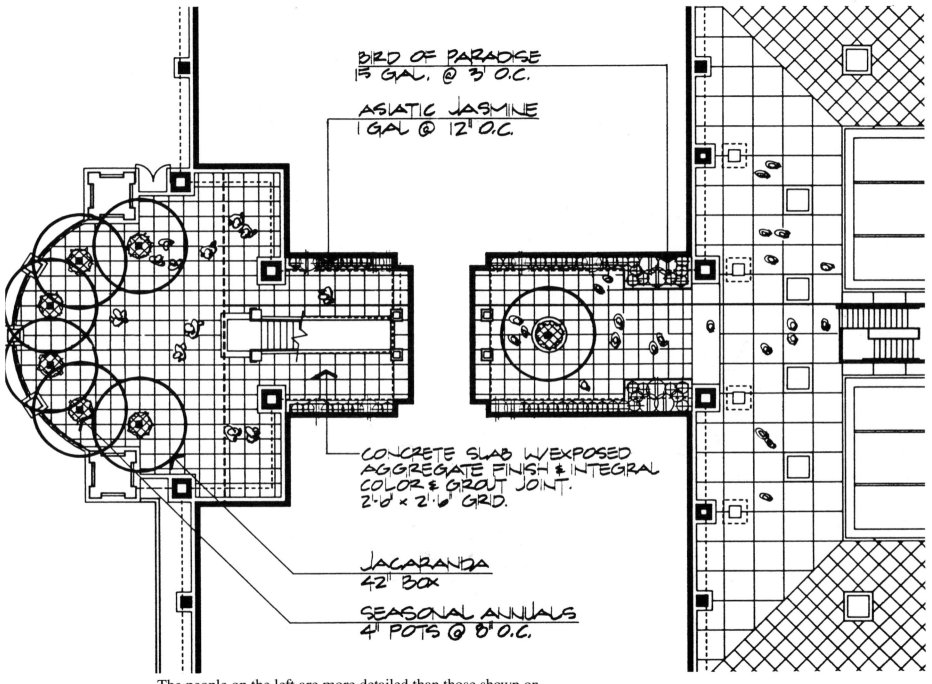

BIRD OF PARADISE
15 GAL. @ 3' O.C.

ASIATIC JASMINE
1 GAL @ 12" O.C.

CONCRETE SLAB W/EXPOSED
AGGREGATE FINISH & INTEGRAL
COLOR & GROUT JOINT.
2'-0" × 2'-6" GRID.

JACARANDA
42" BOX

SEASONAL ANNUALS
4" POTS @ 8" O.C.

The people on the left are more detailed than those shown on
the right.

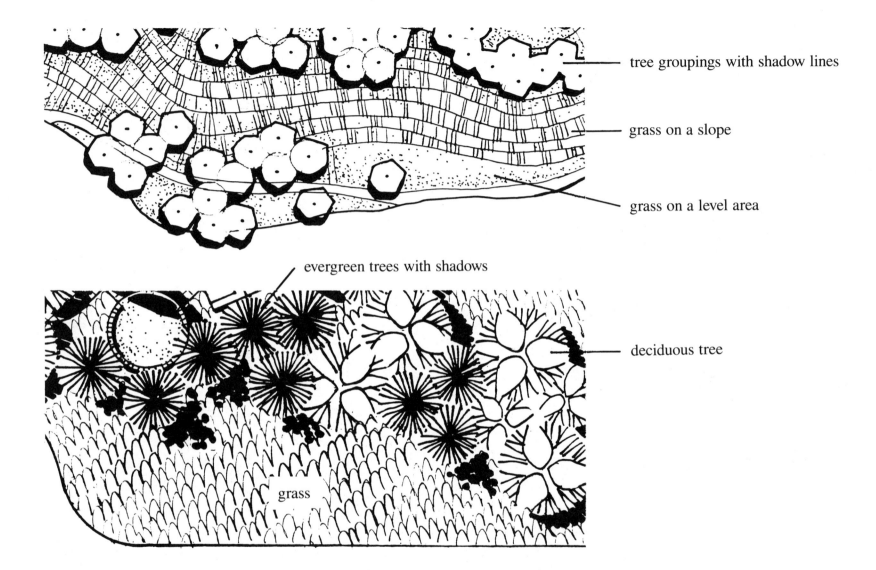

tree groupings with shadow lines

grass on a slope

grass on a level area

evergreen trees with shadows

deciduous tree

grass

Two of several techniques for delineating the use of grass on
a plan. You will find other examples elsewhere in this book.

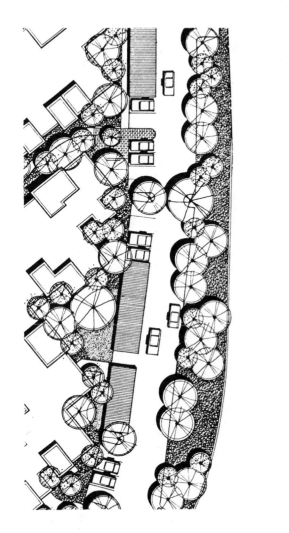

Art
Gallery

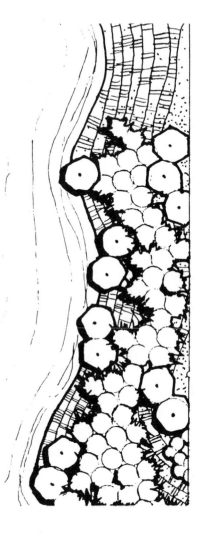

Examples of tree graphics, tree groupings, and the use of
shadows. As you look through this book you will find more
graphic styles for trees and other plants.

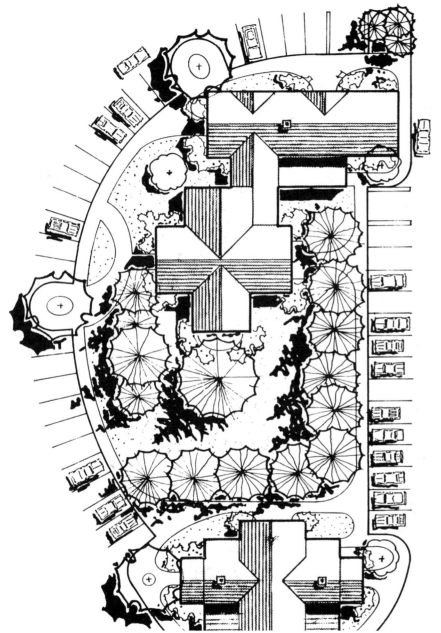
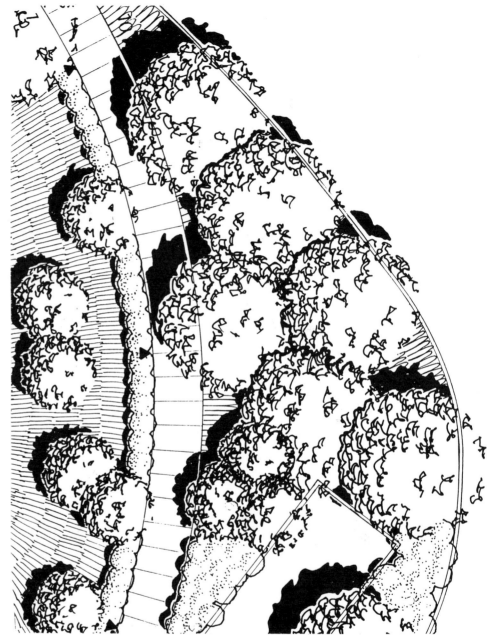

More examples of tree graphics.

Illustrated on the following pages are some techniques for delineating shrub masses with various symbols plus hatching. The centers of some shrubs are marked with a "plus" symbol, others with a large "dot" and still others with a "triangle." The building wall dominates with its bold black line. Garden walls are much less dominant with just two parallel lines with or without hatching. On page 17 groundcovers are identified with a dot pattern type "zip-a-tone," while grass is randomly stippled, "zip-a-tone" is used for grass on page 16.

On this page, rock boulders are identified by using a dark "zip-a-tone" while the groundcover is a lighter "zip-a-tone," and the grass is stippled.

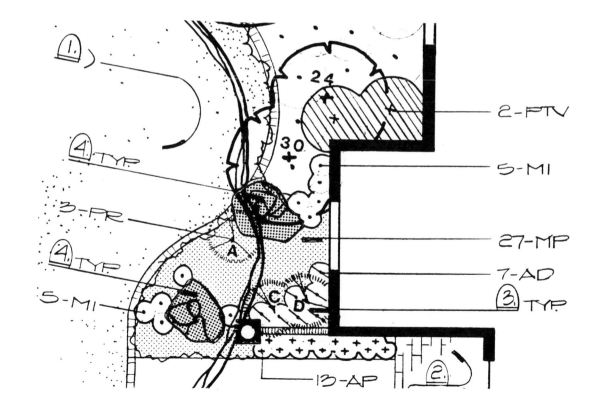

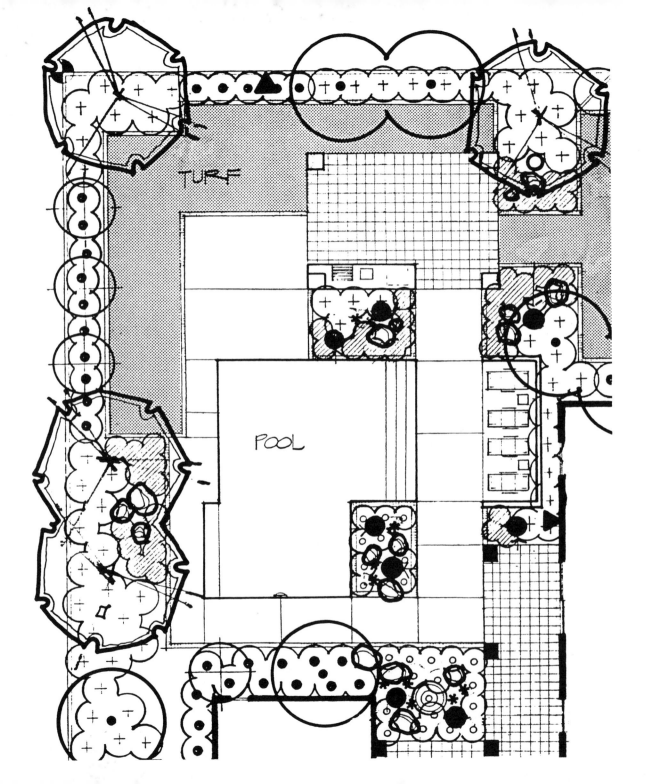

TURF

POOL

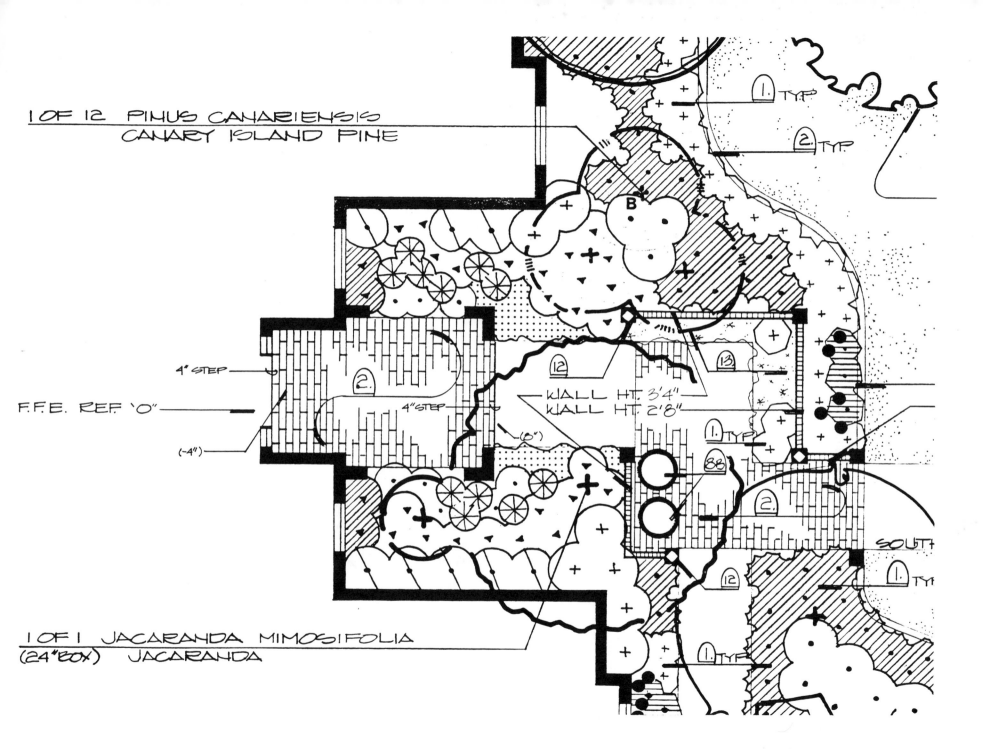

1 OF 12   PINUS CANARIENSIS
CANARY ISLAND PINE

4" STEP

F.F.E. REF. "0"

(-4")

1 OF 1 JACARANDA MIMOSIFOLIA
(24"BOX) JACARANDA

4"STEP

WALL HT. 3'4"
WALL HT. 2'8"

(6")

1. TYP.

2. TYP.

12

13

1. TYP.

88

2.

SOUTH

12

1. TYP.

1. TYP.

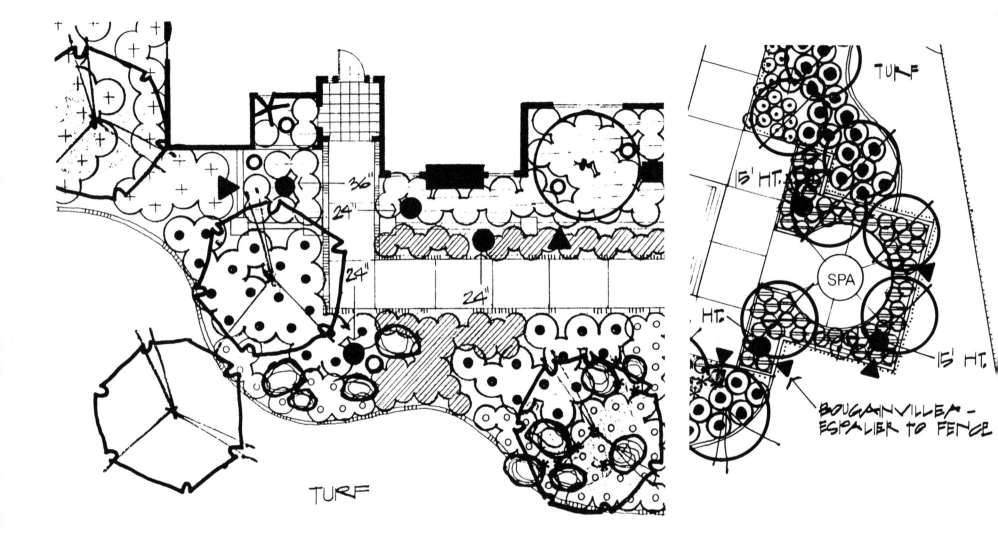

36"

24"

24"

24"

TURF

TURF

15' HT.

SPA

HT.

15' HT.

BOUGAINVILLEA -
ESPALIER TO FENCE

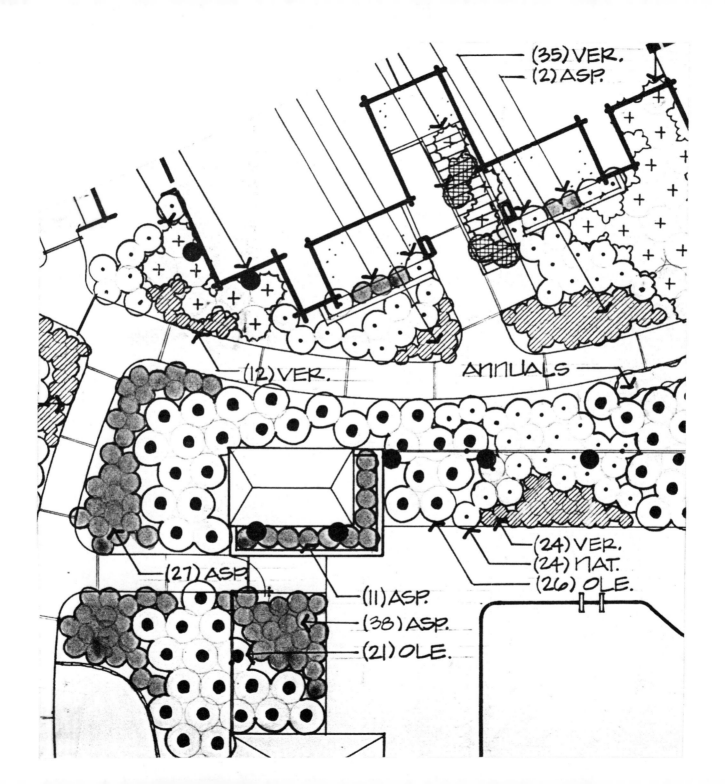

(35) VER.
(2) ASP.

annuals

(12) VER.

(24) VER.
(24) NAT.
(26) OLE.

(27) ASP.

(11) ASP.

(38) ASP.

(21) OLE.

19

CREDITS FOR CHAPTER 1

Page 2
Edward D. Stone Jr. and Associates

Page 3
Browning Day Mullins Dierdorf

Page 4
upper left: Johnson Guthrie Associates by Herb Cockcroft
lower left: Johnson Guthrie Associates by Herb Cockcroft
right: Edward D. Stone Jr. and Associates

Page 5
Post Buckley Schuh and Jernigan

Page 6
left: Post Buckley Schuh and Jernigan
right: Edward D. Stone Jr. and Associates

Page 7
left: Groves and Associates by Walter Heard
right: Johnson Guthrie Associates by Herb Cockcroft

Page 8
left: Browning Day Mullins Dierdorf
upper right: Edward D. Stone Jr. and Associates
lower right: Johnson Guthrie Associates by Herb Cockcroft

Page 9
left: A. Wayne Smith and Associates
right: CR3, inc.

Page 10
left: Edward D. Stone Jr. and Associates
upper right: Groves and Associates by Walter Heard
lower right: William A. Behnke Associates by Russell L. Butler II

Page 11
A. Wayne Smith and Associates

Page 12
top: Bonnell and Associates
bottom: Browning Day Mullins Dierdorf

Page 13
left: Johnson Guthrie Associates by Herb Cockcroft
middle: Johnson Guthrie Associates by Herb Cockcroft
right: Bonnell and Associates

Page 14
left: CR3, inc.
right: CR3, inc.

Page 15
Wendy Scofield

Page 16
A. Wayne Smith and Associates

Page 17
McConaghie/Batt and Associates

Page 18
left: A. Wayne Smith and Associates
right: A. Wayne Smith and Associates

Page 19
A. Wayne Smith and Associates

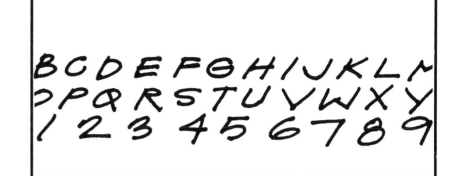

LETTERING

Your main goal when presenting plan graphics is to effectively communicate your ideas and concepts. Part of that communication process is the addition of notes to your plans. The technique for adding handwritten notes is presented in this chapter.

CREDITS FOR CHAPTER 2

Page 24
bottom: A. Wayne Smith & Associates

Page 30
upper left: A. Wayne Smith & Associates
upper right: A. Wayne Smith & Associates
middle right: Johnson Johnson & Roy
bottom: Dan Ray Burnett

Page 31
Griswold Winters Swain and Mullin

Page 32
bottom: Johnson and Dee

Introduction

Most of the plan graphics presented in this book whether they be conceptual, final presentations, or working drawings are a combination of images and notation in the form of graphics and text.

While the images catch our eye first and are regarded with primary importance, the notation adds a level of detail and information the images cannot represent. In most cases, when notation is needed we should think about how to integrate the words or block of words into the entire composition. For example, the positive image a paragraph creates when viewed is of a geometric shape and should be carefully incorporated into the plan graphic. Another example is the possible dual function titles have within the composition. The most important of these functions is to provide project identity, but the second function may be to become an element of the graphic composition. Sometimes, style or color can be used to create effectively a positive first impression.

Throughout this book we have not only illustrated the importance of plan graphics but also of the text within the composition. Although we recognize the value of computer and/or machine generated lettering this chapter will concentrate on increasing your hand- lettering skills.

Before you begin to add hand written notes to your work, take a short amount of time to decide what role your notation has within the plan graphic. Usually, notation on conceptual and presentation style work is loosely drafted, precisely worded, and its placement is a predetermined element of the final composition. Conversely, when preparing construction documents or details, notation is usually firmly drafted with a straightedge consisting of technical information and general notes. Whenever possible its placement should still attempt to complement the overall composition.

Suggested styles

Determine what media is best suited for your purposes. Generally, graphite or plastic lead on mylar or vellum is best when drafting construction documents since it is quickly applied and easily erased. Ink is an effective media for presentation style drawings due to its boldness, crisp lines, and ability to reproduce more clearly than graphite.

Decide which form of hand lettering, freehand or hardline, you should use and what size is appropriate. As a rule, freehand lettering should be used on conceptual and some presentation style drawings since it is quickly applied and will complement a loose style of image. Hardline lettering should be used on all construction documents and details. In either case, your decision should be based on the style of the image, the time allowed, and the specific use of the plan.

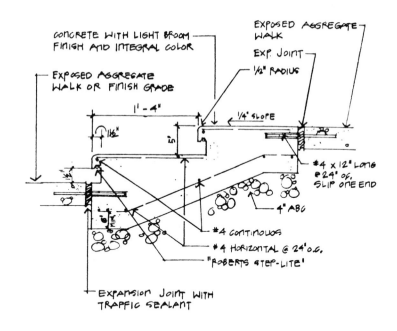

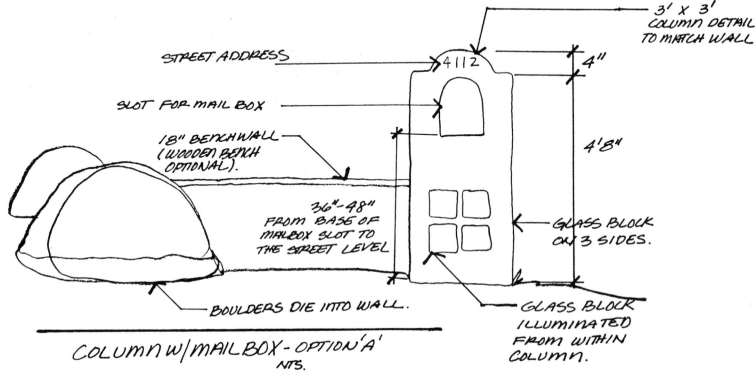

COLUMN W/ MAILBOX - OPTION 'A'
NTS.

The size of the letters will be determined by the designer based on the importance of the notes within the plan.

HEIGHT	EXAMPLES
1/8"	APPROPRIATE SIZE FOR LABELING MOST DETAILS & CONSTRUCTION DOCUMENTS
3/16"	COMFORTABLE SIZE FOR FREEHAND LETTERING & SUBTITLES. ALSO GOOD FOR CONCEPTUAL PLANS WHICH REQUIRE BOLDER TEXT & TITLES.
1/4"	MOST TITLES

NOTE: 1/4" IS GENERALLY REGARDED AS THE UPPER LIMIT FOR HARDLINED LETTERING USING A PENCIL. TO ACHIEVE MORE SUCCESS WITH LARGER LETTERS USE A PEN WITH A THICKER TIP.

The last item of consideration, mainly with presentation work, is what notation is necessary and where it is to be placed. To do this, simply place a piece of tracing paper over the entire plan and map out your notes. By doing this, you can design the layout of notes around the graphic elements strengthening the overall composition.

Remember: Consistency is the key to successful hand lettering. Once you have determined the style, shape, size, and location of notation, maintain these elements throughout the entire plan graphic.

Suggested techniques

Always use the guidelines to achieve clear, consistent lettering. Guidelines are horizontal and vertical lines drawn lightly with a hard lead, 3H or 4H, or non-photo pencils to aid in the construction of letters and numerals. Non-photo pencils work well in situations where it is important that the guidelines do not produce onto the final image.

Use a soft lead pencil, as it will be easier to control than a hard lead and will glide more easily over the surface of the paper or mylar. To start, try an H or HB lead. Later as you become more proficient, experiment with various leads so that you can eventually use the appropriate leads for the different drawing surfaces available.

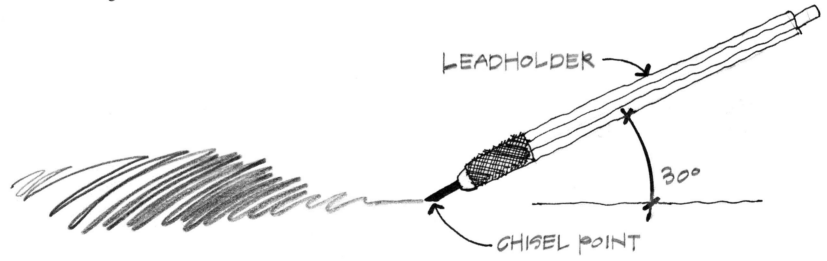

Before you begin, flatten the lead on a scrap piece of paper or sandpaper block to produce a chisel point. You can create both thick and thin lines by twirling the lead holder between your thumb and fingers. The flat edge of the chisel point is used for thick lines and the side edge for thin lines.

One of the most important techniques to remember when hand lettering is to maintain consistent letter dimensions and spacings. Each letter, except for "I," will be of equal height and should have similar width and proportion. To accurately draw each letter with matched heights, always use horizontal guidelines. It also should be noted that hand lettered notation is easier to read when the designer provides adequate spacing between letters, words, and sentences.

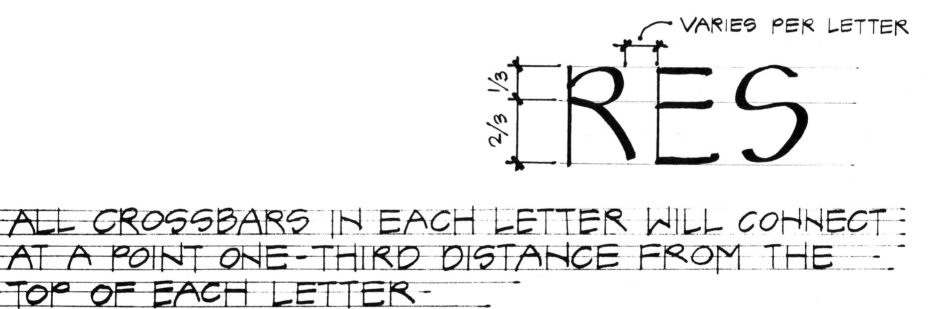

Another very successful technique to remember is that all crossbars will connect at the same point in each letter. To begin, practice using three horizontal guidelines for each line of text. After drawing your upper and lower guidelines, add a third horizontal guideline at a point two-thirds above the base of the letter. All crossbars will connect at points along this guideline.

Your objective when hand lettering is to be sure the notation is accurate and legible. To ensure accuracy you need to understand the content and always check for incorrect spelling. A common problem that compromises legibility is the smearing of letters. To avoid smudging the graphite, it is best to begin at the top of the plan and work down from left to right, when possible. Even when working left to right, it is common to drag your arm or triangle across fresh graphite causing it to smear.

To avoid this problem practice lettering with the guide triangle on the right side of the lead holder as opposed to the left side, which seems so much more natural for right handed persons.

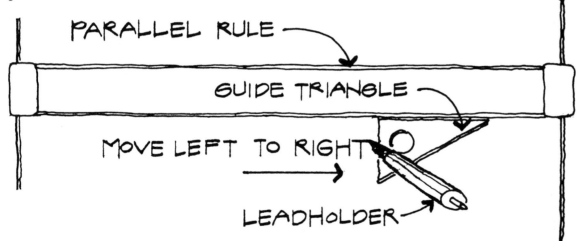

PARALLEL RULE

GUIDE TRIANGLE

MOVE LEFT TO RIGHT

LEADHOLDER

Simply wrap your left arm over the top of the parallel rule and place your thumb and fore finger on the top of the guide triangle gliding it across the parallel rule as you write.

Grouping notes will also strengthen the overall plan graphic. Not only does grouped notes provide mass to the composition, it also makes it easier for the reader to pick out information. The reader does not have to search the entire plan for single floating notes.

In all graphic communications, including hand lettering, the line is a fundamental element. When drafting any line the emphasis is always on the end-points of the line. Avoid letting up or decreasing pressure at the end of your stroke.

||||||||||||||| ||||| |||||||| |TYPICAL SECTION

When lettering, verticals are drawn with a thin line while horizontals are drawn boldly with thick lines. This is achieved by twirling the lead holder as you write. As you gain experience you will notice that when using this technique with a soft lead, and by maintaining the chisel point, sharpening the lead point is minimized.

ABCDEFGHIJKLMNOPQRSTUVWXYZ
0123456789¢#

BANK TO BE ENGULFED IN CASCADING
FLOWERING SHRUBS AND GROUND COVERS.

BOULDER POCKETS TO FORM A SERIES OF
WHITE WATER FALLS AND TRANQUIL POOLS
FROM ABOVE THE SIGNAGE TO A BASIN
BELOW THE FINISHED WALK ELEVATION.

Native vegetation-specimen cactus
always with mesquite or palo verde
shrubbery in natural massing, groups
of 10-30 plants with sympathetic
combinations.

ABCDEFGHIJKLM
NOPQRSTUVWXYZ
0123456789

NOTE: ALL REDWOOD SURFACES TO
RECEIVE 2 COATS THOMPSONS
CLEAR SEALANT WATERPROOFING.

SMOOTH MASONRY FINISH. PAINT
TO MATCH SIGNAGE & PLANTER
WALL. COLOR TO BE APPROVED
BY LANDSCAPE ARCH/OWNER

abcdefghijklmnopqrstuvwxyz 123456789
american society of landscape architects

ABCDEFGHIJKLMNOPQRSTUVWXYZ   123456789
AMERICAN SOCIETY OF LANDSCAPE ARCHITECTS

ABCDEFGHIJKLMNOPQRSTUVWXYZ 1234567891
AMERICAN Society of LANDSCAPE ARCHITECTS

ABCDEFGHIJKLMNOPQRSTUVWXYZ
1234567890   ¢ ₵ $ ¢ #   and/or

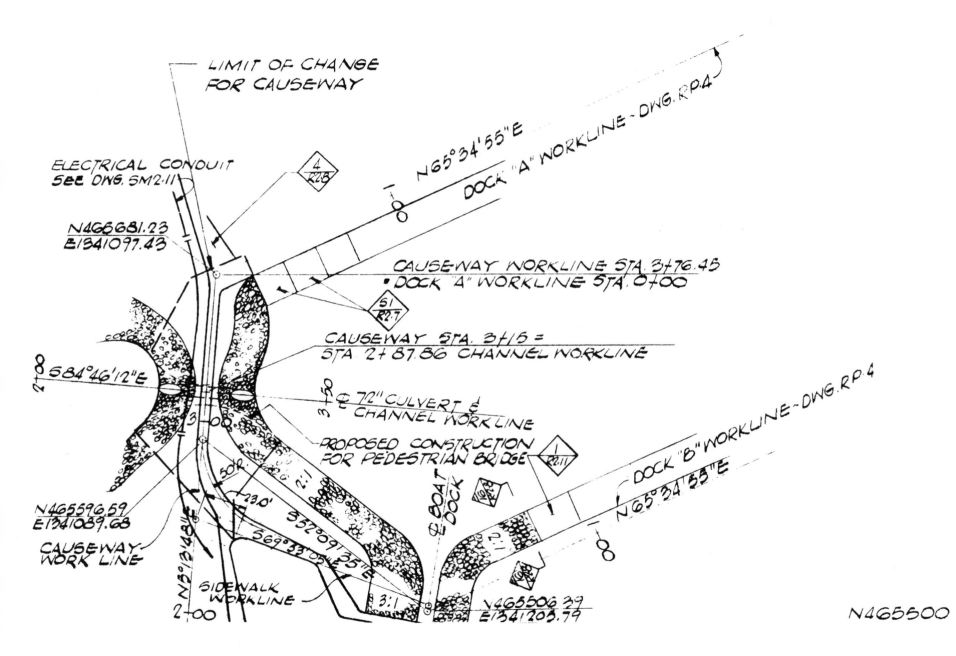

LIMIT OF CHANGE
FOR CAUSEWAY

N65°34'55"E

DOCK "A" WORKLINE - DWG. RP.4

4 R28

ELECTRICAL CONDUIT
SEE DWG. SM2·11

N465681.23
E1341097.43

CAUSEWAY WORKLINE STA. 3+76.45
• DOCK "A" WORKLINE STA. 0+00

51 R2.7

CAUSEWAY STA. 3+15 =
STA. 2+87.86 CHANNEL WORKLINE

S84°46'12"E

€ 72" CULVERT &
CHANNEL WORKLINE

PROPOSED CONSTRUCTION
FOR PEDESTRIAN BRIDGE

1 R2.11

DOCK "B" WORKLINE - DWG. RP.4

N65°34'55"E

N465596.59
E1341089.68

CAUSEWAY
WORK LINE

SIDEWALK
WORKLINE

S69°53'05"E

N465506.39
E1341205.79

N465500

31

● MILLER RESIDENCE ③

Canton Public Library

COLLINSVILLE , CONNECTICUT

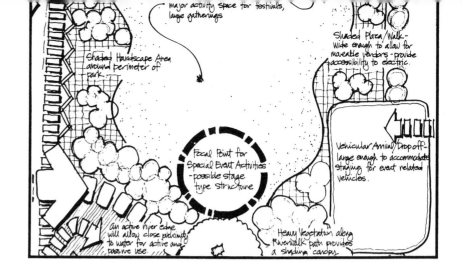

major activity space for festivals, large gatherings

Shaded Plaza/Walk - Wide enough to allow for moveable vendors - provide accessibility to electric.

Shaded Hardscape Area around perimeter of park.

Focal Point for Special Event Activities - possible stage type structure

Vehicular Arrival/Drop off - large enough to accommodate staging for event related vehicles.

an active river edge will allow close proximity to water for active and passive use.

Heavy Vegetation along Riverwalk path provides a shading canopy.

SITE ANALYSIS

On many design projects, the first phase of the design process is analyzing the project site and its surroundings. The importance of an accurate analysis is crucial to the success of the design solution. When creating a graphic representation of the analysis information, the same degree of accuracy must be followed. Since the site analysis graphics are often accompanied with a more thorough written analysis, the graphic representations should illustrate all pertinent physical benefits, constraints, and characteristics.

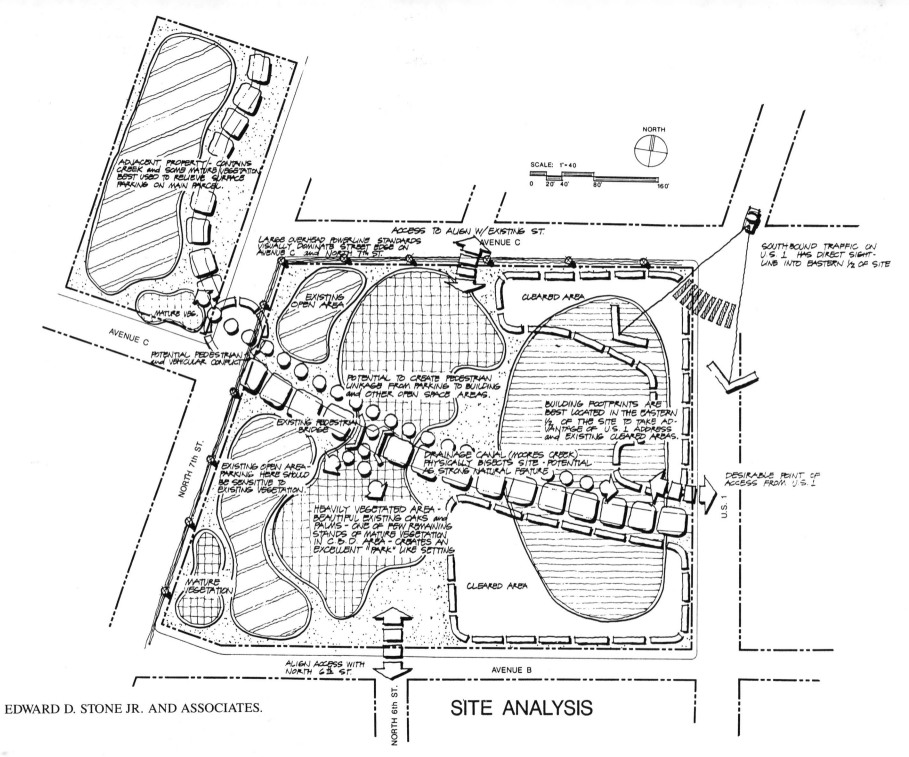

NORTH

SCALE: 1"=40
0 20' 40' 80'   160'

ADJACENT PROPERTY - CONTAINS
CREEK and SOME MATURE VEGETATION
BEST USED TO RELIEVE SURFACE
PARKING ON MAIN PARCEL.

ACCESS TO ALIGN W/ EXISTING ST.
AVENUE C

LARGE OVERHEAD POWERLINE STANDARDS
VISUALLY DOMINATE STREET EDGE ON
AVENUE C and NORTH 7th ST.

SOUTHBOUND TRAFFIC ON
U.S. 1 HAS DIRECT SIGHT-
LINE INTO EASTERN ½ OF SITE

AVENUE C

MATURE VEG.

EXISTING
OPEN AREA

CLEARED AREA

POTENTIAL PEDESTRIAN
and VEHICULAR CONFLICT

POTENTIAL TO CREATE PEDESTRIAN
LINKAGE FROM PARKING TO BUILDING
and OTHER OPEN SPACE AREAS.

BUILDING FOOTPRINTS ARE
BEST LOCATED IN THE EASTERN
½ OF THE SITE TO TAKE AD-
VANTAGE OF U.S. 1 ADDRESS
and EXISTING CLEARED AREAS.

EXISTING PEDESTRIAN
BRIDGE

DRAINAGE CANAL (MOORES CREEK)
PHYSICALLY BISECTS SITE - POTENTIAL
AS. STRONG NATURAL FEATURE

DESIRABLE POINT OF
ACCESS FROM U.S. 1

NORTH 7th ST.

EXISTING OPEN AREA -
PARKING HERE SHOULD
BE SENSITIVE TO
EXISTING VEGETATION.

U.S. 1

HEAVILY VEGETATED AREA -
BEAUTIFUL EXISTING OAKS and
PALMS - ONE OF FEW REMAINING
STANDS OF MATURE VEGETATION
IN C.B.D. AREA - CREATES AN
EXCELLENT "PARK" LIKE SETTING

MATURE
VEGETATION

CLEARED AREA

ALIGN ACCESS WITH
NORTH 6 ST.

AVENUE B

NORTH 6th ST.

EDWARD D. STONE JR. AND ASSOCIATES.

SITE ANALYSIS

34

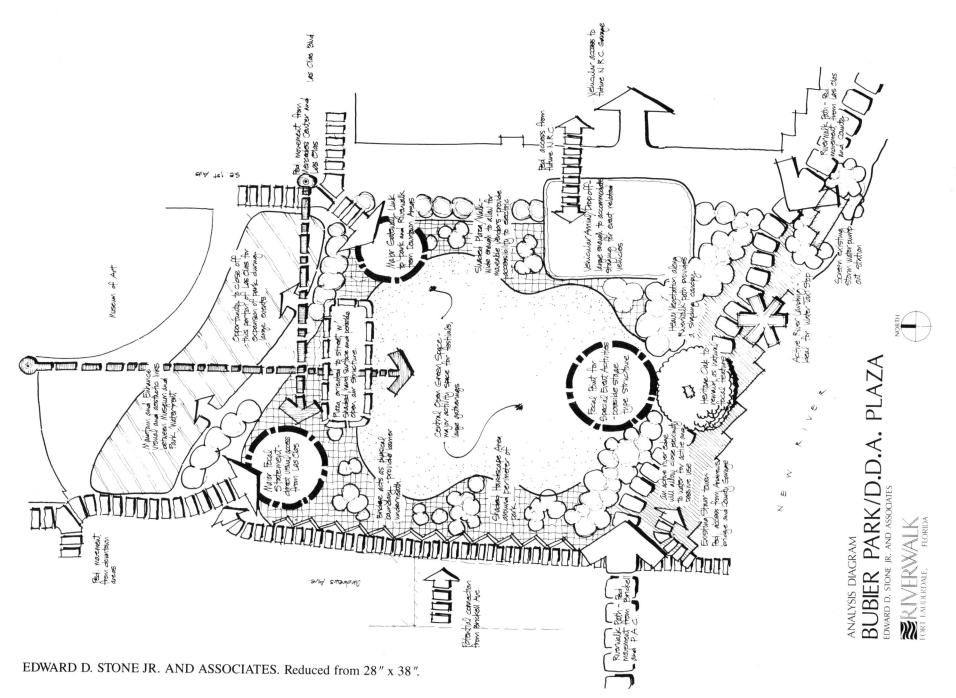

ANALYSIS DIAGRAM
BUBIER PARK/D.D.A. PLAZA
EDWARD D. STONE JR. AND ASSOCIATES

RIVERWALK
FORT LAUDERDALE,   FLORIDA

NORTH

EDWARD D. STONE JR. AND ASSOCIATES. Reduced from 28″ x 38″.

35

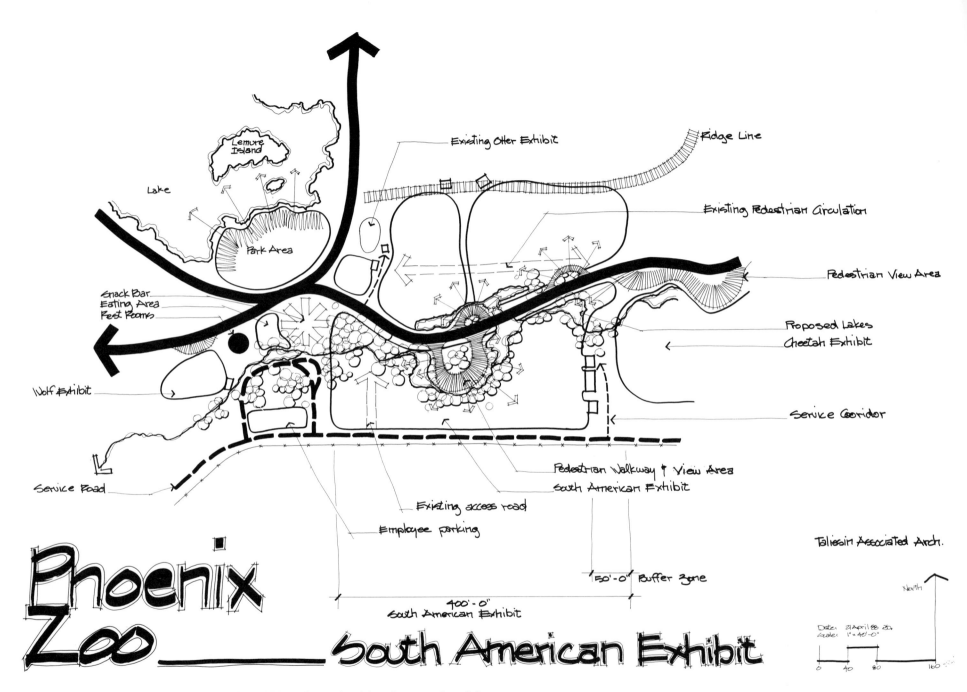

Existing Otter Exhibit

Ridge Line

Lemure Island

Lake

Existing Pedestrian Circulation

Park Area

Pedestrian View Area

Snack Bar
Eating Area
Rest Rooms

Proposed Lakes
Cheetah Exhibit

Wolf Exhibit

Service Corridor

Service Road

Pedestrian Walkway & View Area
South American Exhibit

Existing access road

Employee parking

Taliesin Associated Arch.

North

50'-0" Buffer Zone

400'-0"
South American Exhibit

Date: 21 April 88 20.
Scale: 1" = 40'-0"

0   40   80   160

Phoenix Zoo _____ South American Exhibit

TALIESIN/ALLEN GROSS/JOHNN STERZER. Ink on sketching tissue, reduced from
24" x 36".

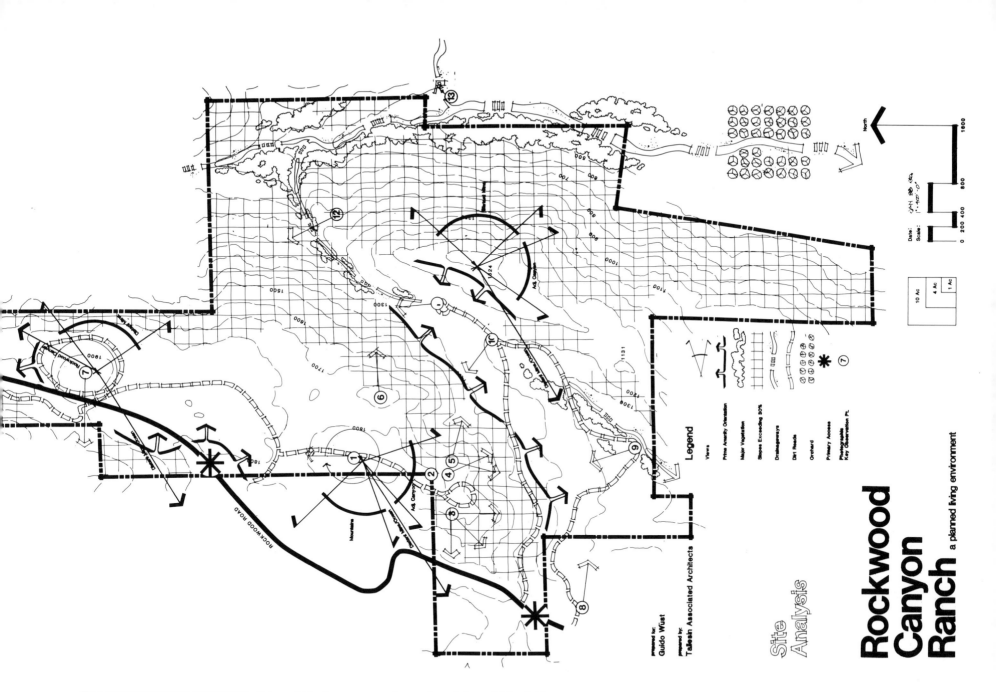

TALIESIN/JOHNN STERZER. Ink and black tape on mylar, reduced from 24″ x 36″.

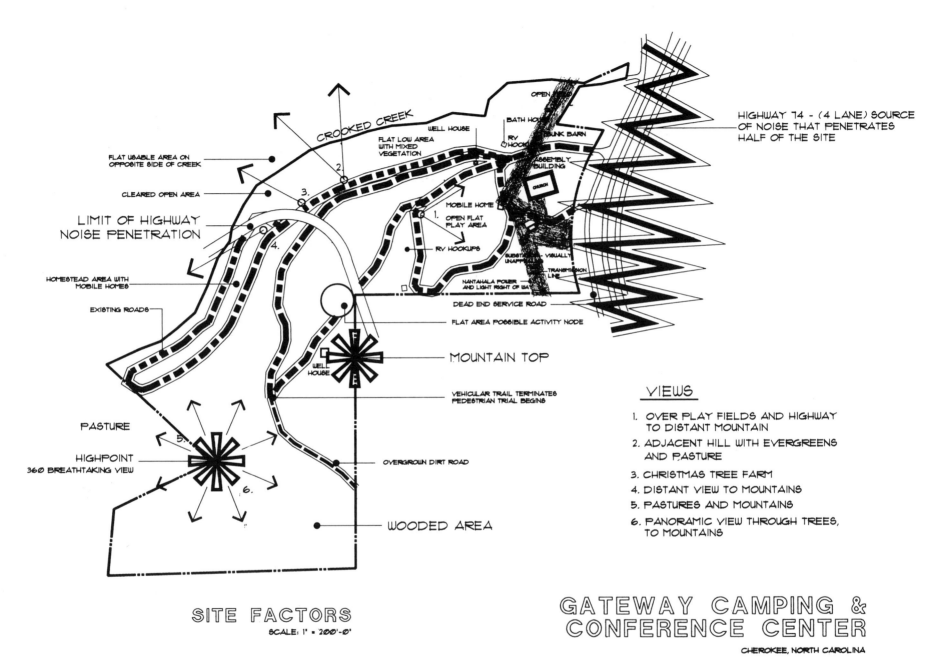

FLAT USABLE AREA ON
OPPOSITE SIDE OF CREEK

CLEARED OPEN AREA

LIMIT OF HIGHWAY
NOISE PENETRATION

HOMESTEAD AREA WITH
MOBILE HOMES

EXISTING ROADS

PASTURE

HIGHPOINT
360 BREATHTAKING VIEW

CROOKED CREEK

FLAT LOW AREA
WITH MIXED
VEGETATION

WELL HOUSE

BATH HOUSE

RV HOOKUP

OPEN

BUNK BARN

ASSEMBLY
BUILDING

CABIN

MOBILE HOME

OPEN FLAT
PLAY AREA

RV HOOKUPS

SUBSTATION - VISUALLY
UNAPPEALING

TRANSMISSION
LINE

NANTAHALA POWER
AND LIGHT RIGHT OF WAY

DEAD END SERVICE ROAD

FLAT AREA POSSIBLE ACTIVITY NODE

MOUNTAIN TOP

WELL
HOUSE

VEHICULAR TRAIL TERMINATES
PEDESTRIAN TRIAL BEGINS

OVERGROWN DIRT ROAD

WOODED AREA

HIGHWAY 74 - (4 LANE) SOURCE
OF NOISE THAT PENETRATES
HALF OF THE SITE

VIEWS

1. OVER PLAY FIELDS AND HIGHWAY
   TO DISTANT MOUNTAIN
2. ADJACENT HILL WITH EVERGREENS
   AND PASTURE
3. CHRISTMAS TREE FARM
4. DISTANT VIEW TO MOUNTAINS
5. PASTURES AND MOUNTAINS
6. PANORAMIC VIEW THROUGH TREES,
   TO MOUNTAINS

SITE FACTORS
SCALE: 1" = 200'-0"

GATEWAY CAMPING &
CONFERENCE CENTER

CHEROKEE, NORTH CAROLINA

KENDALL-VERSON/LAND DESIGN GROUP. This plan prepared by using CAD.

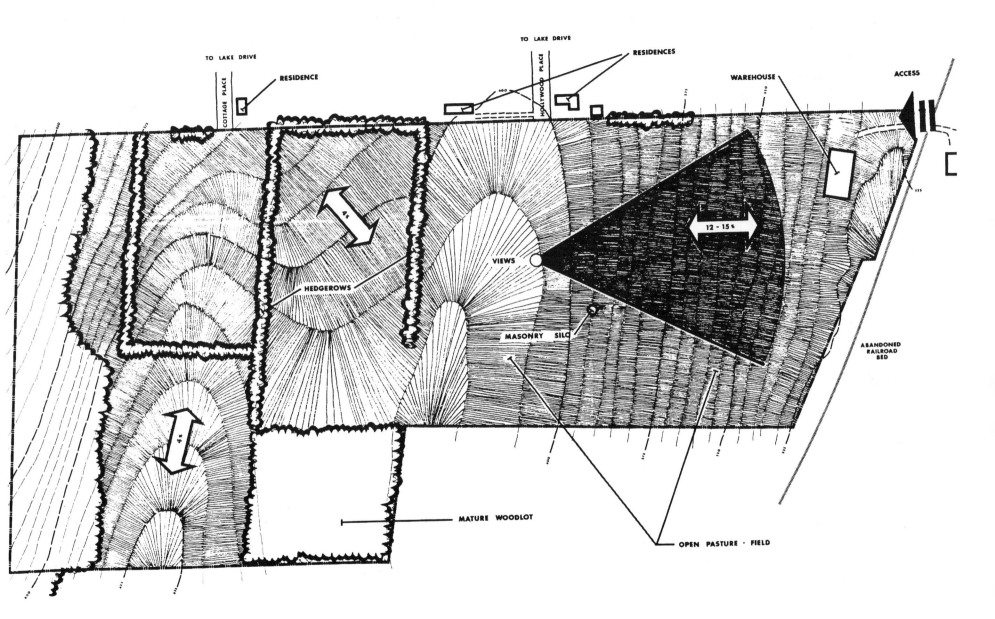

TO LAKE DRIVE

RESIDENCE

TO LAKE DRIVE

RESIDENCES

WAREHOUSE

ACCESS

HEDGEROWS

VIEWS

12 - 15 %

MASONRY SILO

ABANDONED RAILROAD BED

MATURE WOODLOT

OPEN PASTURE · FIELD

THE SARATOGA ASSOCIATES. Site Analysis for Somers, UDC.

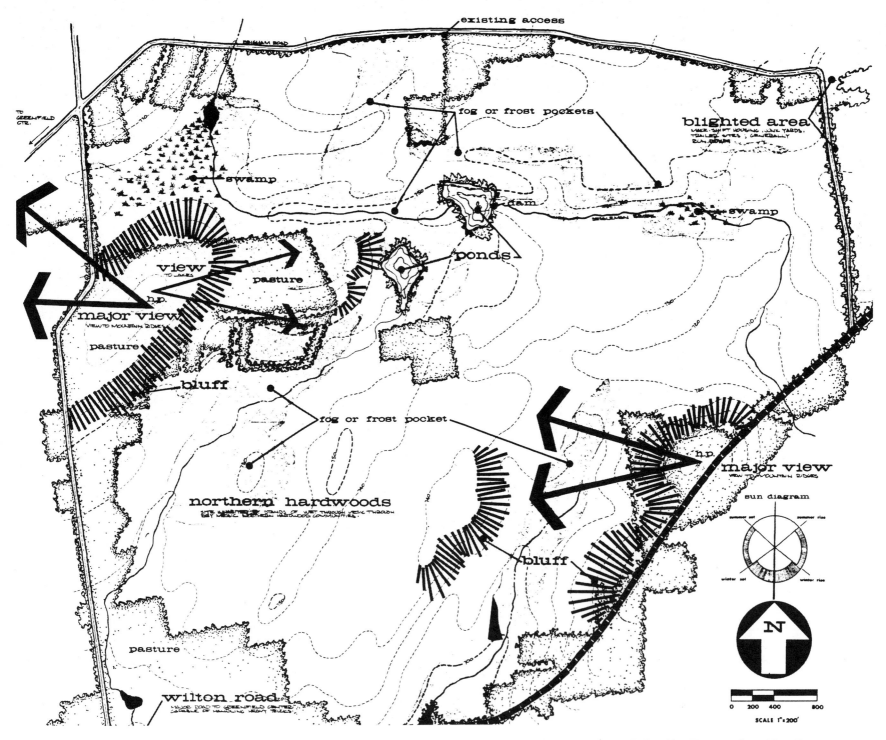

existing access

fog or frost pockets

blighted area
LAKE SHIFT HOUSING, JUNK YARDS,
TRAILER SITES, GENERALLY
RUN-DOWN

swamp

dam

swamp

view
TO LAKES

pasture

ponds

major view
VIEW TO MOUNTAIN 2 DECS

pasture

bluff

fog or frost pocket

h.p.

major view
VIEW TO MOUNTAIN RIDGES

northern hardwoods
SITE UNPROTECTED STANDS OF WET THROUGH MESIC THROUGH
DRY MESIC NORTHERN HARDWOOD COMMUNITIES.

bluff

sun diagram

TO
GREENFIELD
CTR.

pasture

wilton road
MAJOR ROAD TO GREENFIELD CENTER
CAPABLE OF HANDLING HEAVY TRUCKS

N

0 200 400 800

SCALE 1"=200'

40   THE SARATOGA ASSOCIATES. Existing Site Features for a New Town.

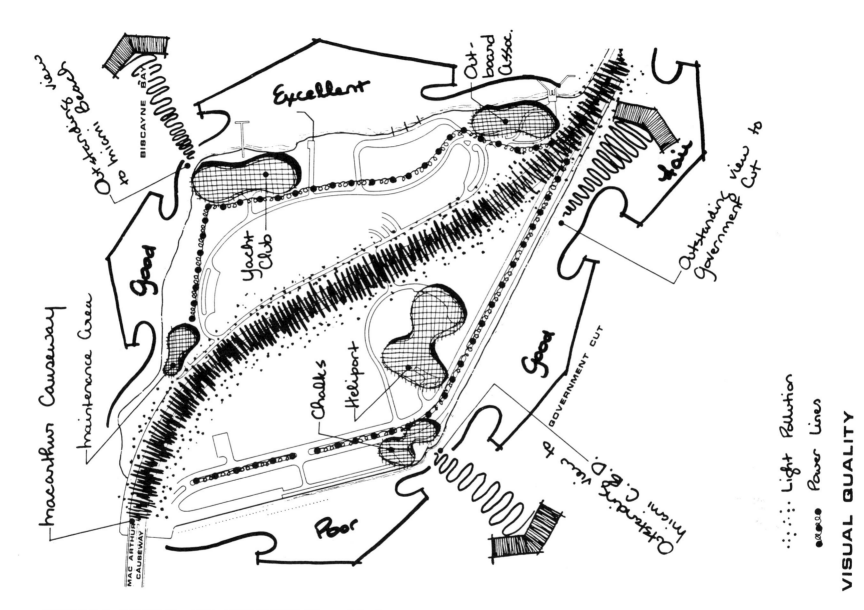

Outstanding view to miami Beach

BIBCAYNE BAY

Excellent

Out-board Assoc.

Good

Yacht Club

Macarthur Causeway

Maintenance Area

Chalks Heliport

MAC ARTHUR CAUSEWAY

Poor

Good

GOVERNMENT CUT

Outstanding view to Government Cut

Stair

Outstanding view to miami C.B.D.

∴∴∴ Light Pollution

⊶⊶⊶ Power Lines

VISUAL QUALITY

EDWARD D. STONE JR. AND ASSOCIATES. Watson Island.

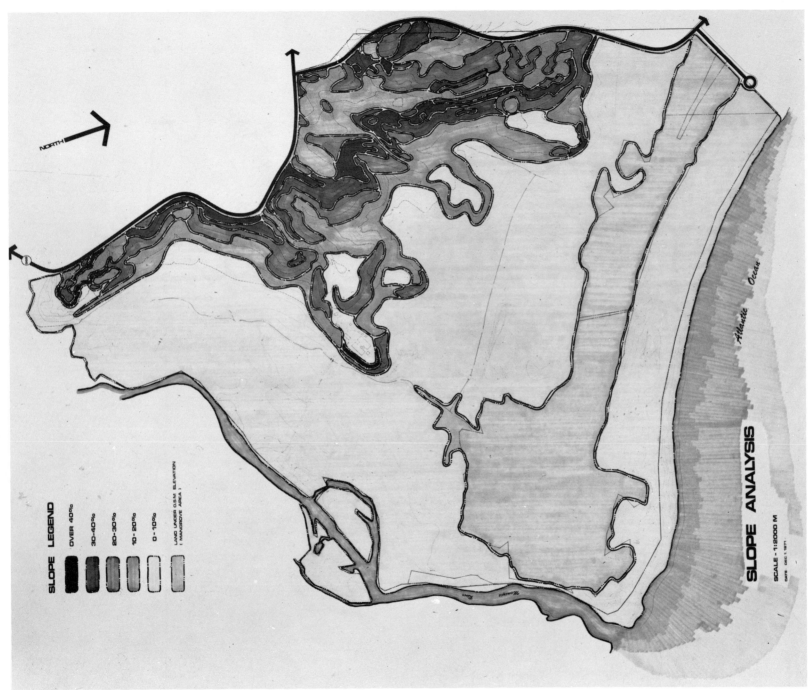

SLOPE LEGEND

OVER 40%
30-40%
20-30%
10-20%
0-10%
LAND UNDER 0.5M ELEVATION
(MANGROVE AREA)

NORTH

Atlantic Ocean

SLOPE ANALYSIS

SCALE - 1:12000 M

DATE: DEC. 1 1971

EDWARD D. STONE JR. AND ASSOCIATES. Palmer Resort.

42

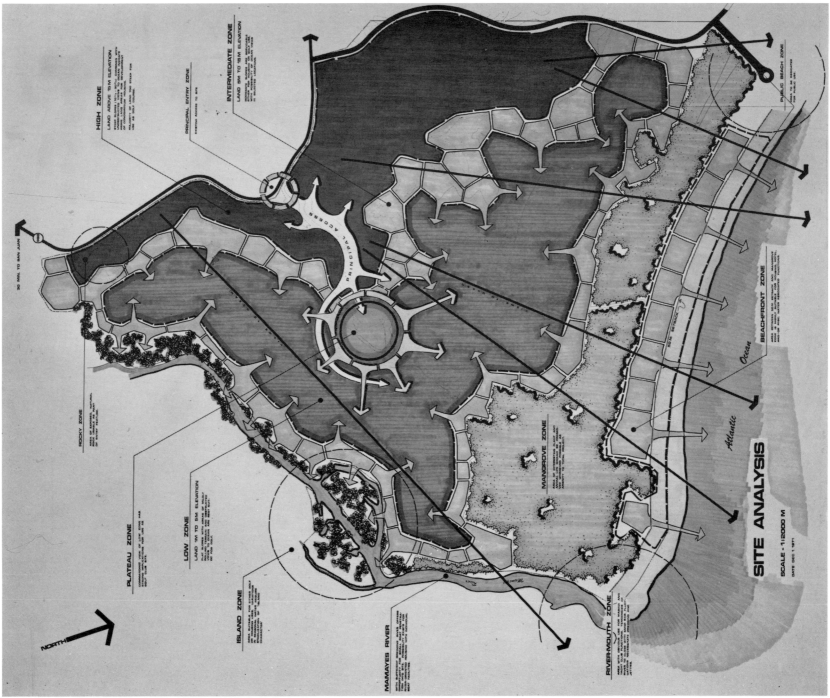

EDWARD D. STONE JR. AND ASSOCIATES. Palmer Resort.

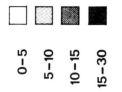

0-5
5-10
10-15
15-30

PERCENT OF SLOPE

44

CR3, inc., by Jeffrey A. Gebrian. Western Connecticut State College.

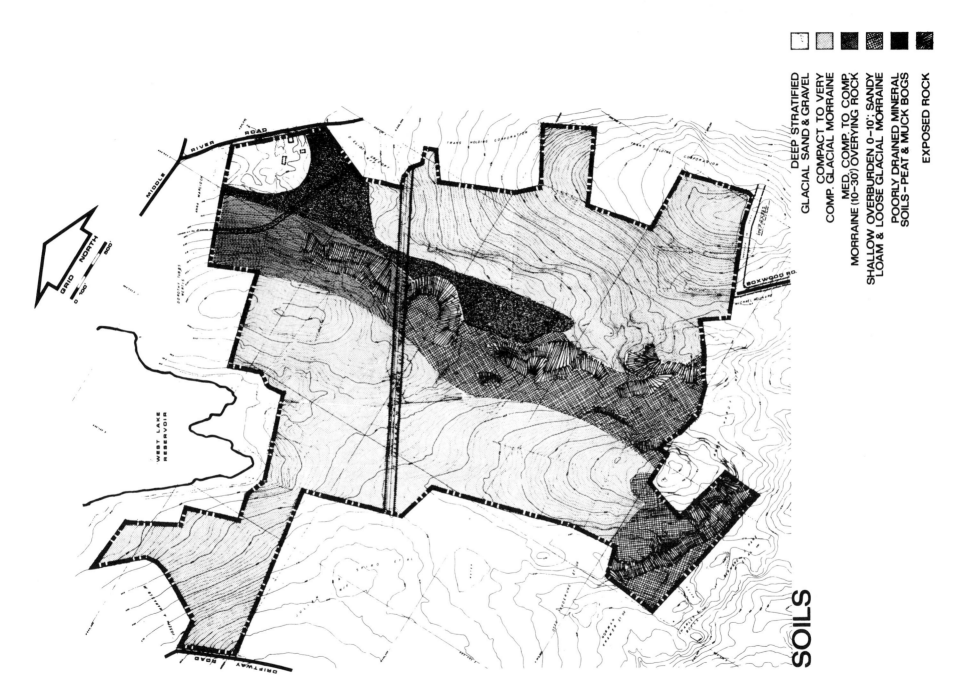

SOILS

Legend:
- DEEP STRATIFIED GLACIAL SAND & GRAVEL
- COMPACT TO VERY COMP. GLACIAL MORRAINE
- MED. COMP. TO COMP. MORRAINE (10-30') OVERYING ROCK
- SHALLOW OVERBURDEN 0-10': SANDY LOAM & LOOSE GLACIAL MORRAINE
- POORLY DRAINED MINERAL SOILS-PEAT & MUCK BOGS
- EXPOSED ROCK

WEST LAKE RESERVOIR

CR3, inc., by Jeffrey A. Gebrian. Western Connecticut State College.

DRAINAGE - ELEVATIONS

BELOW 600
600 - 650
650 - 700
ABOVE 700
PEAT BOG
STREAM

CR3, inc., by Jeffrey A. Gebrian. Western Connecticut State College.

46

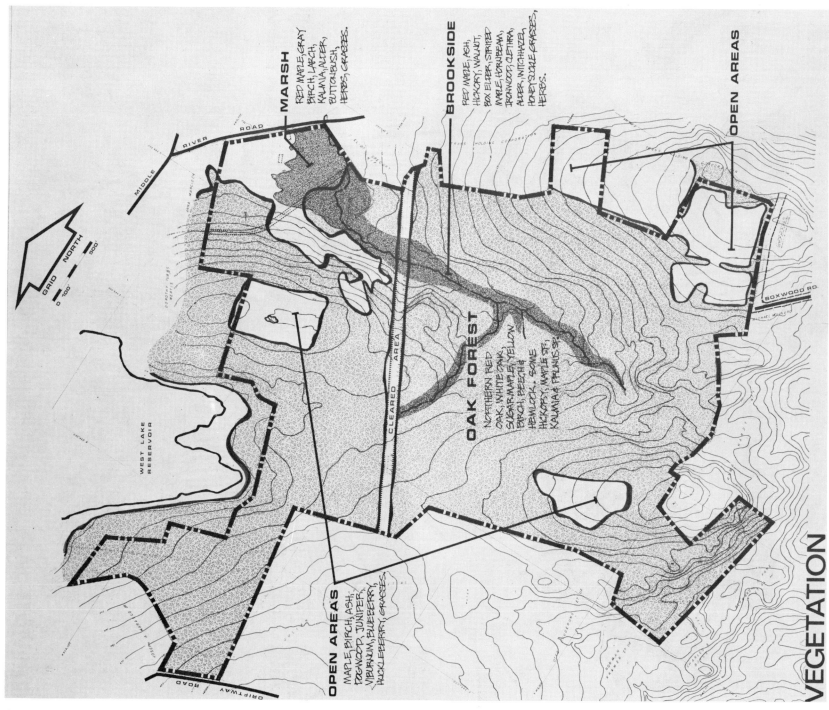

MARSH

RED MAPLE, GRAY BIRCH, LARCH, KALMIA, ALDER, BUTTON-BUSH, HERBS, GRASSES.

BROOKSIDE

RED MAPLE, ASH, HICKORY, WALNUT, BOX ELDER, STRIPED MAPLE, HORNBEAM, IRONWOOD, CLETHRA, ALDER, WITCHHAZEL, HONEYSUCKLE GRASSES, HERBS.

OPEN AREAS

OAK FOREST

NORTHERN RED OAK, WHITE OAK, SUGAR MAPLE, YELLOW BIRCH, BEECH & HEMLOCK. SOME HICKORY, MAPLE SP., KALMIA & PRUNUS SP.

OPEN AREAS

MAPLE, BIRCH, ASH, DOGWOOD, JUNIPER, VIBURNUM, BLUEBERRY, HUCKLEBERRY, GRASSES.

GRID NORTH
0 100' 300'

MIDDLE RIVER ROAD

WEST LAKE RESERVOIR

DRIFTWAY ROAD

CLEARED AREA

BOXWOOD RD.

VEGETATION

CR3, inc., by Jeffrey A. Gebrian. Western Connecticut State College.

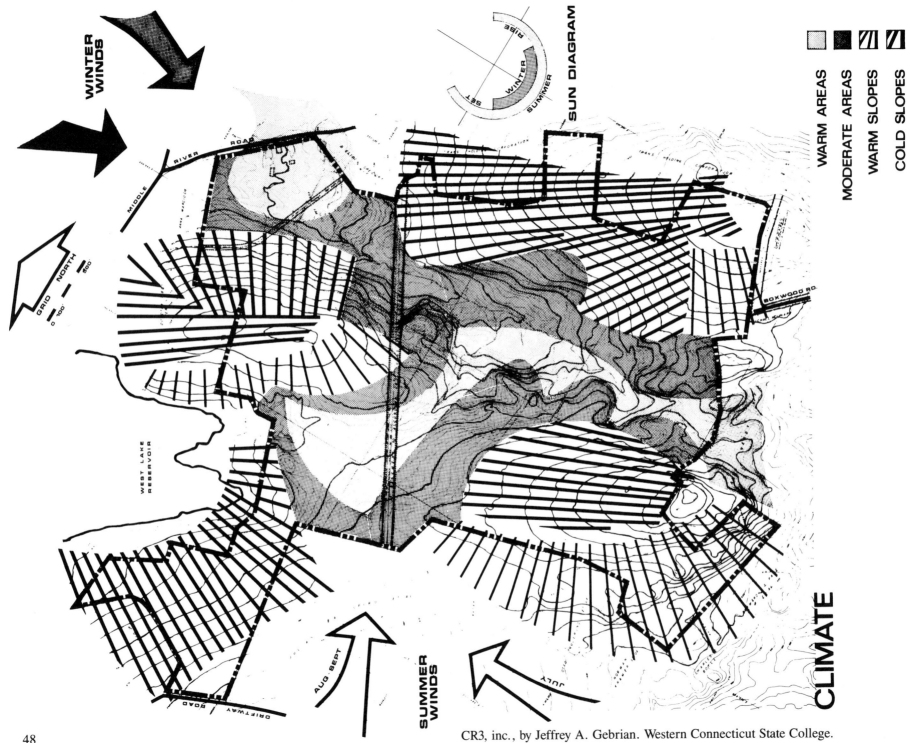

WINTER WINDS

SUN DIAGRAM

RISE

WINTER
SET
SUMMER

WARM AREAS
MODERATE AREAS
WARM SLOPES
COLD SLOPES

GRID NORTH
0 100'   500'

MIDDLE RIVER ROAD

WEST LAKE RESERVOIR

DRIFTWAY ROAD

AUG · SEPT

SUMMER WINDS

JULY

BOXWOOD RD.

CLIMATE

CR3, inc., by Jeffrey A. Gebrian. Western Connecticut State College.

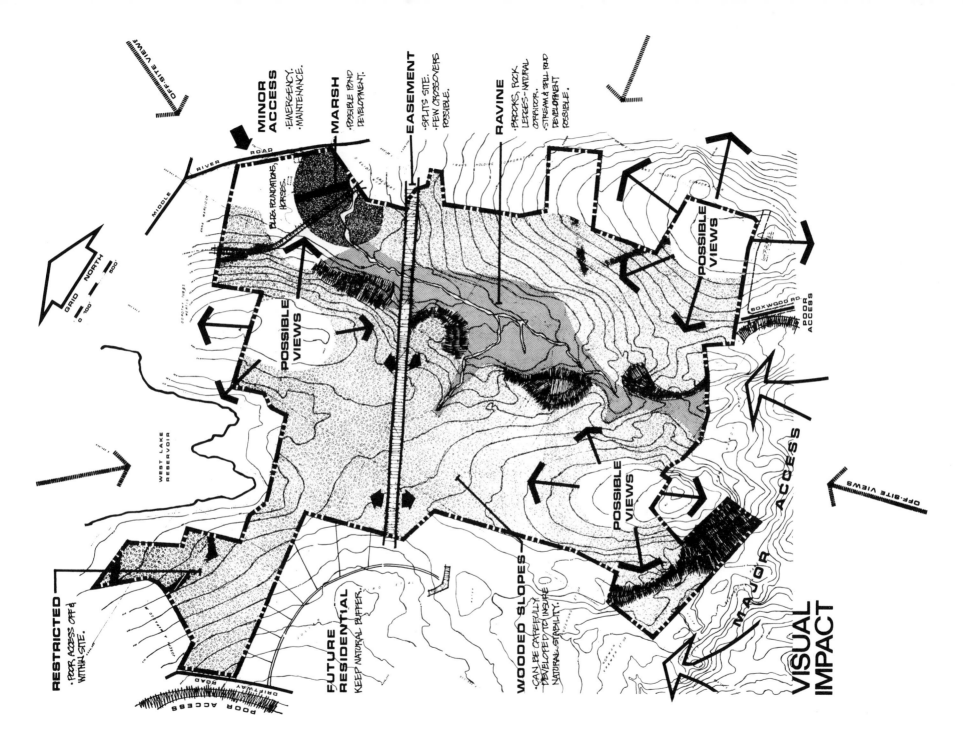

MINOR ACCESS
· EMERGENCY.
· MAINTENANCE.

MARSH
· POSSIBLE POND DEVELOPMENT.

EASEMENT
· SPLITS SITE.
· FEW CROSSOVERS POSSIBLE.

RAVINE
· BROOKS, ROCK LEDGES - NATURAL CORRIDOR.
· STREAM & SPILL POND DEVELOPMENT POSSIBLE.

OFF-SITE VIEW

POSSIBLE VIEWS

POSSIBLE VIEWS

POSSIBLE VIEWS

POSSIBLE VIEWS

GRID NORTH
0 100' 500'

WEST LAKE RESERVOIR

OFF-SITE VIEWS

POOR ACCESS

MAJOR ACCESS

VISUAL IMPACT

RESTRICTED
· POOR ACCESS OFF & WITHIN SITE.

FUTURE RESIDENTIAL
KEEP NATURAL BUFFER.

WOODED SLOPES
· CAN BE CAREFULLY DEVELOPED TO INSURE NATURAL STABILITY.

POOR ACCESS

CR3, inc., by Jeffrey A. Gebrian. Western Connecticut State College.

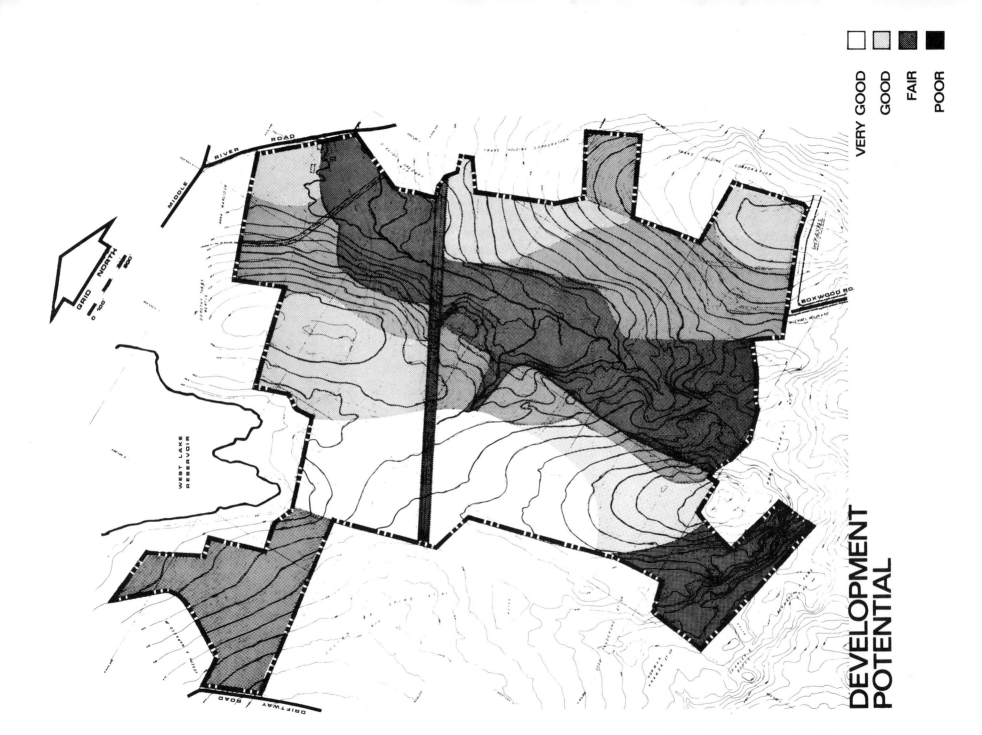

DEVELOPMENT POTENTIAL

VERY GOOD

GOOD

FAIR

POOR

CR3, inc., by Jeffrey A. Gebrian. Western Connecticut State College.

50

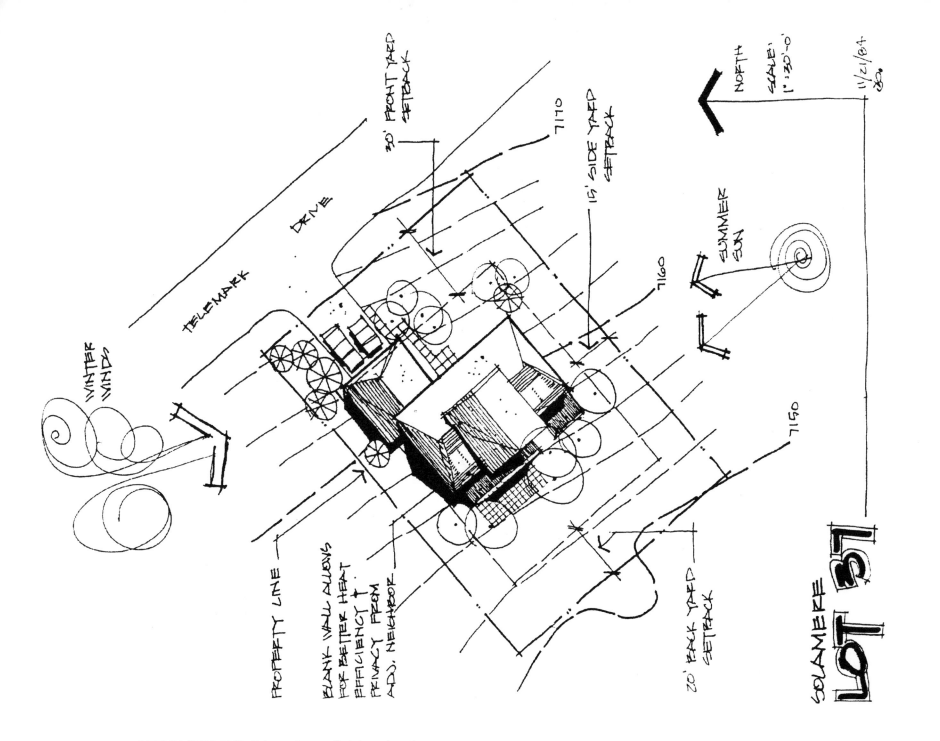

NORTH

SCALE: 1":30'-0"

11/21/84

30' FRONT YARD SETBACK

7170

15' SIDE YARD SETBACK

SUMMER SUN

7160

TELEMARK DRIVE

WINTER WINDS

7150

PROPERTY LINE

BLANK WALL ALLOWS FOR BETTER HEAT EFFICIENCY + PRIVACY FROM ADJ. NEIGHBOR

20' BACK YARD SETBACK

SOLAMERE LOT 37

JOHNN STERZER. Ink on tissue, slightly reduced.

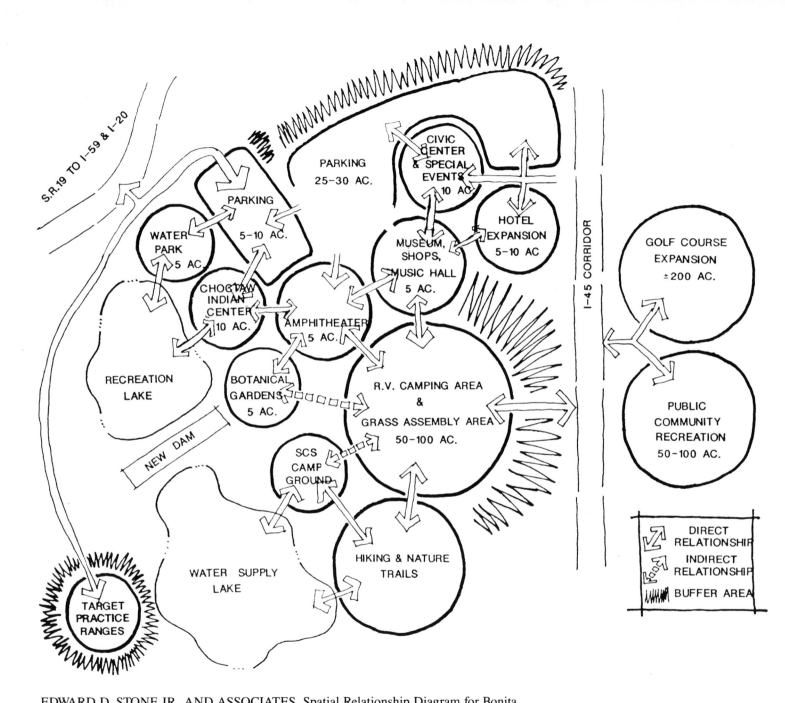

EDWARD D. STONE JR. AND ASSOCIATES. Spatial Relationship Diagram for Bonita
Lakes/Long Creek Master Plan, reduced from 17″ x 19″.

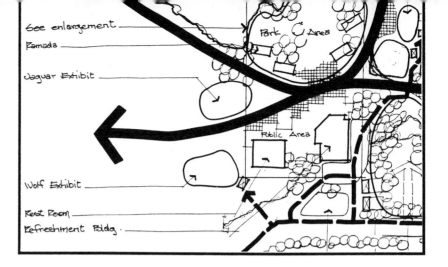

See enlargement

Ramada

Jaguar Exhibit

Wolf Exhibit

Rest Room

Refreshment Bldg.

Park Area

Public Area

DESIGN CONCEPTS

In the design process, site analysis may be followed by the preparation of design concepts. Conceptual plans often represent a broad range of ideas allowing the viewer to visualize the potential design solutions. Four different design concepts are illustrated for each of the first two projects presented in this chapter.

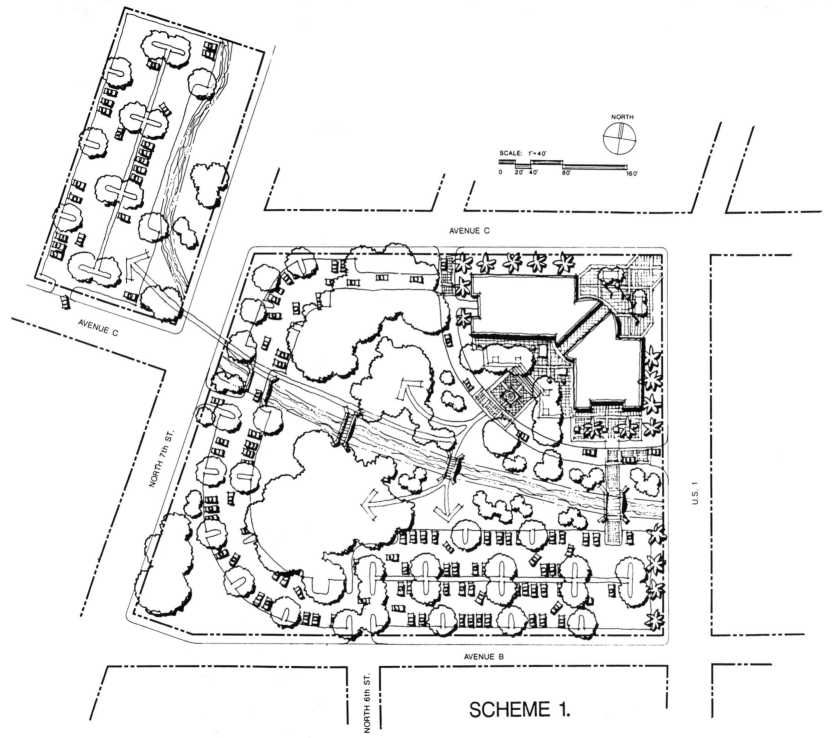

NORTH

SCALE: 1" = 40'
0   20' 40'   80'   160'

AVENUE C

AVENUE C

NORTH 7th ST.

U.S. 1

AVENUE B

NORTH 6th ST.

SCHEME 1.

54   EDWARD D. STONE JR. AND ASSOCIATES. See the site analysis plan for this same
project on page 34.

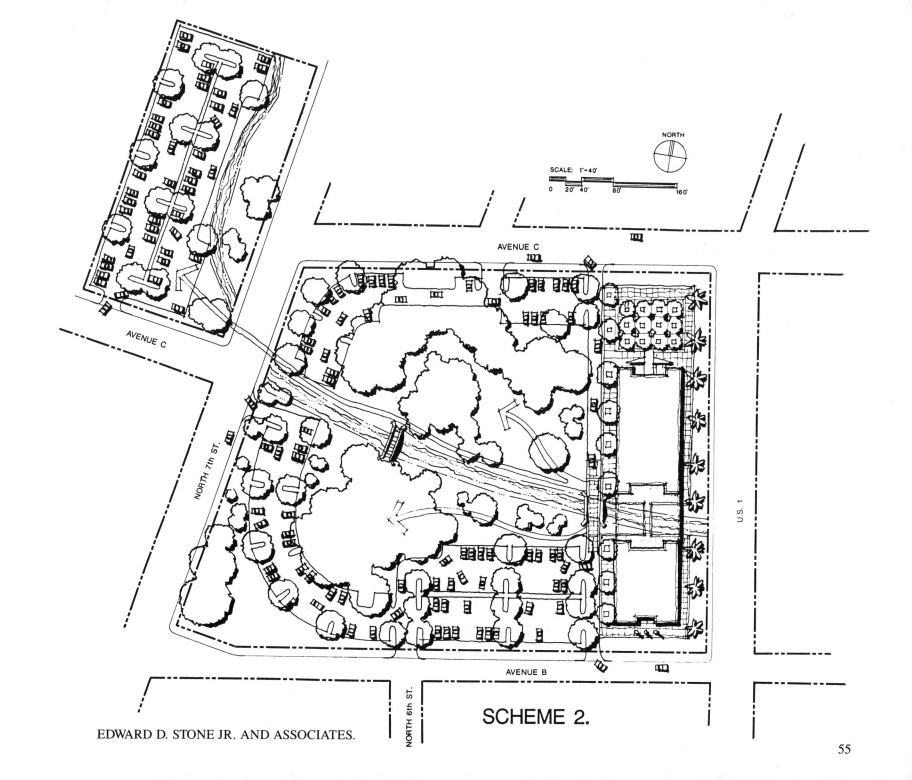

NORTH

SCALE: 1"=40'

0   20' 40'   80'   160'

AVENUE C

AVENUE C

NORTH 7th ST.

U.S. 1

AVENUE B

NORTH 6th ST.

EDWARD D. STONE JR. AND ASSOCIATES.

SCHEME 2.

55

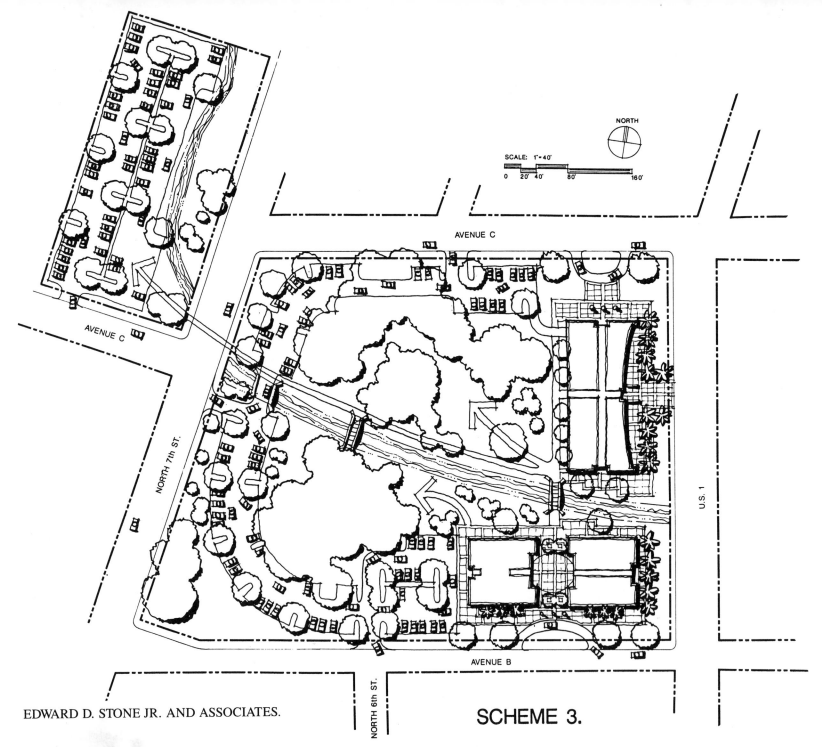

NORTH

SCALE: 1"=40'

0 20' 40'   80'   160'

AVENUE C

AVENUE C

NORTH 7th ST.

NORTH 6th ST.

AVENUE B

U.S. 1

EDWARD D. STONE JR. AND ASSOCIATES.

SCHEME 3.

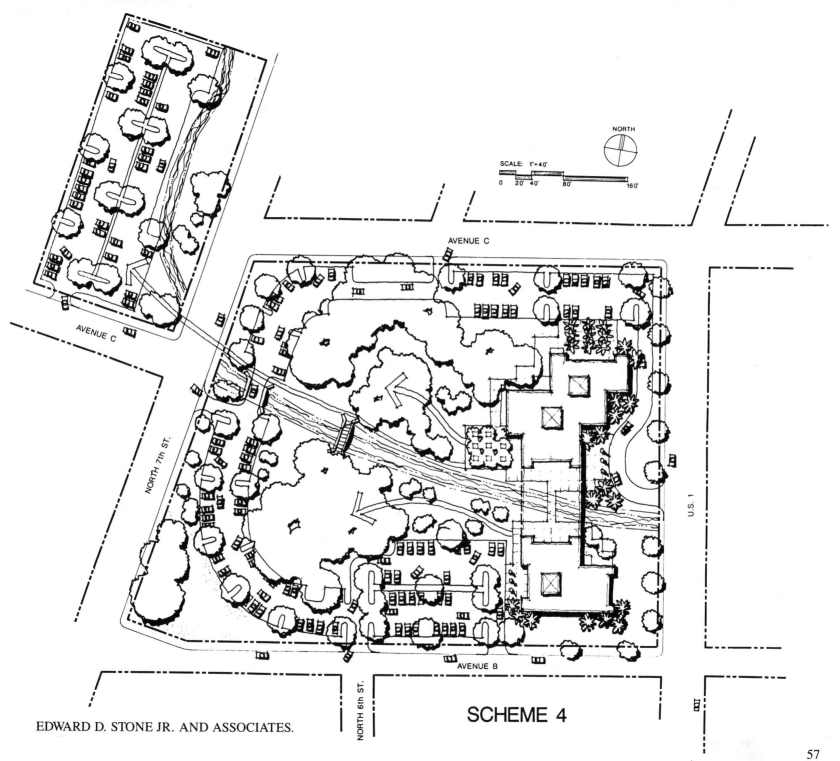

NORTH

SCALE: 1"=40'

0 20' 40' 80'   160'

AVENUE C

AVENUE C

NORTH 7th ST.

U.S. 1

AVENUE B

NORTH 6th ST.

EDWARD D. STONE JR. AND ASSOCIATES.

SCHEME 4

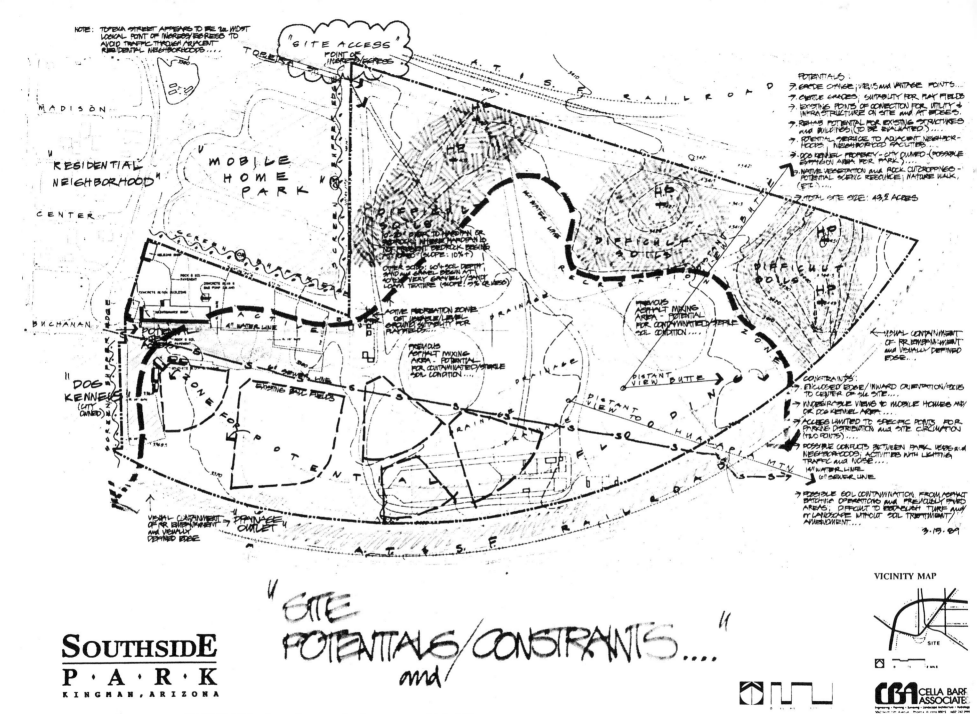

CELLA BARR ASSOCIATES. This plan relates to the four pages which follow.

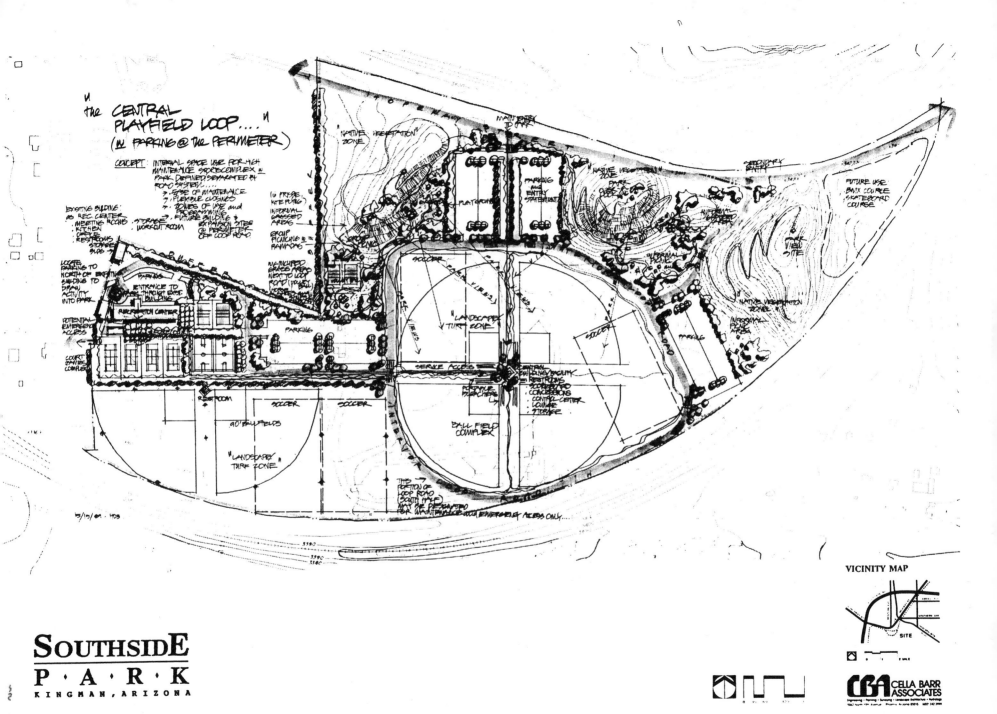

"the CENTRAL
PLAYFIELD LOOP...."
(w/ PARKING @ the PERIMETER)

SOUTHSIDE
P·A·R·K
KINGMAN, ARIZONA

CELLA BARR ASSOCIATES.

VICINITY MAP

CELLA BARR
ASSOCIATES

59

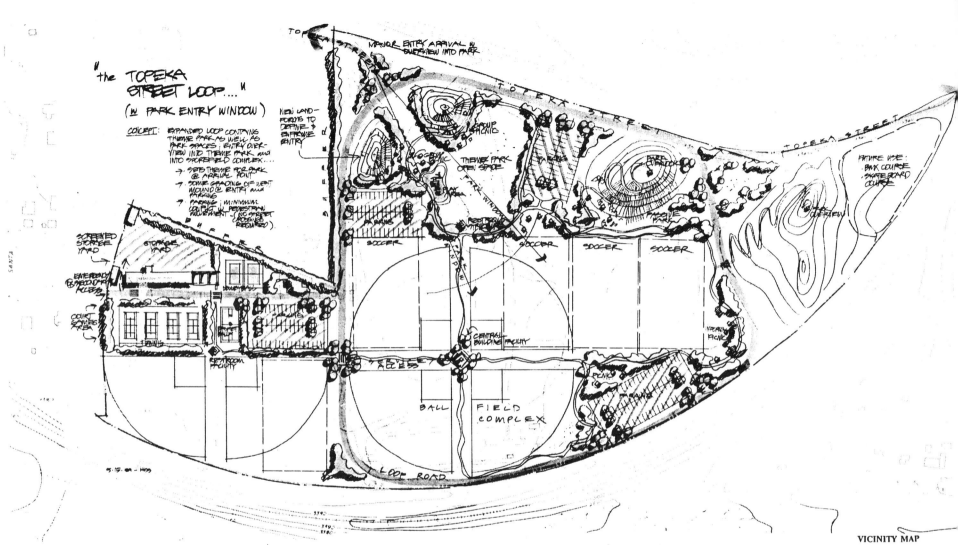

"the TOPEKA
STREET LOOP...."
(w/ PARK ENTRY WINDOW)

CONCEPT: EXPANDED LOOP CONTAINS
THEME PARK AS WELL AS
PARK SPACES; ENTRY OVER-
VIEW INTO THEME PARK AND
INTO SPORTFIELD COMPLEX....
→ SETS THEME FOR PARK
@ ARRIVAL POINT
→ SOME GRADING OF WEST
MOUND @ ENTRY AND
PARKING
→ PARKING: MINIMAL
COMPLEX W/ PEDESTRIAN
MOVEMENT (NO STREET
ACCESS REQUIRED)

SOUTHSIDE
P·A·R·K
KINGMAN, ARIZONA

CELLA BARR ASSOCIATES.

VICINITY MAP

60

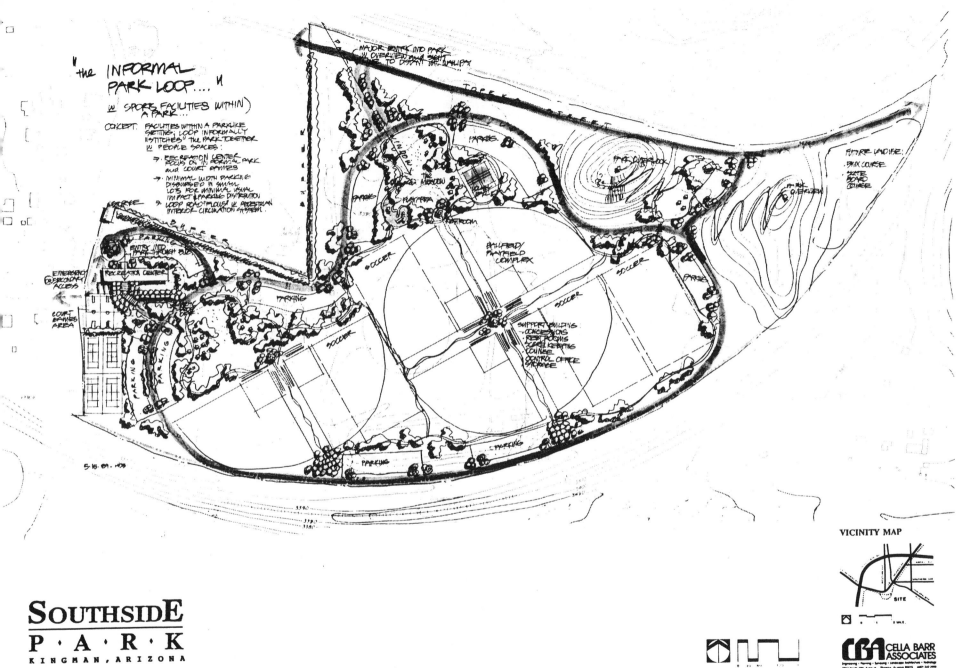

"the INFORMAL PARK LOOP.... "

(w SPORTS FACILITIES WITHIN)
A PARK...

CONCEPT: FACILITIES WITHIN A PARKLIKE
SETTING; LOOP INFORMALLY
"STITCHES" THE PARK TOGETHER
W PEOPLE SPACES:

→ RECREATION CENTER
FOCUS ON 'IN FORMAL PARK
AND COURT GAMES

→ MINIMAL WIDTH PARKLINE
DISPERSED IN SMALL
LOTS FOR MINIMAL VISUAL
IMPACT PARKING DISTRIBUTION

→ LOOP ROAD "PLOWS" W PEDESTRIAN
INTERIOR CIRCULATION SYSTEM

MAJOR ENTRY INTO PARK
W OVERVIEW DOWN SIGHT
LINE TO DISTANT VIEW

PARKING

PARK OVERLOOK

FUTURE LAND USE:
BMX COURSE
SKATE
BOARD
COURSE

PARK
OVERVIEW

PARKING

SOCCER

BALLFIELD
PLAYFIELD
COMPLEX

SOCCER

PARKING

SOCCER

SOCCER

SUPPORT BUILDING:
CONCESSIONS
RESTROOMS
SCORE KEEPING
LOUNGE
CONTROL OFFICE
STORAGE

SERVICE

ENTRY INTO
PARK THROUGH

RECREATION CENTER

EMERGENCY
SECONDARY
ACCESS

COURT
GAMES
AREA

PARKING

PARKING

PARKING

RESTROOM

PLAYAREA

THE MEADOW

5.16.89

PARKING

PARKING

VICINITY MAP

SITE

SOUTHSIDE
P·A·R·K
KINGMAN, ARIZONA

CELLA BARR ASSOCIATES.

CELLA BARR
ASSOCIATES

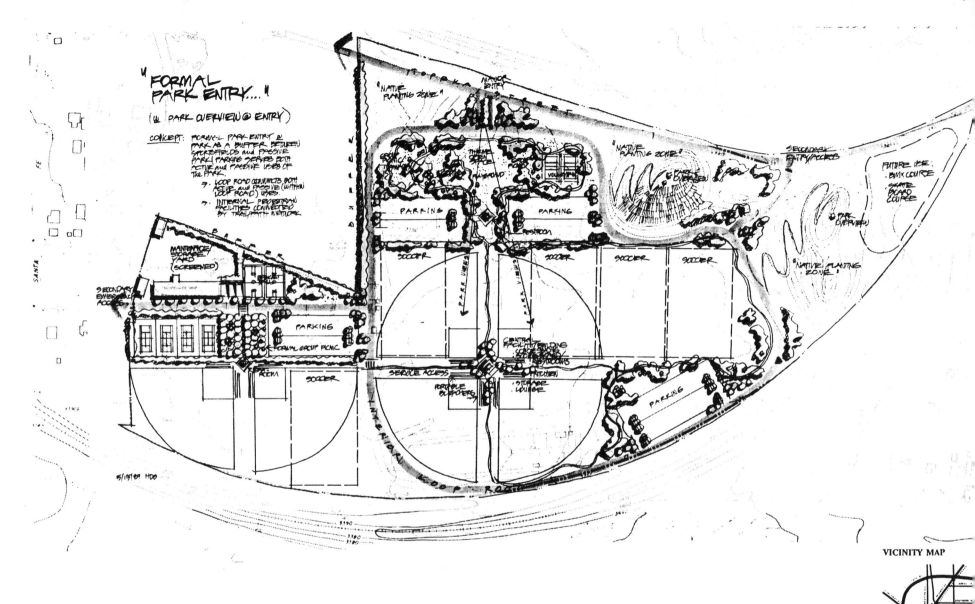

"FORMAL PARK ENTRY..."

(w PARK OVERVIEW @ ENTRY)

CONCEPT: FORMAL PARK ENTRY @ PARK AS A BUFFER BETWEEN SPORTSFIELDS AND PASSIVE PARK; PARKING SERVES BOTH ACTIVE AND PASSIVE USERS OF THE PARK.

→ LOOP ROAD CONNECTS BOTH ACTIVE AND PASSIVE (WITHIN LOOP ROAD) USERS.

→ INTERNAL PEDESTRIAN FACILITIES CONNECTED BY TRAIL/PATH NETWORK

SOUTHSIDE
P·A·R·K
KINGMAN, ARIZONA

CELLA BARR ASSOCIATES.

VICINITY MAP

62

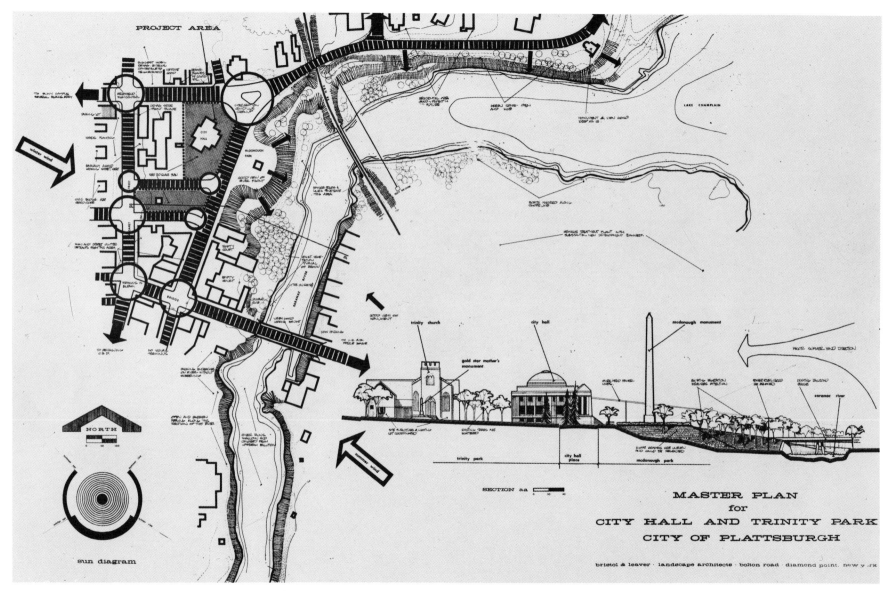

PROJECT AREA

LAKE CHAMPLAIN

NORTH

sun diagram

SECTION aa

trinity church

gold star mother's
monument

city hall

mcdonough monument

trinity park

city hall
place

mcdonough park

saranac river

MASTER PLAN
for
CITY HALL AND TRINITY PARK
CITY OF PLATTSBURGH

bristol & leaver · landscape architects · bolton road · diamond point, new york

THE SARATOGA ASSOCIATES.

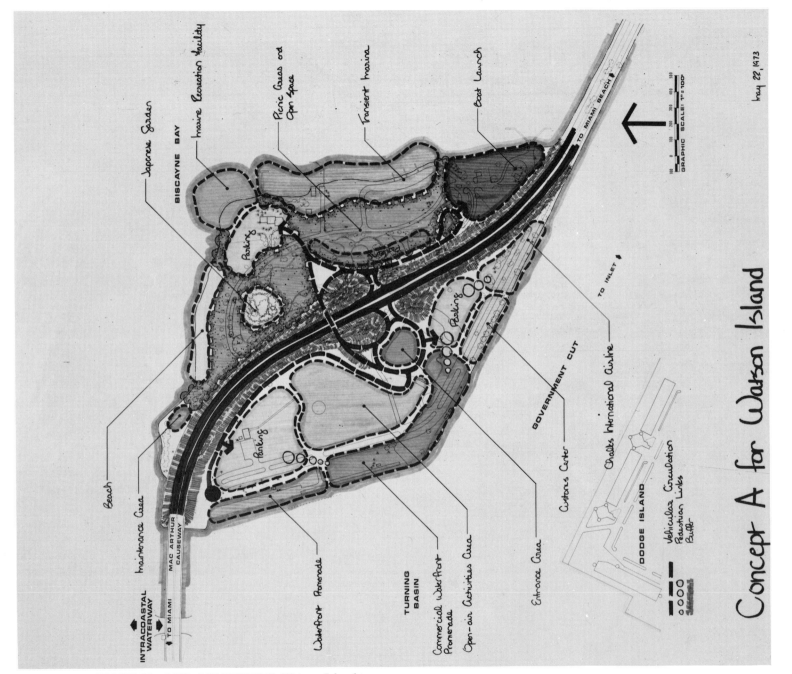

Japanese Garden

BISCAYNE BAY

Marine Recreation facility

Picnic Areas and Open Space

Transient Marina

Boat Launch

Parking

Parking

Parking

TO MIAMI BEACH

TO INLET

GOVERNMENT CUT

Challes International Airline

Customs Center

Entrance Area

Open-air Activities Area

Commercial Waterfront Promenade

TURNING BASIN

Waterfront Promenade

Parking

Beach

Maintenance Area

MAC ARTHUR CAUSEWAY

TO MIAMI

INTRACOASTAL WATERWAY

GRAPHIC SCALE: 1":100'

May 22, 1973

Concept A for Watson Island

DODGE ISLAND

Vehicular Circulation
Pedestrian Links
Buffer

EDWARD D. STONE JR. AND ASSOCIATES. Watson Island.

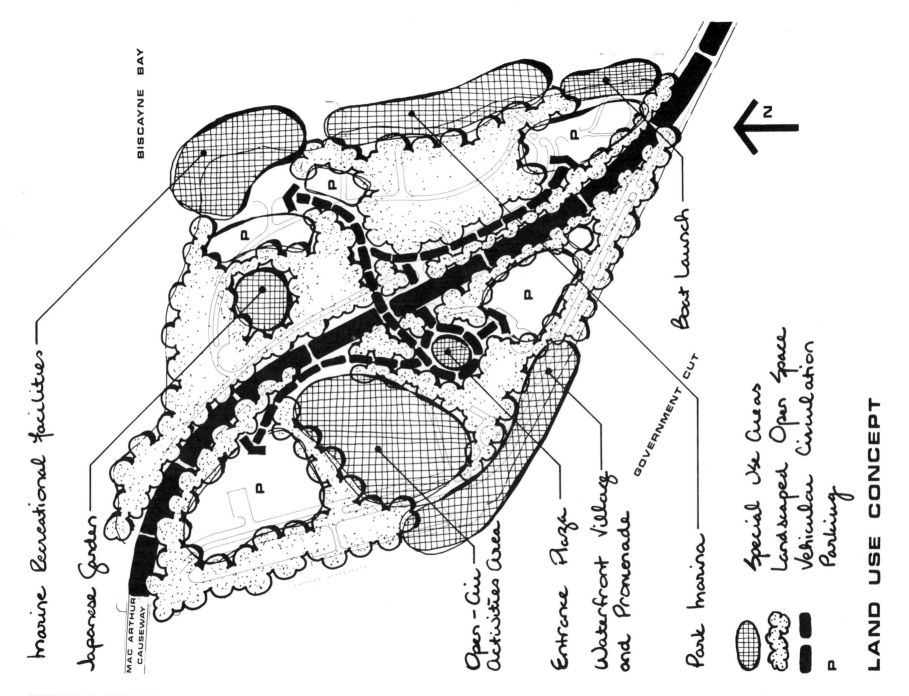

BISCAYNE BAY

Marine Recreational Facilities

Japanese Garden

MAC ARTHUR CAUSEWAY

Open-Air Activities Area

Entrance Plaza

Waterfront Village and Promenade

Park Marina

GOVERNMENT CUT

Boat Launch

Special Use Areas

Landscaped Open Space

Vehicular Circulation

P Parking

N

LAND USE CONCEPT

EDWARD D. STONE JR. AND ASSOCIATES. Watson Island.

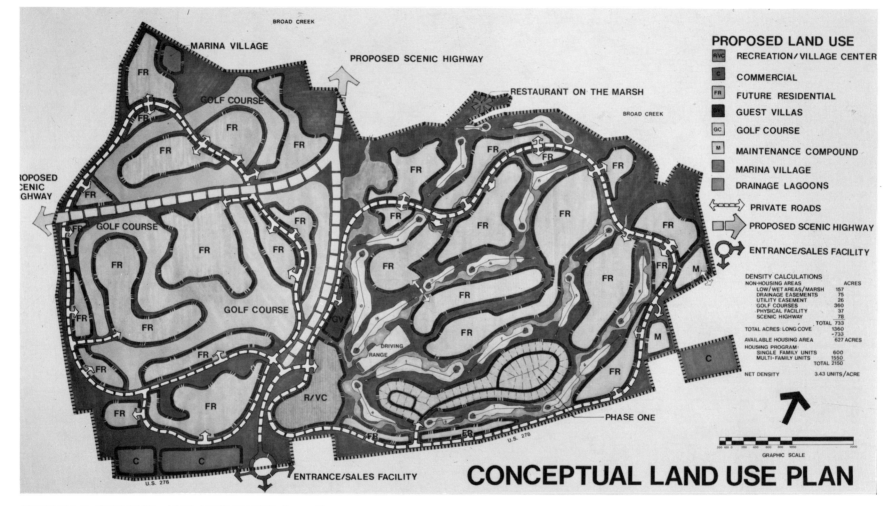

PROPOSED LAND USE

RVC RECREATION/VILLAGE CENTER
C COMMERCIAL
FR FUTURE RESIDENTIAL
GV GUEST VILLAS
GC GOLF COURSE
M MAINTENANCE COMPOUND
MARINA VILLAGE
DRAINAGE LAGOONS
PRIVATE ROADS
PROPOSED SCENIC HIGHWAY
ENTRANCE/SALES FACILITY

DENSITY CALCULATIONS
NON-HOUSING AREAS   ACRES
    LOW/WET AREAS/MARSH   157
    DRAINAGE EASEMENTS   75
    UTILITY EASEMENT   26
    GOLF COURSES   360
    PHYSICAL FACILITY   37
    SCENIC HIGHWAY   78
                            TOTAL 733
TOTAL ACRES: LONG COVE   1360
                                          -733
AVAILABLE HOUSING AREA   627 ACRES
HOUSING PROGRAM:
    SINGLE FAMILY UNITS   600
    MULTI-FAMILY UNITS   1550
                            TOTAL 2150

NET DENSITY   3.43 UNITS/ACRE

BROAD CREEK
MARINA VILLAGE
PROPOSED SCENIC HIGHWAY
RESTAURANT ON THE MARSH
BROAD CREEK
PROPOSED SCENIC HIGHWAY
GOLF COURSE
GOLF COURSE
GOLF COURSE
DRIVING RANGE
R/VC
PHASE ONE
U.S. 278
ENTRANCE/SALES FACILITY
U.S. 278

GRAPHIC SCALE

CONCEPTUAL LAND USE PLAN

EDWARD D. STONE JR. AND ASSOCIATES. Long Cove.

66

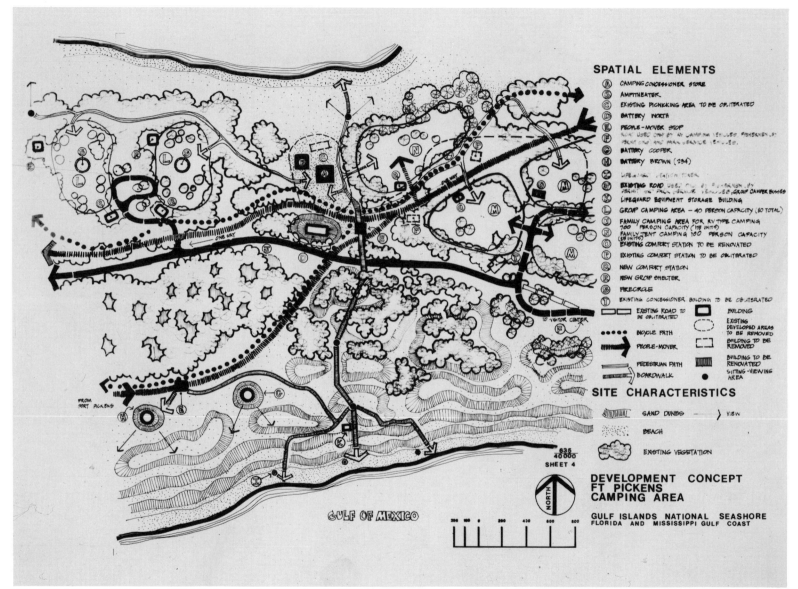

SPATIAL ELEMENTS

- (A) CAMPING CONCESSIONER STORE
- (B) AMPITHEATER
- (C) EXISTING PICNICKING AREA TO BE OBLITERATED
- (D) BATTERY NORTH
- (E) PEOPLE-MOVER STOP
  - ALSO USED ONLY BY CAMPING VEHICLES, FISHERMEN, BY PERMIT ONLY AND PARK SERVICE VEHICLES.
- (F) BATTERY COOPER
- (G) BATTERY BROWN (234)
- (H) LIFEGUARD STATION TOWER
- (I) EXISTING ROAD USED MO. BY PASSENGER BY PERMIT INC PARK SERVICE VEHICLES, GROUP CAMPER BUSSES
- (J) LIFEGUARD EQUIPMENT STORAGE BUILDING
- (K) GROUP CAMPING AREA — 40 PERSON CAPACITY (80 TOTAL)
- (L) FAMILY CAMPING AREA FOR RV TYPE CAMPING 700 PERSON CAPACITY (175 UNITS)
- (M) FAMILY TENT CAMPING 100 PERSON CAPACITY (25 UNITS)
- (N) EXISTING COMFORT STATION TO BE RENOVATED
- (O) EXISTING COMFORT STATION TO BE OBLITERATED
- (P) NEW COMFORT STATION
- (Q) NEW GROUP SHELTER
- (R) FIRECIRCLE
- (T) EXISTING CONCESSIONER BUILDING TO BE OBLITERATED

▭▭ EXISTING ROAD TO BE OBLITERATED	▭ BUILDING
•••• BICYCLE PATH	⌁ EXISTING DEVELOPED AREAS TO BE REMOVED
⟩⟩⟩ PEOPLE-MOVER	⌐ BUILDING TO BE REMOVED
⟩ PEDESTRIAN PATH	▦ BUILDING TO BE RENOVATED
⟩ BOARDWALK	• SITTING-VIEWING AREA

SITE CHARACTERISTICS

- ⟩ SAND DUNES — ⟩ VIEW
- BEACH
- EXISTING VEGETATION

635
40000
SHEET 4

DEVELOPMENT CONCEPT
FT PICKENS
CAMPING AREA

GULF ISLANDS NATIONAL SEASHORE
FLORIDA AND MISSISSIPPI GULF COAST

ONE WAY

TO VISITOR CENTER

FROM FORT PICKENS

GULF OF MEXICO

NORTH

200 100 0   200   400   600   800

REYNOLDS, SMITH AND HILLS. In consultation with the National Park Service. Gulf
Islands National Seashore.

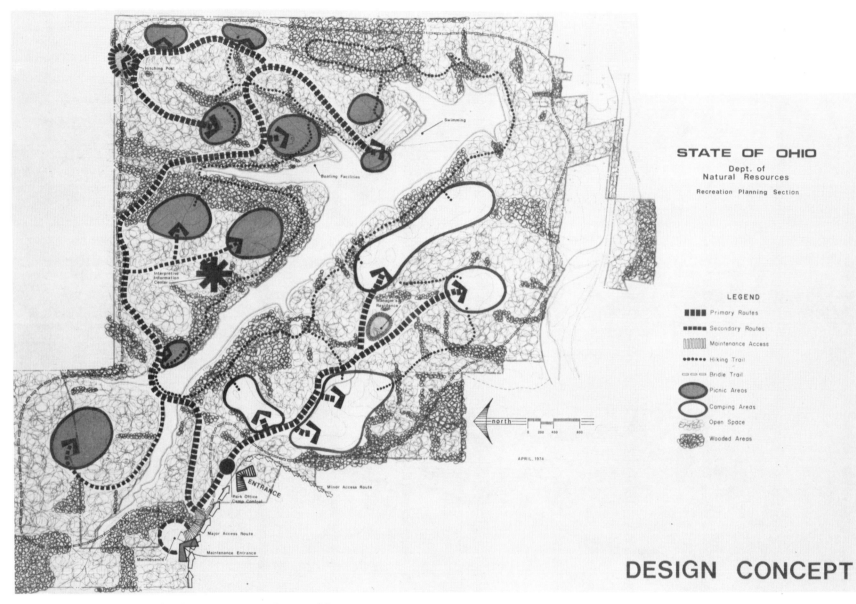

Swimming

Hitching Post

Boating Facilities

Interpretive
Information
Center

Manager's
Residence

ENTRANCE

Park Office
Camp Control

Minor Access Route

Major Access Route

Maintenance Entrance

Maintenance

north

0   200   400   800

APRIL, 1974

STATE OF OHIO
Dept. of
Natural Resources

Recreation Planning Section

LEGEND

Primary Routes
Secondary Routes
Maintenance Access
Hiking Trail
Bridle Trail
Picnic Areas
Camping Areas
Open Space
Wooded Areas

DESIGN CONCEPT

Plans contracted by State of Ohio, Department of Natural Resources.

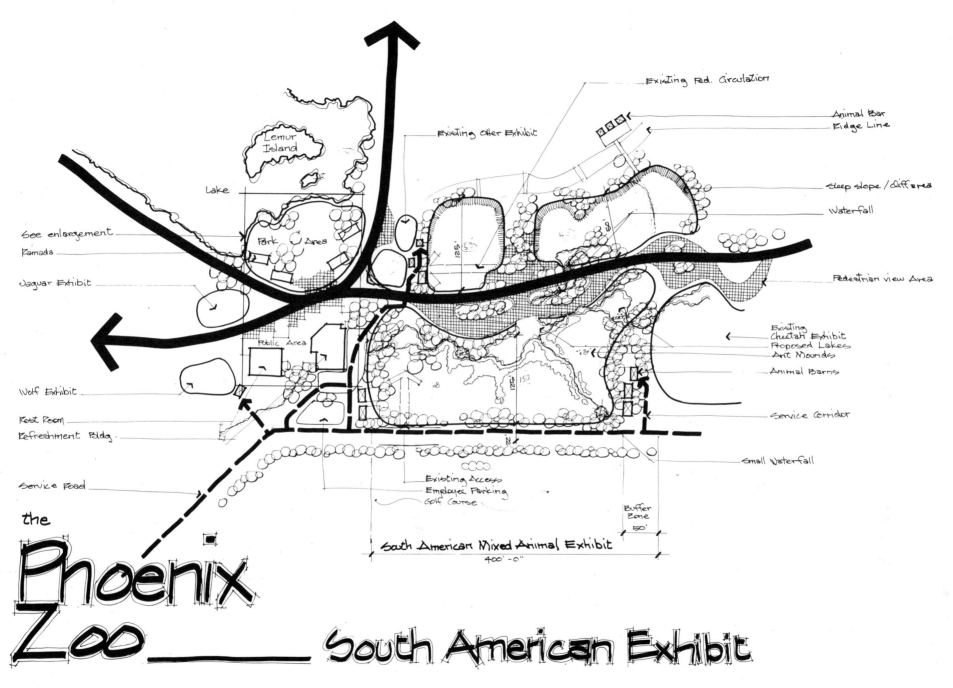

Existing Ped. Circulation

Animal Bar
Ridge Line

Steep slope / Cliff area

Waterfall

Existing Otter Exhibit

Lemur
Island

Lake

See enlargement

Ramada

Jaguar Exhibit

Park Area

Public Area

Wolf Exhibit

Rest Room

Refreshment Bldg.

Service Road

Pedestrian view Area

Existing
Cheetah Exhibit
Proposed Lakes
Ant Mounds

Animal Barns

Service Corridor

Small Waterfall

Existing Access
Employee Parking
Golf Course

Buffer
Zone
50'

South American Mixed Animal Exhibit
400'-0"

the

Phoenix Zoo _____ South American Exhibit

TALIESIN/ALLEN GROSS/JOHN STERZER. Ink on sketching tissue, reduced from
24" x 36".

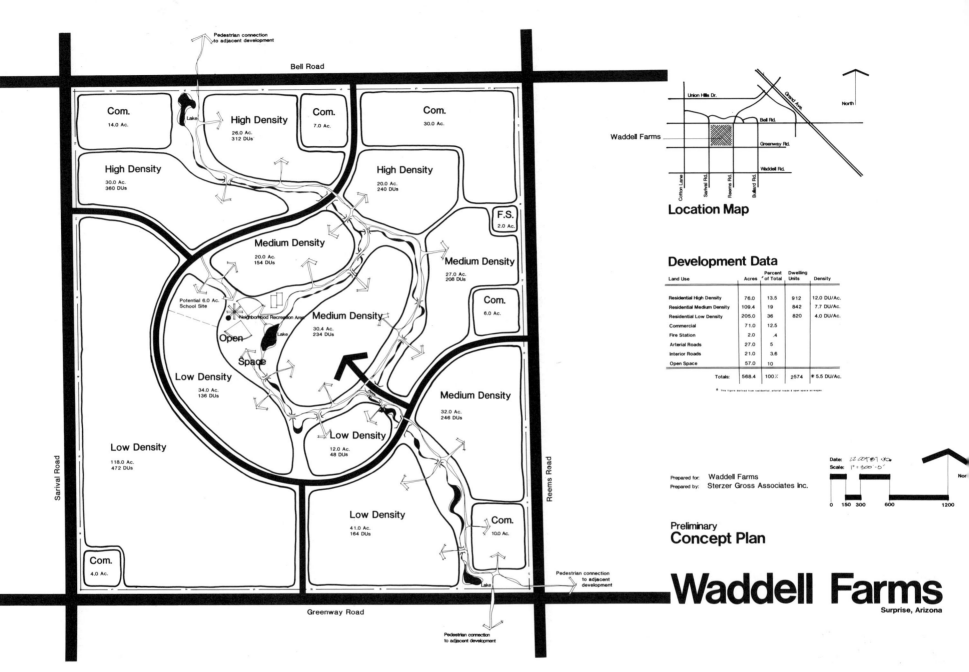

Location Map

- Union Hills Dr.
- Bell Rd.
- Greenway Rd.
- Waddell Rd.
- Grand Ave.
- Cotton Lane
- Sarival Rd.
- Reems Rd.
- Bullard Rd.
- Waddell Farms
- North

Development Data

Land Use	Acres	Percent of Total	Dwelling Units	Density
Residential High Density	76.0	13.5	912	12.0 DU/Ac.
Residential Medium Density	109.4	19	842	7.7 DU/Ac.
Residential Low Density	205.0	36	820	4.0 DU/Ac.
Commercial	71.0	12.5		
Fire Station	2.0	.4		
Arterial Roads	27.0	5		
Interior Roads	21.0	3.6		
Open Space	57.0	10		
Totals:	568.4	100%	2574	* 5.5 DU/Ac.

* This figure derived from residential, interior roads & open space acreages

Prepared for: Waddell Farms
Prepared by: Sterzer Gross Associates Inc.

Date: 22 OCT 87
Scale: 1" = 300'-0"

0 150 300 600 1200

North

Preliminary
Concept Plan

Waddell Farms
Surprise, Arizona

Within the concept plan (map labels):

Bell Road

Pedestrian connection to adjacent development

Com. 14.0 Ac.

High Density 26.0 Ac. 312 DUs

Com. 7.0 Ac.

Com. 30.0 Ac.

Lake

High Density 30.0 Ac. 360 DUs

High Density 20.0 Ac. 240 DUs

F.S. 2.0 Ac.

Medium Density 20.0 Ac. 154 DUs

Medium Density 27.0 Ac. 208 DUs

Com. 6.0 Ac.

Potential 6.0 Ac. School Site

Neighborhood Recreation Area

Medium Density 30.4 Ac. 234 DUs

Open Space

Lake

Low Density 34.0 Ac. 136 DUs

Low Density 12.0 Ac. 48 DUs

Medium Density 32.0 Ac. 246 DUs

Low Density 118.0 Ac. 472 DUs

Sarival Road

Reems Road

Low Density 41.0 Ac. 164 DUs

Com. 10.0 Ac.

Com. 4.0 Ac.

Lake

Pedestrian connection to adjacent development

Greenway Road

Pedestrian connection to adjacent development

STERZER GROSS ASSOCIATES. Ink and black tape on mylar, reduced from 24" x 36".

MASTER PLANS

The master plans represented in this chapter range in size from one-acre residential sites to master planned communities of several thousand acres. Examples featuring community parks, office parks, school campuses, hospitals, churches, resorts, and industrial complexes are illustrated. Chapter six will contain color examples of master plan graphics.

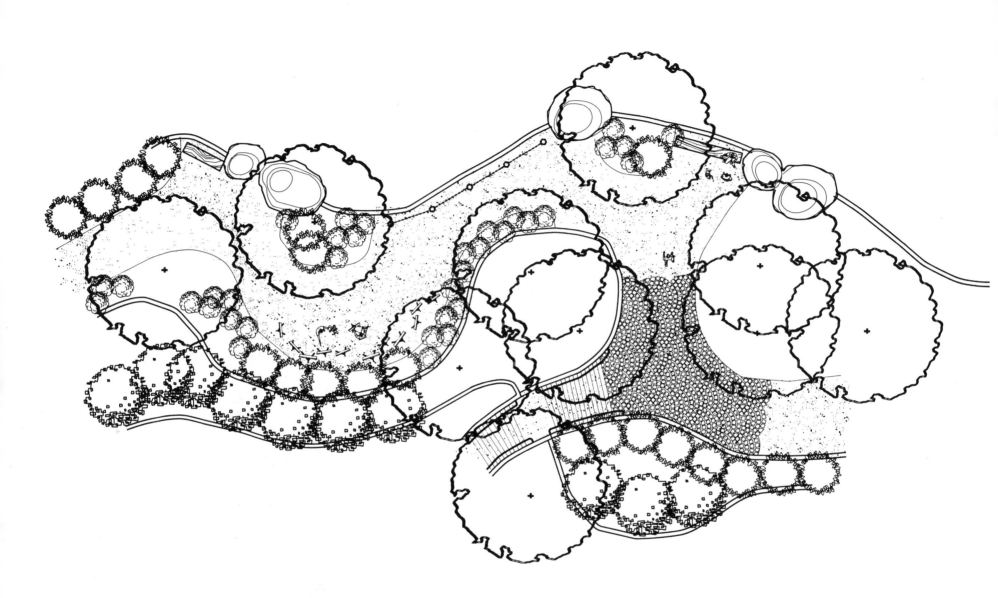

GROVES AND ASSOCIATES by Walter H. Heard. A drawing prepared by CAD, reduced
from 13″ x 23″.

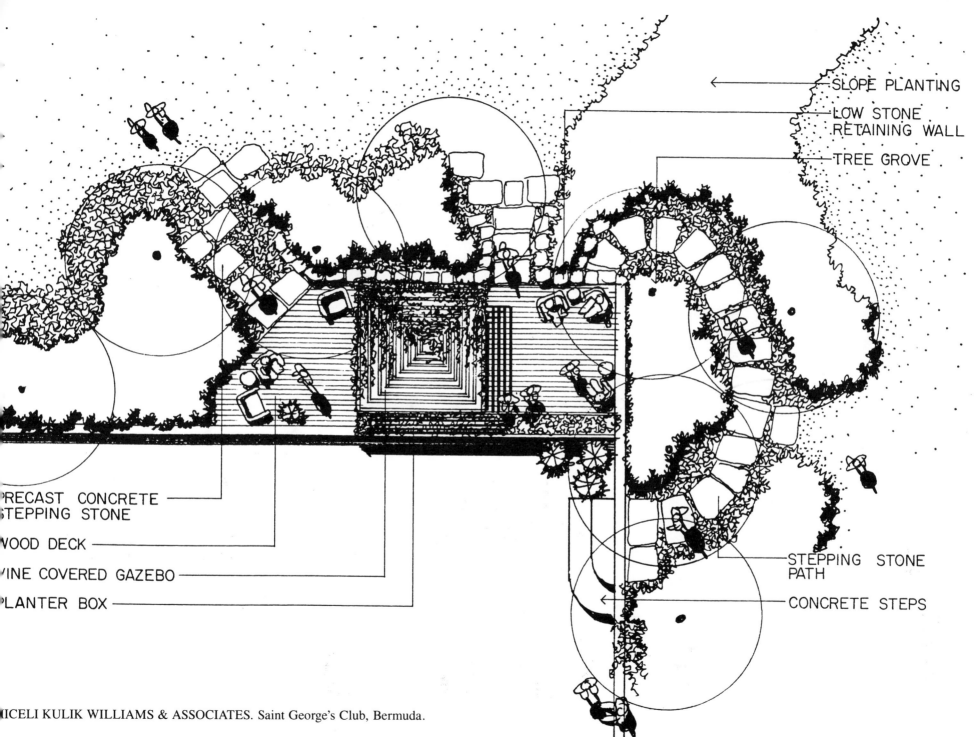

SLOPE PLANTING

LOW STONE
RETAINING WALL

TREE GROVE

PRECAST CONCRETE
STEPPING STONE

WOOD DECK

VINE COVERED GAZEBO

PLANTER BOX

STEPPING STONE
PATH

CONCRETE STEPS

MICELI KULIK WILLIAMS & ASSOCIATES. Saint George's Club, Bermuda.

underground parking

underground parking

restaurants

lodging

lodging

lodging

Amenities:

Adolph's Restaurant
Hotel Restaurant
Fondue Restaurant
Pool /Plaza Area
Lounge/Bar
Lodge

A Swiss Lodge
featuring Adolph's Restaurant

principal designer: J.J. Johnson & Assoc.
architect: Brighton / Walker Assoc.

north
date:

J. J. JOHNSON & ASSOCIATES/JOHN STERZER. Reduced from 24″ x 36″.

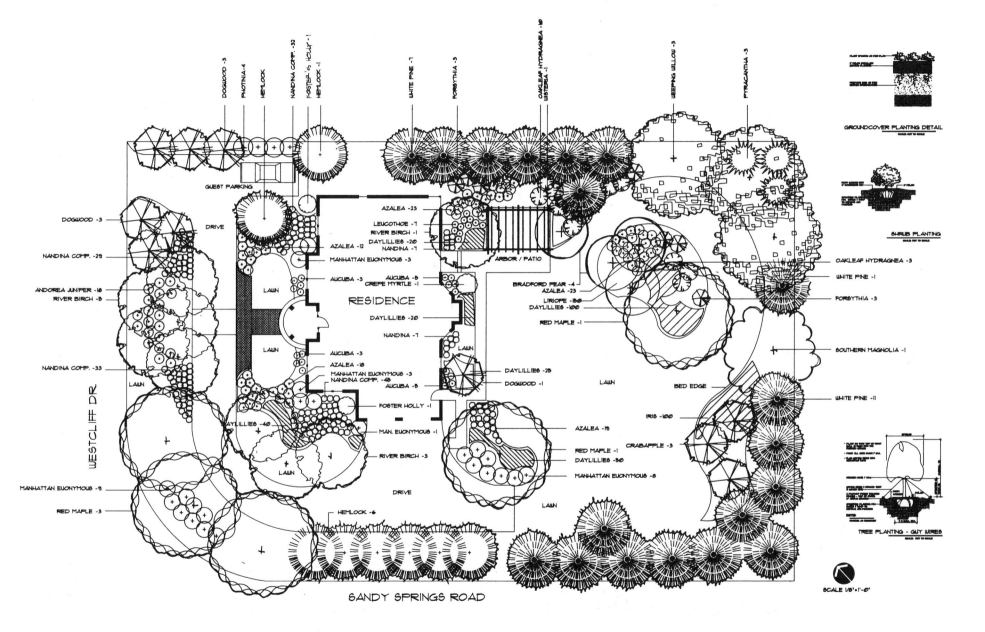

KENDALL-VERSON/LAND DESIGN GROUP. A drawing prepared by CAD. Reduced from 24″ x 36″.

77

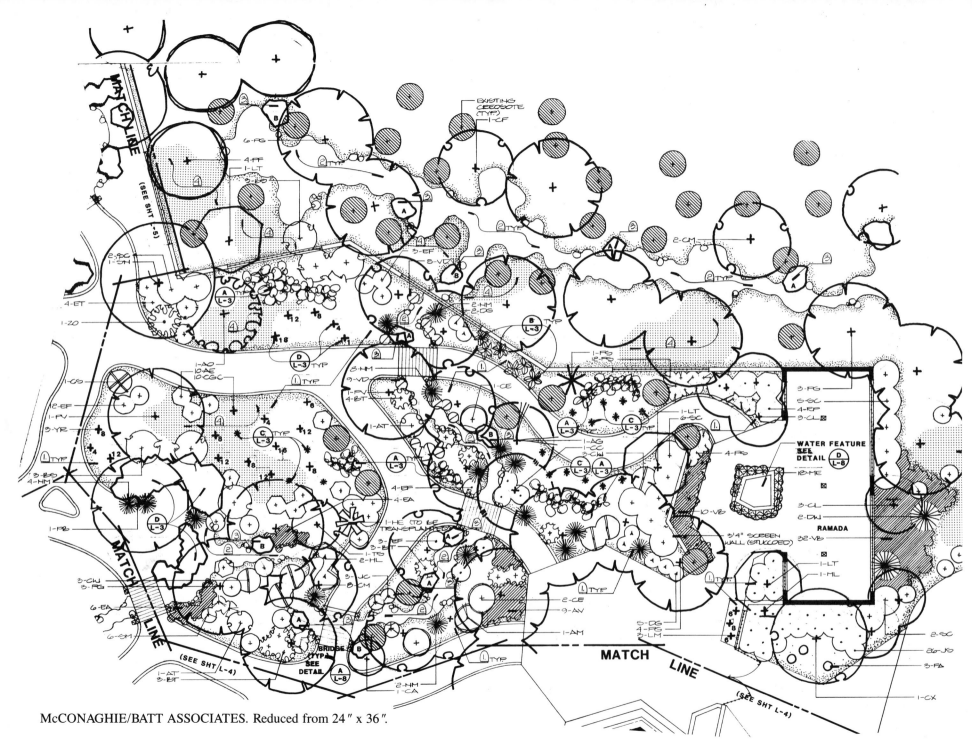

McCONAGHIE/BATT ASSOCIATES. Reduced from 24" x 36".

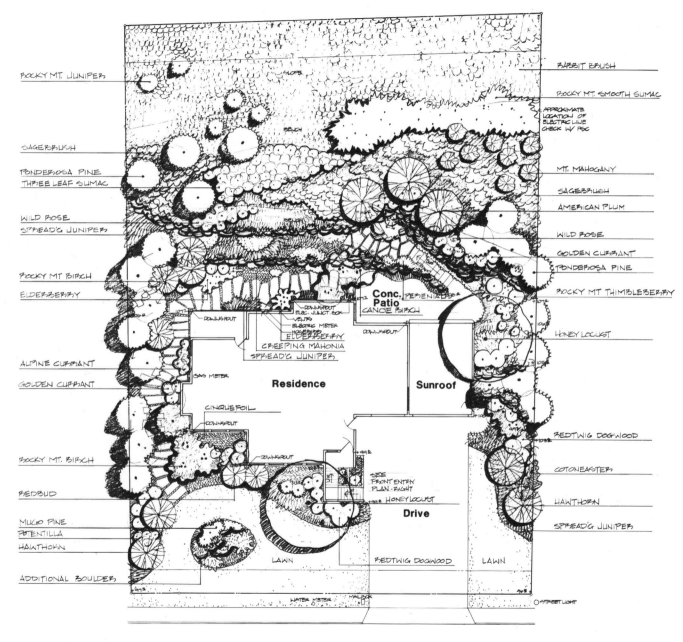

ROCKY MT. JUNIPER

SAGEBRUSH

PONDEROSA PINE
THREE LEAF SUMAC

WILD ROSE
SPREAD'G JUNIPER

ROCKY MT. BIRCH
ELDERBERRY

ALPINE CURRANT
GOLDEN CURRANT

ROCKY MT. BIRCH

REDBUD

MUGO PINE
POTENTILLA
HAWTHORN

ADDITIONAL BOULDER

RABBIT BRUSH

ROCKY MT. SMOOTH SUMAC

APPROXIMATE
LOCATION OF
ELECTRIC LINE
CHECK W/ PSC

MT. MAHOGANY

SAGEBRUSH
AMERICAN PLUM

WILD ROSE

GOLDEN CURRANT
PONDEROSA PINE

ROCKY MT THIMBLEBERRY

HONEY LOCUST

REDTWIG DOGWOOD

COTONEASTER

HAWTHORN

SPREAD'G JUNIPER

SLOPE
BIRCH
BENCH
PERENNIALS

**Conc.
Patio**
CANOE BIRCH

DOWNSPOUT
ELEC. JUNCT. BOX
VENTS
ELECTRIC METER
HOSEBIBB
ELDERBERRY
CREEPING MAHONIA
SPREAD'G JUNIPER

DOWNSPOUT

DOWNSPOUT

Residence

GAS METER

CINQUEFOIL

DOWNSPOUT

DOWNSPOUT

Sunroof

SEE
FRONT ENTRY
PLAN - RIGHT
HONEY LOCUST

Drive

LAWN

REDTWIG DOGWOOD

LAWN

WATER METER
MAILBOX
STREET LIGHT

West 70th Drive

EDAW inc. by Herb Schaal. Pencil on mylar, reduced from 24″ x 36″.

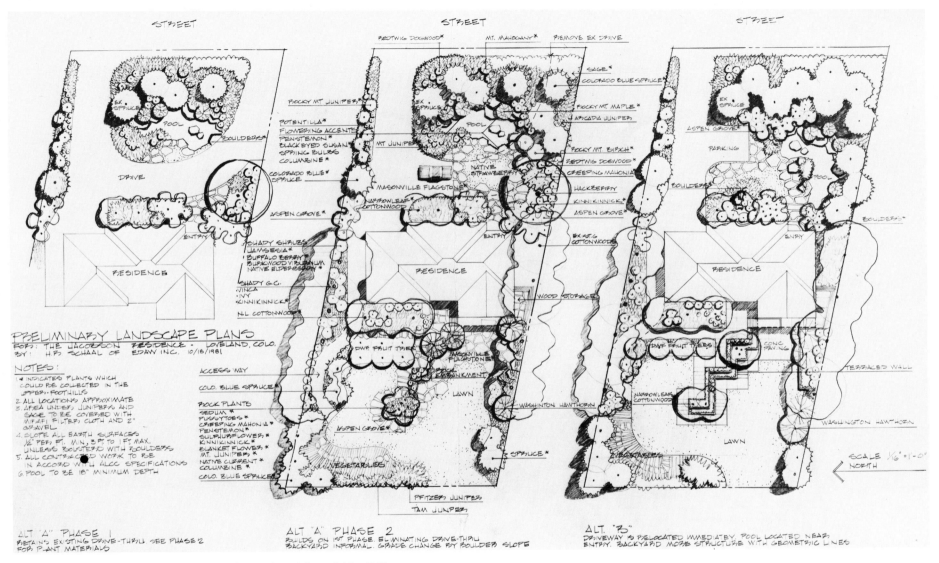

STREET   STREET   STREET

PRELIMINARY LANDSCAPE PLANS
FOR: THE JACOBSON RESIDENCE - LOVELAND, COLO.
BY: H.B. SCHAAL OF EDAW INC. 10/18/1981

NOTES:
1. * INDICATES PLANTS WHICH
   COULD BE COLLECTED IN THE
   UPPER FOOTHILLS
2. ALL LOCATIONS APPROXIMATE
3. AREA UNDER JUNIPERS AND
   SAGE TO BE COVERED WITH
   MIRAFI FILTER CLOTH AND 2"
   GRAVEL
4. SLOPE ALL EARTH SURFACES
   1/2" PER FT. MIN., 3FT. TO 1 FT. MAX.
   UNLESS BOLSTERED WITH BOULDERS
5. ALL CONTRACTED WORK TO BE
   IN ACCORD WITH ALCC SPECIFICATIONS
6. POOL TO BE 18" MINIMUM DEPTH

ALT "A" PHASE 1
RETAINS EXISTING DRIVE-THRU. SEE PHASE 2
FOR PLANT MATERIALS

ALT "A" PHASE 2
BUILDS ON 1ST PHASE. ELIMINATING DRIVE-THRU
BACKYARD INFORMAL. GRADE CHANGE BY BOULDER SLOPE

ALT "B"
DRIVEWAY IS RELOCATED IMMEDIATELY. POOL LOCATED NEAR
ENTRY. BACKYARD MORE STRUCTURED WITH GEOMETRIC LINES

EDAW inc. by Herb Schaal. Pencil on mylar, reduced from 24″ x 36″.

LANDSCAPE PLAN

Carl and Jeanne Judson Residence
Livermore, Colorado

EDAW inc.

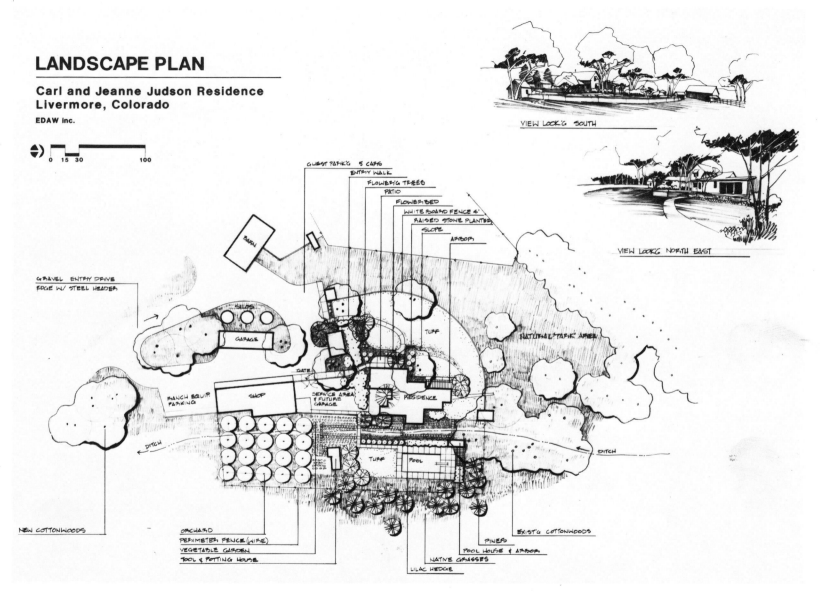

0 15 30   100

GUEST PARK'G 5 CARS
ENTRY WALK
FLOWER'G TREES
PATIO
FLOWERBED
WHITE BOARD FENCE 4'
RAISED STONE PLANTER
SLOPE
ARBOR

GRAVEL ENTRY DRIVE
EDGE W/ STEEL HEADER

BARN

SILOS

GARAGE

TURF

NATURAL "PARK" AREA

GATE

RANCH EQUIP PARKING

SHOP

SERVICE AREA & FUTURE GARAGE

RESIDENCE

DITCH

DITCH

TURF

POOL

NEW COTTONWOODS

ORCHARD
PERIMETER FENCE (WIRE)
VEGETABLE GARDEN
TOOL & POTTING HOUSE

LILAC HEDGE

NATIVE GRASSES

PINES

POOL HOUSE & ARBOR

EXIST'G COTTONWOODS

VIEW LOOK'G SOUTH

VIEW LOOK'G NORTH EAST

EDAW inc. by Herb Schaal. Pencil on mylar, reduced from 24″ x 36″.

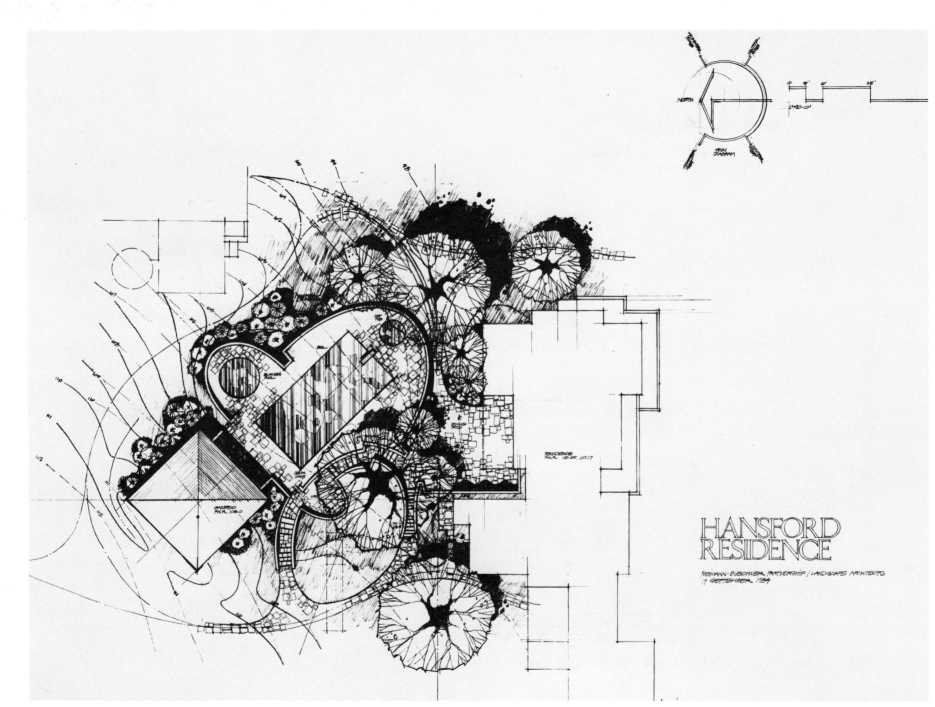

HANSFORD
RESIDENCE

REIMANN-BUECHNER PARTNERSHIP.

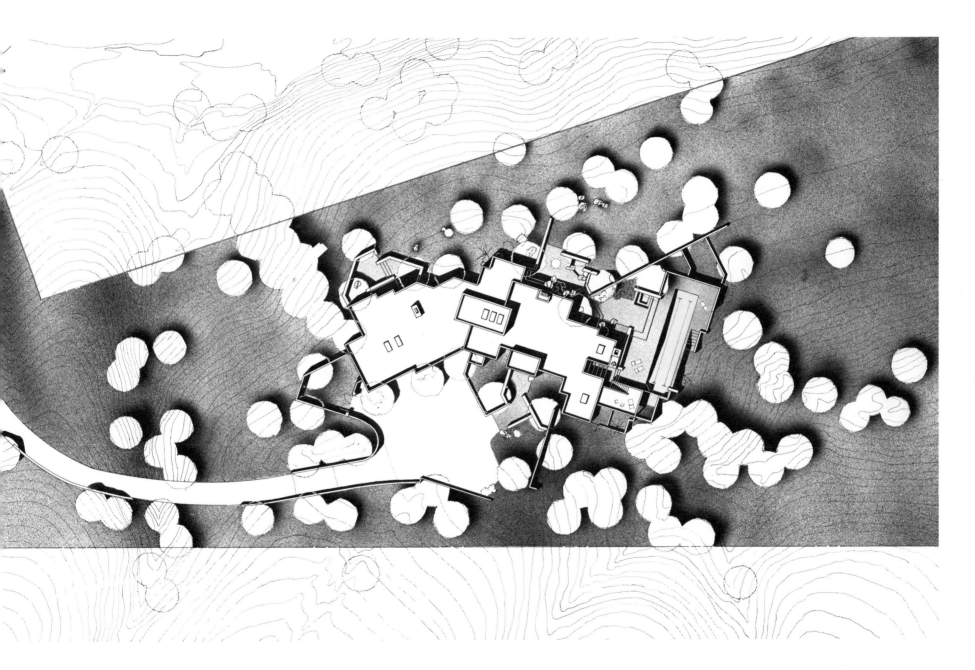

STEVE MARTINO & ASSOCIATES. Air brush.

WILLIAM A. BEHNKE ASSOCIATES by Russell L. Butler II. Residential project. Ink
and pencil on yellow tracing paper.

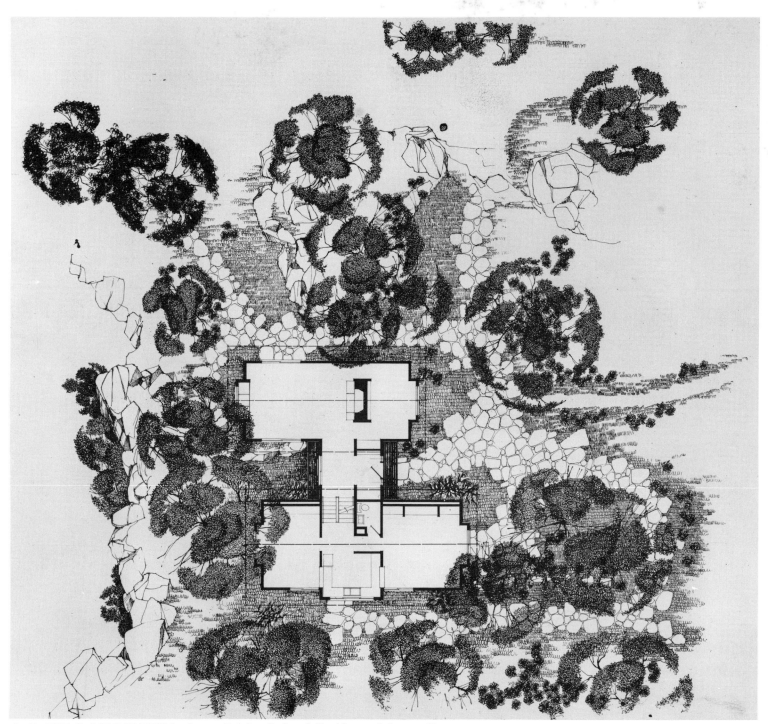

A. E. BYE & ASSOCIATES by James Balsley. Leitzsch Residence. Ink on vellum.

A. E. BYE & ASSOCIATES by A. E. Bye. Residential project. Ink on vellum.

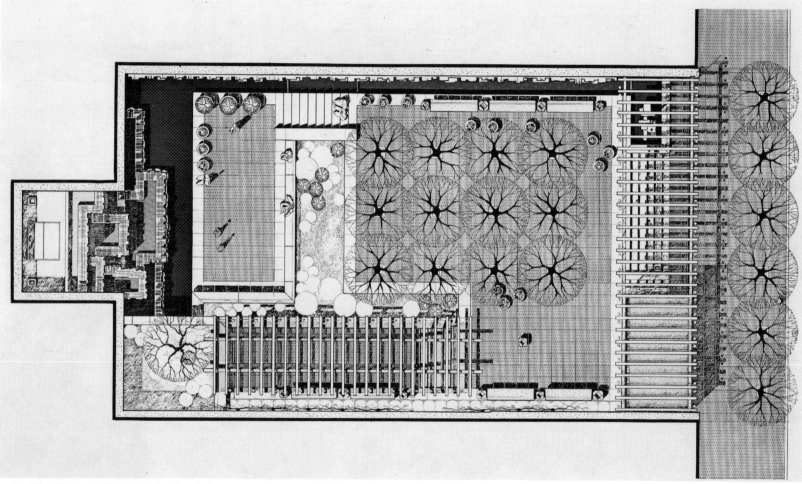

SASAKI ASSOCIATES INC. by Ron Wortman. Greenacre Park.

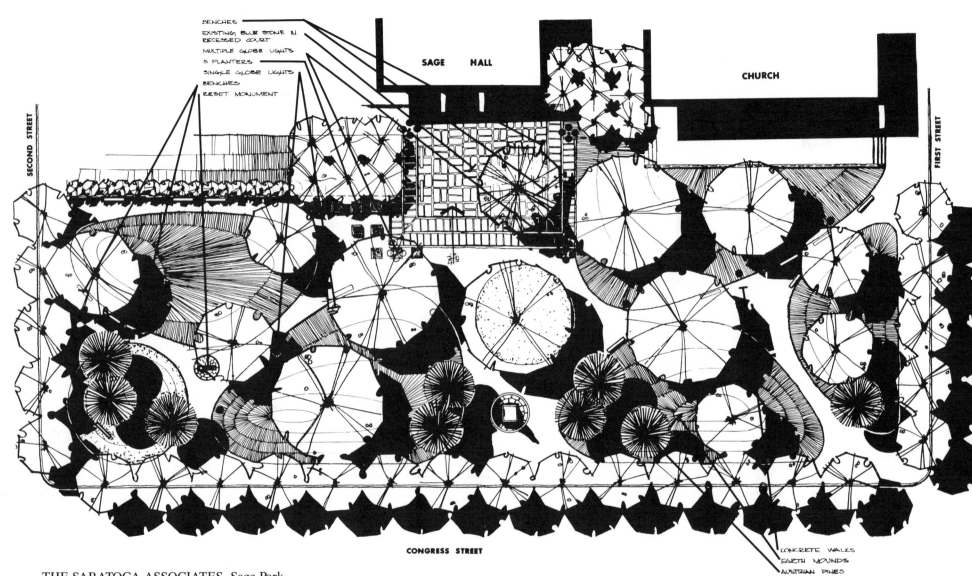

BENCHES
EXISTING BLUE STONE IN RECESSED COURT
MULTIPLE GLOBE LIGHTS
5 PLANTERS
SINGLE GLOBE LIGHTS
BENCHES
RESET MONUMENT

SAGE HALL

CHURCH

SECOND STREET

FIRST STREET

CONGRESS STREET

CONCRETE WALKS
EARTH MOUNDS
AUSTRIAN PINES

THE SARATOGA ASSOCIATES. Sage Park.

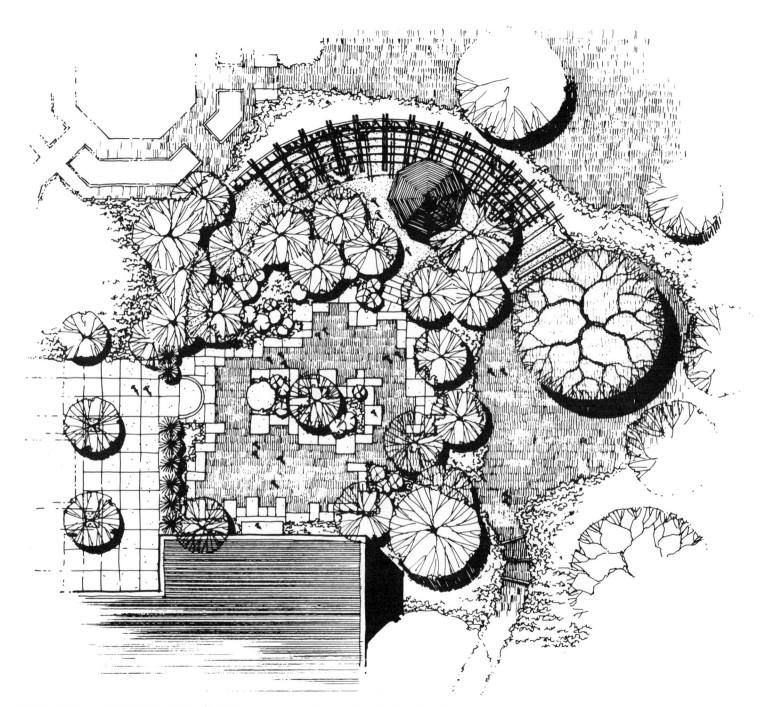

WILLIAM A. BEHNKE ASSOCIATES by Russell L. Butler II. Reading Garden in
Cleveland, Ohio. Ink and pencil on mylar.

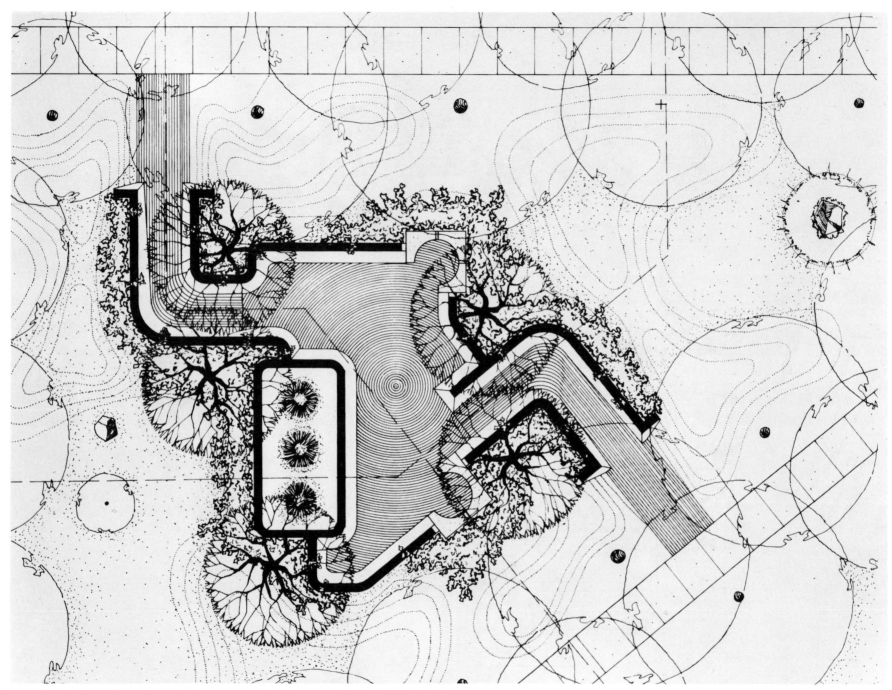

WILLIAM A. BEHNKE ASSOCIATES/JAMES H. NESS. Dauch Memorial Park.

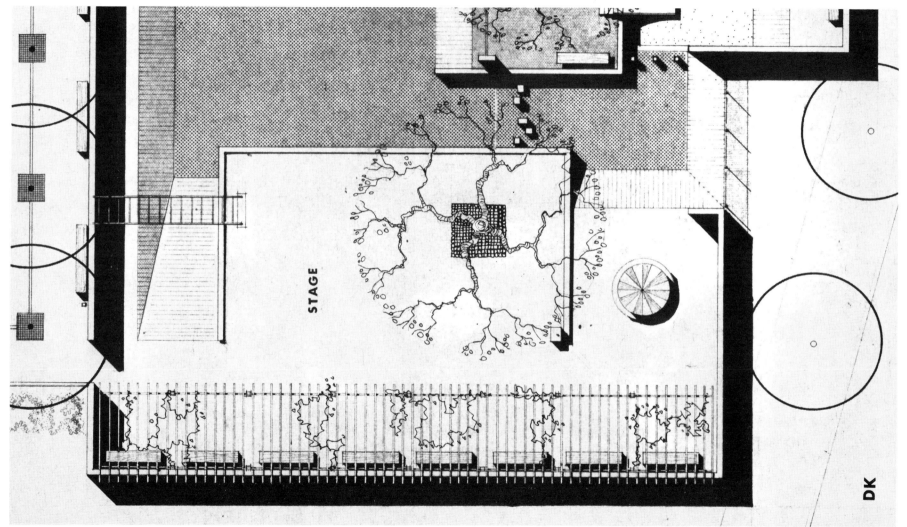

STAGE

DK

DAN KILEY AND PARTNERS.

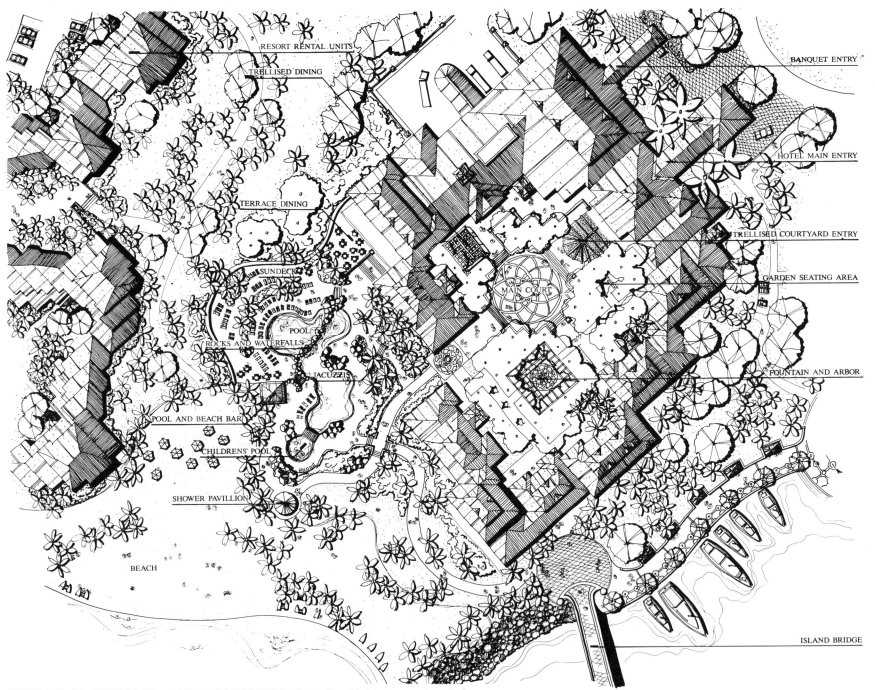

RESORT RENTAL UNITS

TRELLISED DINING

BANQUET ENTRY

HOTEL MAIN ENTRY

TERRACE DINING

TRELLISED COURTYARD ENTRY

SUNDECK

MAIN COURT

GARDEN SEATING AREA

POOL

ROCKS AND WATERFALLS

JACUZZIS

FOUNTAIN AND ARBOR

POOL AND BEACH BAR

CHILDRENS' POOL

SHOWER PAVILLION

BEACH

ISLAND BRIDGE

EDWARD D. STONE JR. AND ASSOCIATES. Port De Plaisance, reduced from
32″ x 40″.

92

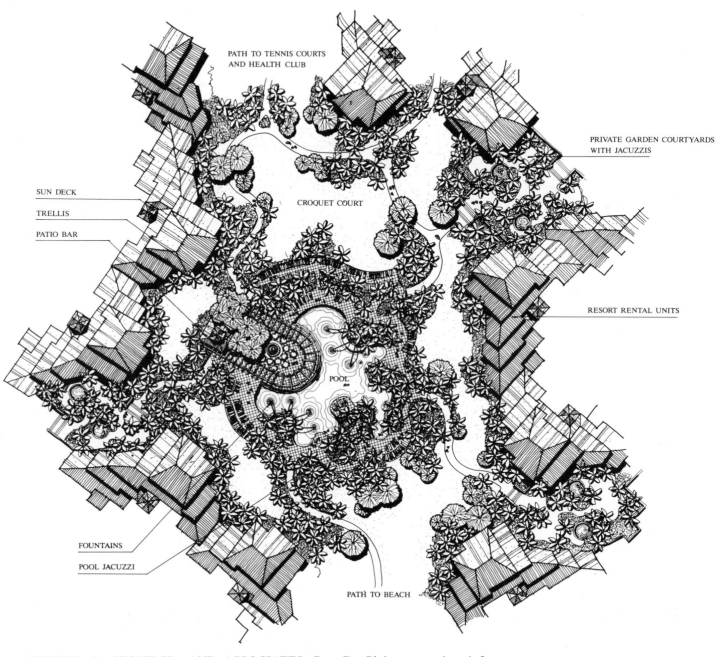

PATH TO TENNIS COURTS
AND HEALTH CLUB

PRIVATE GARDEN COURTYARDS
WITH JACUZZIS

SUN DECK

CROQUET COURT

TRELLIS

PATIO BAR

RESORT RENTAL UNITS

POOL

FOUNTAINS

POOL JACUZZI

PATH TO BEACH

EDWARD D. STONE JR. AND ASSOCIATES. Port De Plaisance, reduced from
32″ x 40″.

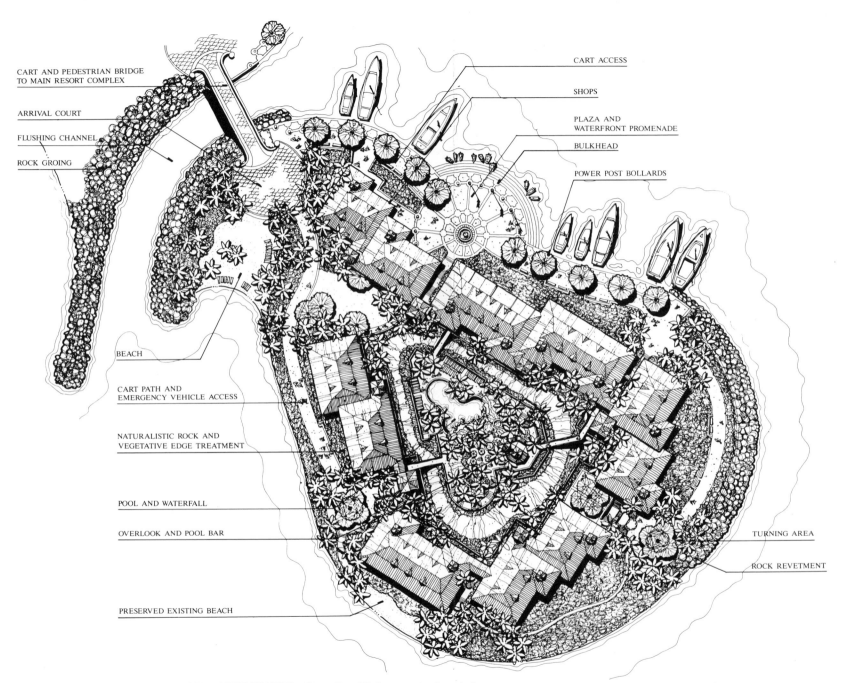

CART AND PEDESTRIAN BRIDGE
TO MAIN RESORT COMPLEX

ARRIVAL COURT

FLUSHING CHANNEL

ROCK GROING

BEACH

CART PATH AND
EMERGENCY VEHICLE ACCESS

NATURALISTIC ROCK AND
VEGETATIVE EDGE TREATMENT

POOL AND WATERFALL

OVERLOOK AND POOL BAR

PRESERVED EXISTING BEACH

CART ACCESS

SHOPS

PLAZA AND
WATERFRONT PROMENADE

BULKHEAD

POWER POST BOLLARDS

TURNING AREA

ROCK REVETMENT

EDWARD D. STONE JR. AND ASSOCIATES. Port De Plaisance, reduced from
32″ x 40″.

94

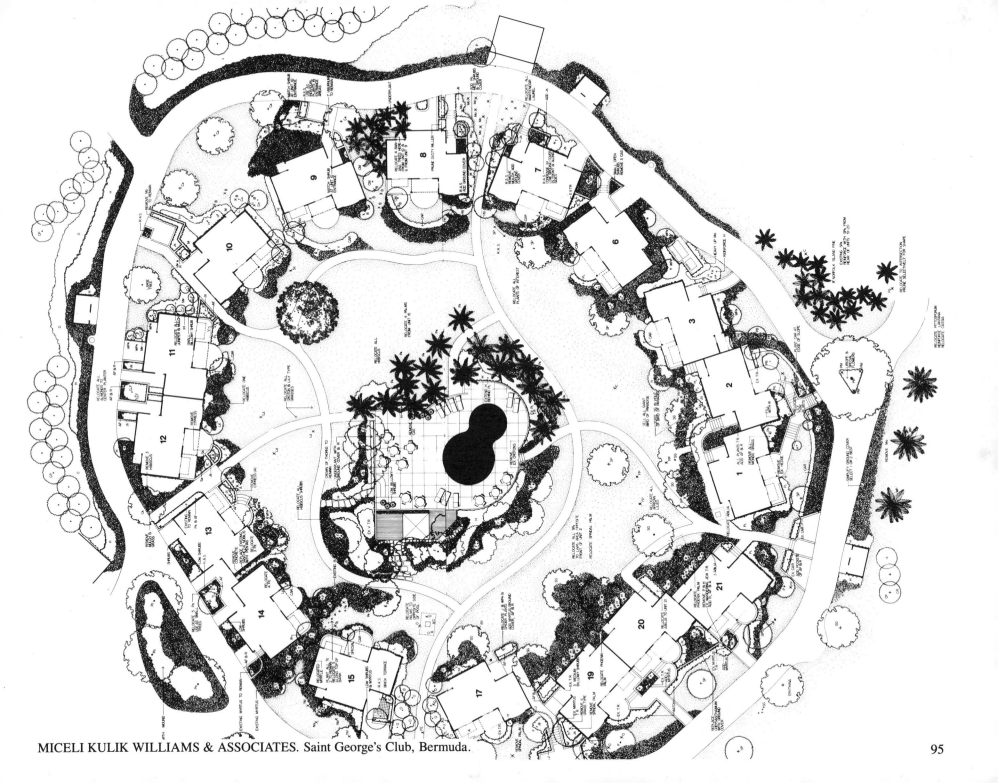

MICELI KULIK WILLIAMS & ASSOCIATES. Saint George's Club, Bermuda.

95

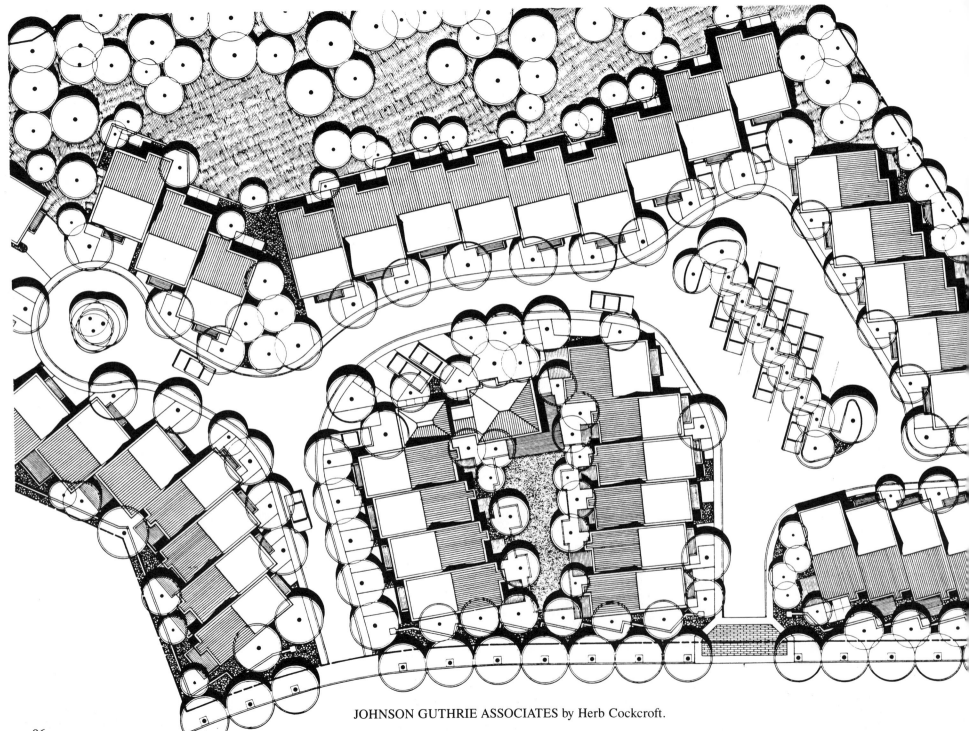

JOHNSON GUTHRIE ASSOCIATES by Herb Cockcroft.

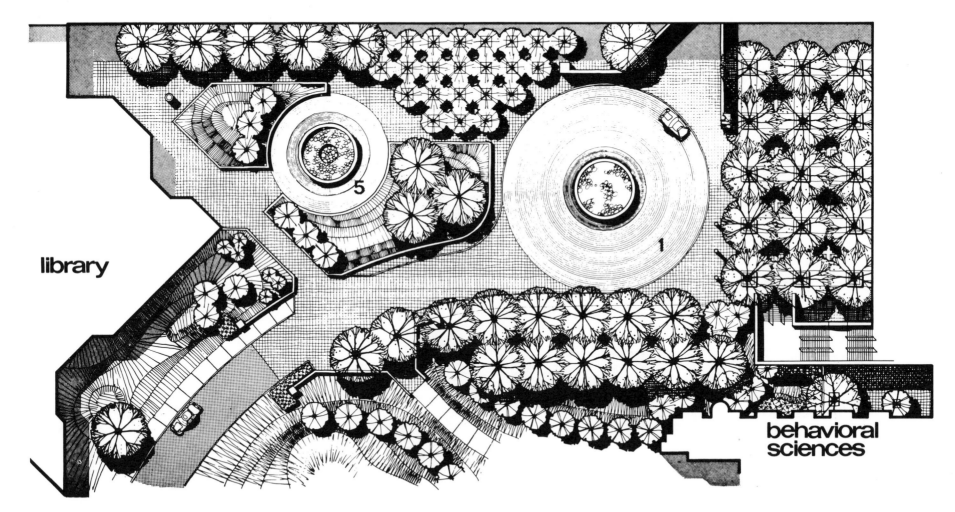

library

behavioral
sciences

CR3 inc. by Kenneth Kay. Western Connecticut State College.

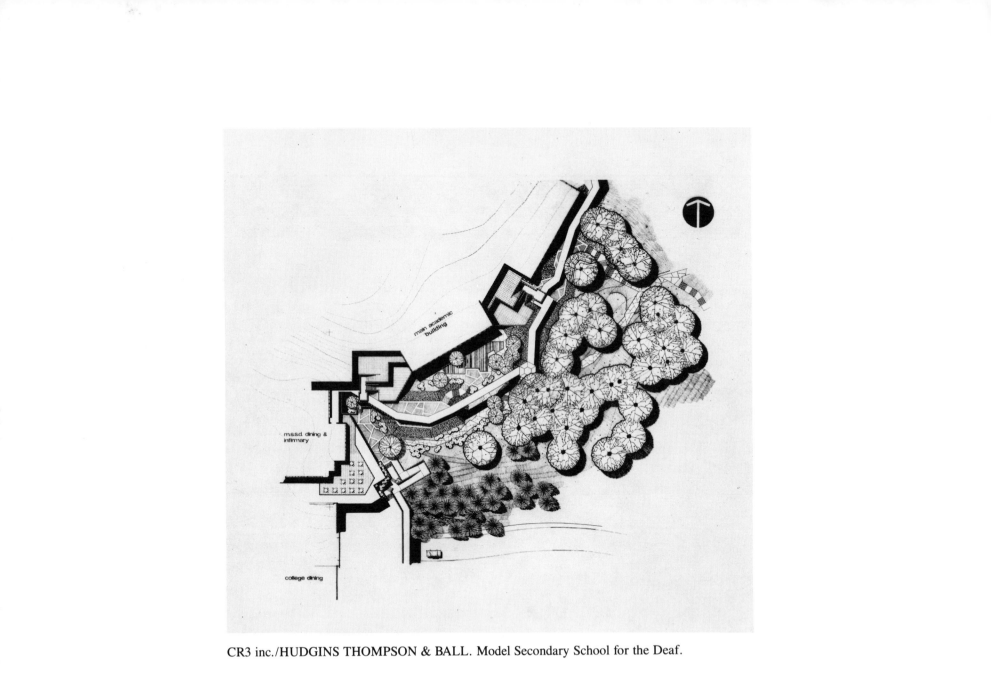

CR3 inc./HUDGINS THOMPSON & BALL. Model Secondary School for the Deaf.

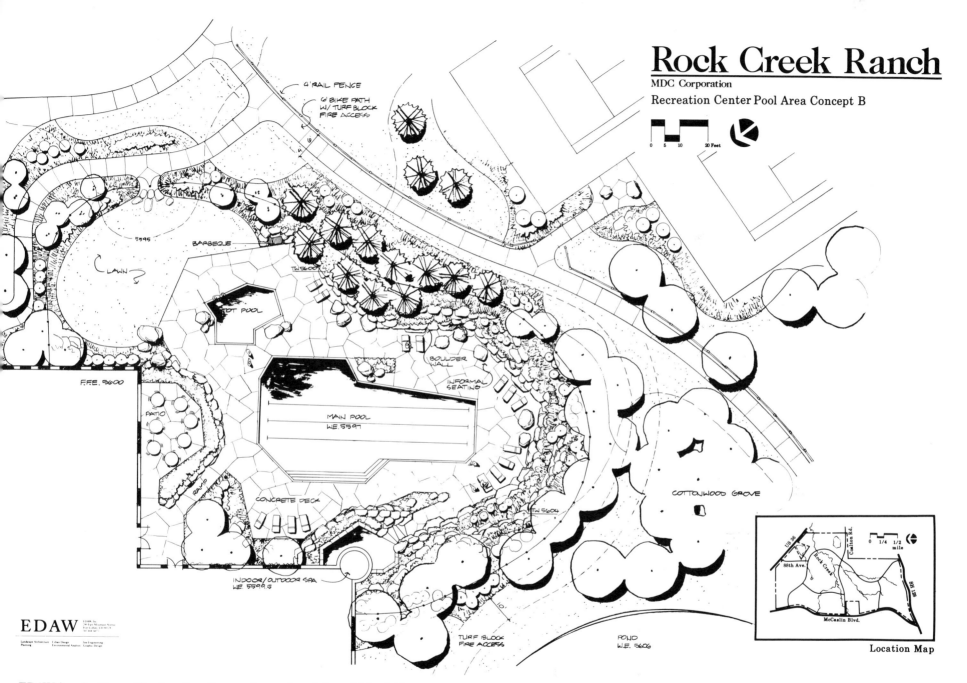

Rock Creek Ranch

MDC Corporation

Recreation Center Pool Area Concept B

0   5   10   20 Feet

4' RAIL FENCE

6' BIKE PATH
W/ TURF BLOCK
FIRE ACCESS

5595

BARBEQUE

LAWN

TW 5600

TOT POOL

BOULDER
WALL

INFORMAL
SEATING

F.F.E. 5600

PATIO

MAIN POOL
W.E. 5597

COTTONWOOD GROVE

CONCRETE DECK

TW 5604

INDOOR/OUTDOOR SPA
W.E. 5599.5

TURF BLOCK
FIRE ACCESS

POND
W.E. 5606

Location Map

US 36

88th Ave.

Coalton Rd.

Rock Creek

SH 128

McCaslin Blvd.

0   1/4   1/2
mile

EDAW

Landscape Architecture   Urban Design
Planning   Site Engineering
                         Environmental Analysis   Graphic Design

EDAW inc. by Bruce Hendee. Pencil on mylar, reduced from 24″ x 36″.

99

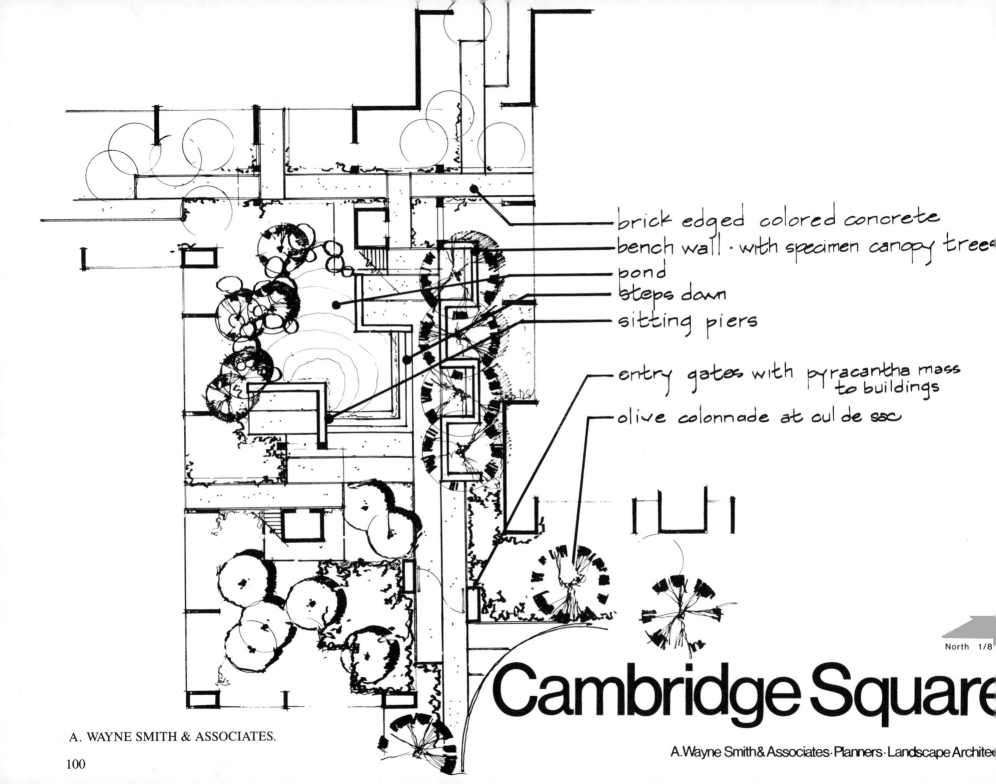

brick edged colored concrete
bench wall · with specimen canopy trees
pond
steps down
sitting piers

entry gates with pyracantha mass
to buildings

olive colonnade at cul de sac

North 1/8

Cambridge Square

A. WAYNE SMITH & ASSOCIATES.

100

A. Wayne Smith & Associates · Planners · Landscape Architec

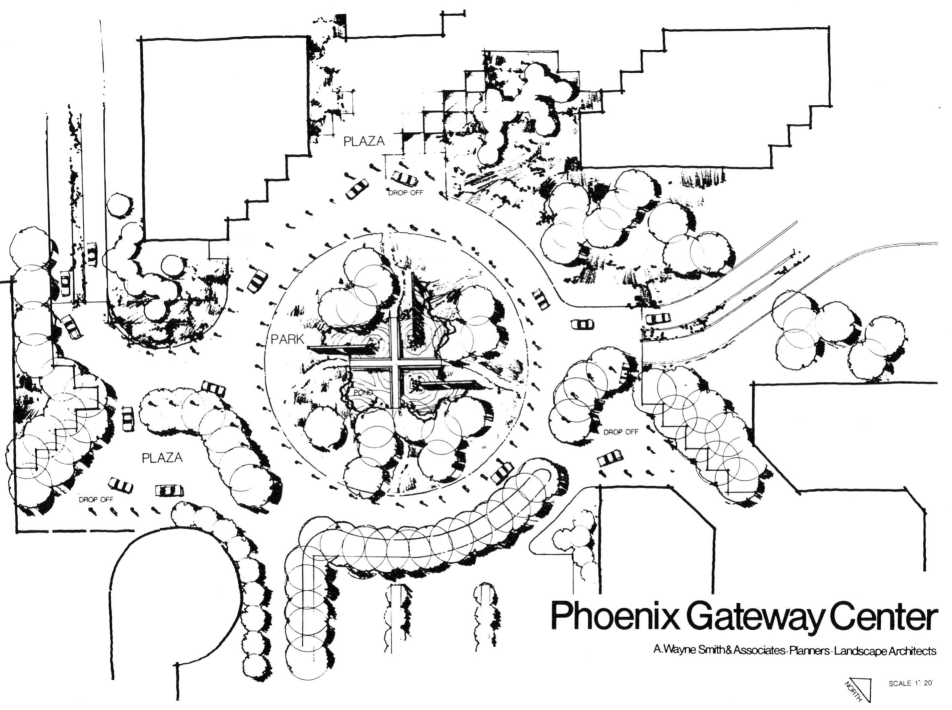

PLAZA

DROP OFF

PARK

POND

PLAZA

DROP OFF

DROP OFF

Phoenix Gateway Center

A. Wayne Smith & Associates · Planners · Landscape Architects

NORTH

SCALE 1" : 20'

A. WAYNE SMITH & ASSOCIATES. Ink on vellum, reduced from 30" x 42".

101

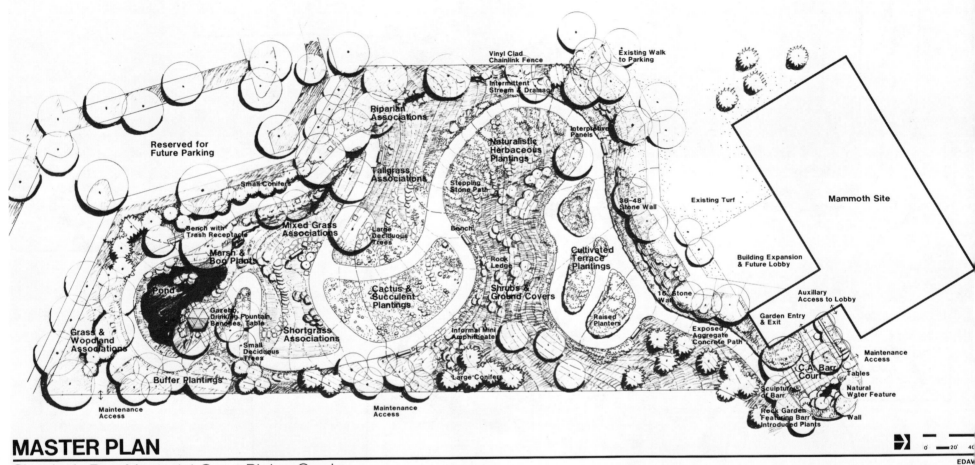

Reserved for
Future Parking

Small Conifers

Bench with
Trash Receptacle

Mixed Grass
Associations

Marsh &
Bog Plants

Pond

Gazebo,
Drinking Fountain,
Benches, Table

Grass &
Woodland
Associations

Small
Deciduous
Trees

Shortgrass
Associations

Buffer Plantings

Maintenance
Access

Riparian
Associations

Tallgrass
Associations

Large
Deciduous
Trees

Cactus &
Succulent
Plantings

Informal Mini
Amphitheater

Large Conifers

Maintenance
Access

Vinyl Clad
Chainlink Fence

Existing Walk
to Parking

Intermittent
Stream & Drainage

Naturalistic
Herbaceous
Plantings

Interpretive
Panels

Stepping
Stone Path

Bench

Rock
Ledge

Shrubs &
Ground Covers

Cultivated
Terrace
Plantings

36-48"
Stone Wall

Existing Turf

16" Stone
Wall

Raised
Planters

Exposed
Aggregate
Concrete Path

Mammoth Site

Building Expansion
& Future Lobby

Auxillary
Access to Lobby

Garden Entry
& Exit

C.A. Barr
Court

Sculpture
of Barr

Rock Garden
Featuring Barr's
Introduced Plants

Maintenance
Access

Tables

Natural
Water Feature

Wall

MASTER PLAN

Claude A. Barr Memorial Great Plains Garden

0'   20'   40'

EDAW

EDAW inc. by Herb Schaal. Pencil on mylar, reduced from 24″ x 36″.

102

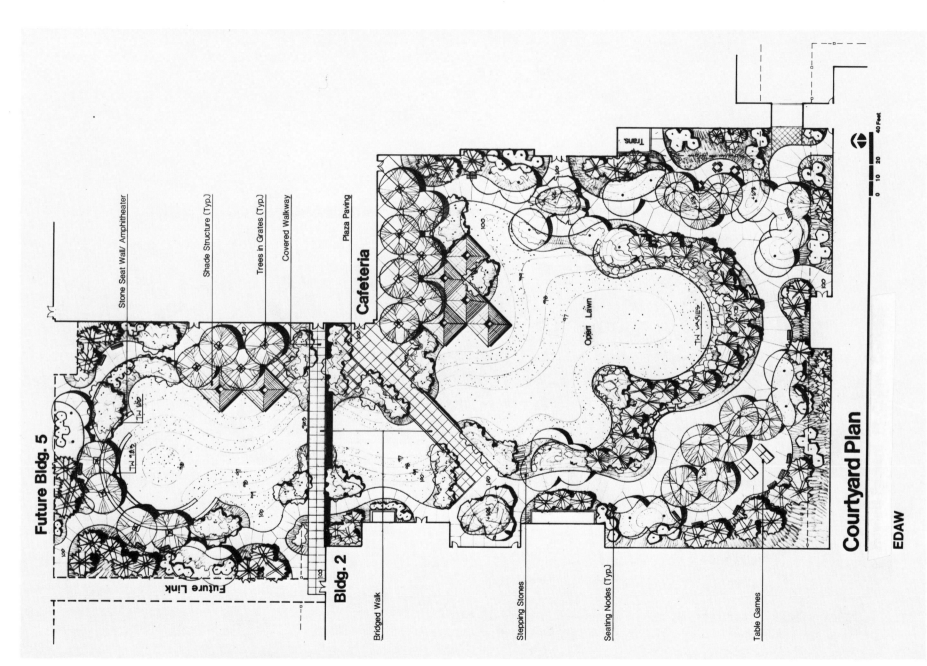

Future Bldg. 5

Future Link

Bldg. 2

Stone Seat Wall/ Amphitheater

Shade Structure (Typ.)

Trees in Grates (Typ.)

Covered Walkway

Plaza Paving

Cafeteria

Open Lawn

Trans.

Bridged Walk

Stepping Stones

Seating Nodes (Typ.)

Table Games

Courtyard Plan

EDAW

0 10 20   40 Feet

EDAW inc. by Joe McGrane. Pencil on mylar, reduced from 24″ x 36″.

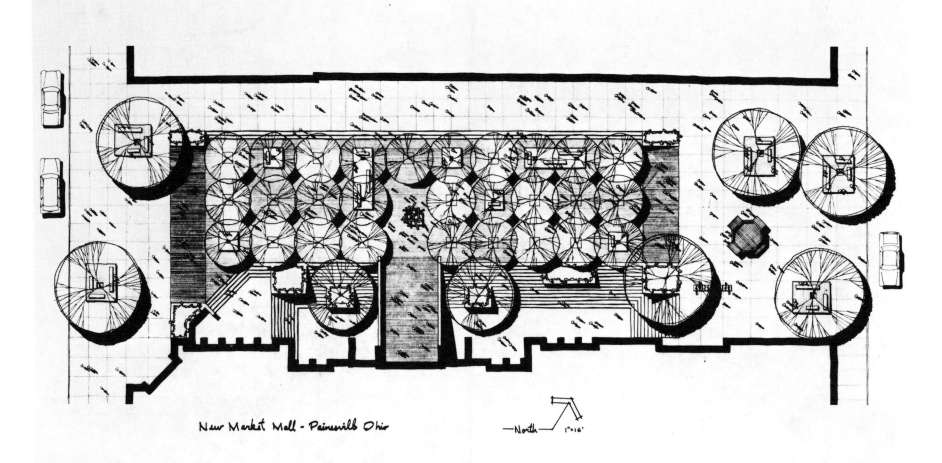

New Market Mall - Painesville Ohio

—North— 1"=16'

WILLIAM A. BEHNKE ASSOCIATES, by Russell L. Butler II. New Market Mall,
Painesville, Ohio. Ink and pencil on mylar.

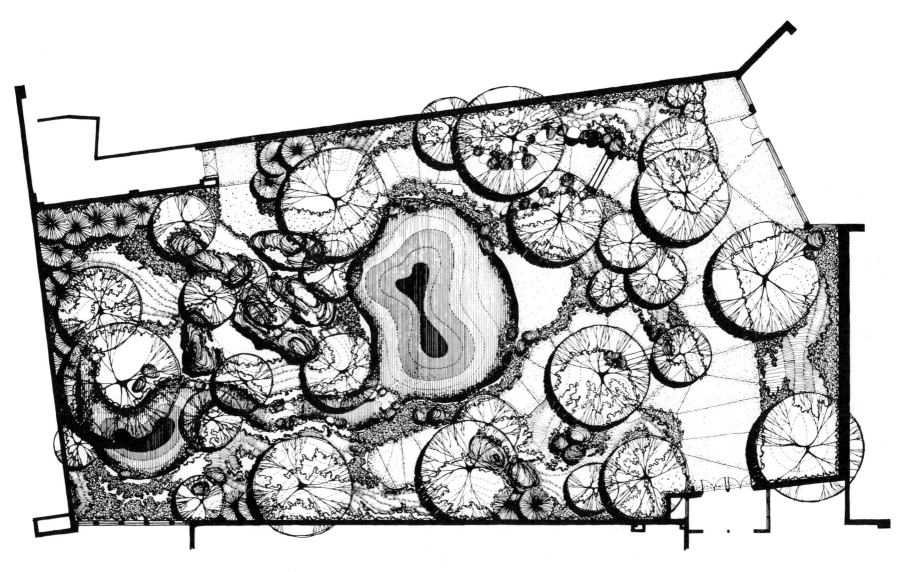

WILLIAM A. BEHNKE ASSOCIATES by Russell L. Butler II. Cleveland Museum of
Natural History Courtyard. Ink on yellow tracing paper.

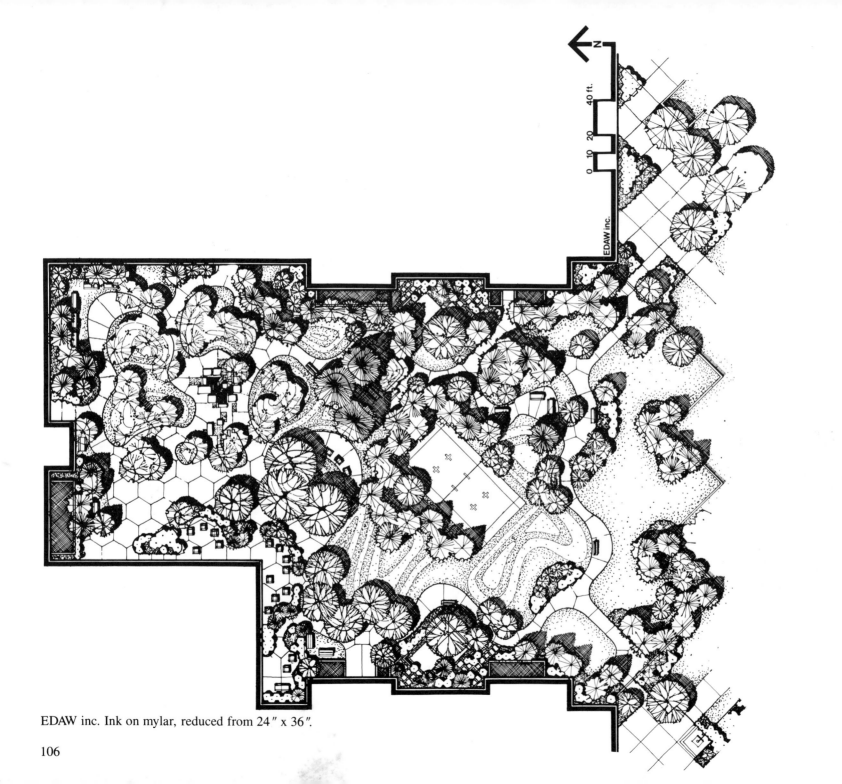

EDAW inc. Ink on mylar, reduced from 24″ x 36″.

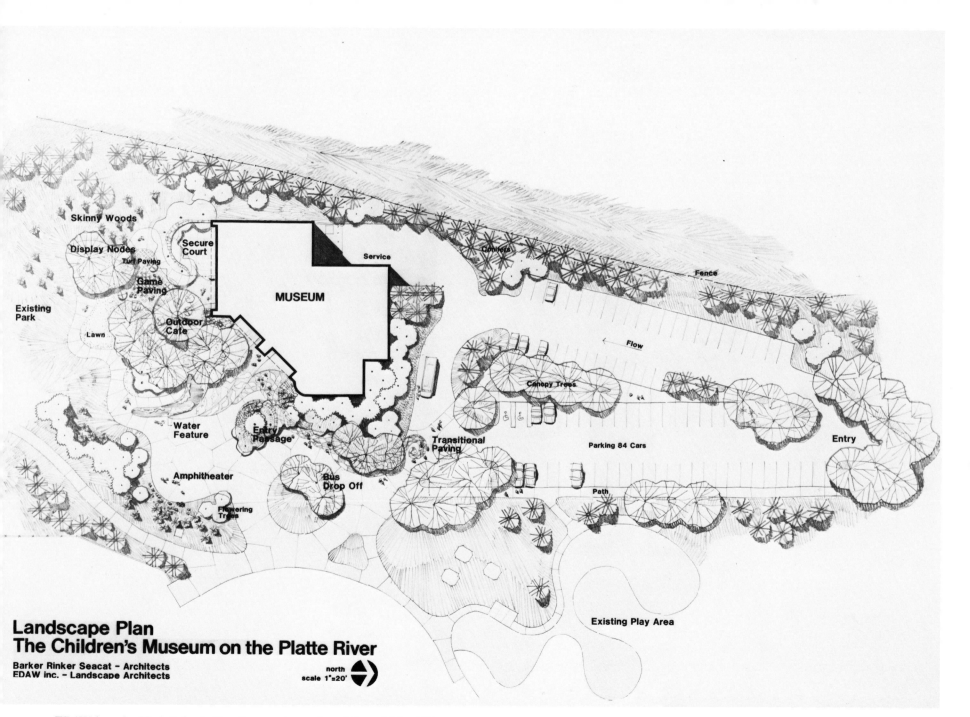

Skinny Woods

Display Nodes

Turf Paving

Secure Court

Game Paving

Outdoor Cafe

Existing Park

Lawn

Water Feature

Amphitheater

Flowering Trees

MUSEUM

Service

Entry Passage

Bus Drop Off

Conifers

Fence

Flow

Canopy Trees

Transitional Paving

Parking 84 Cars

Path

Entry

Existing Play Area

Landscape Plan
The Children's Museum on the Platte River

Barker Rinker Seacat - Architects
EDAW inc. - Landscape Architects

north
scale 1"=20'

EDAW inc., by Herb Schaal. Pencil on mylar, reduced from 24″ x 36″.

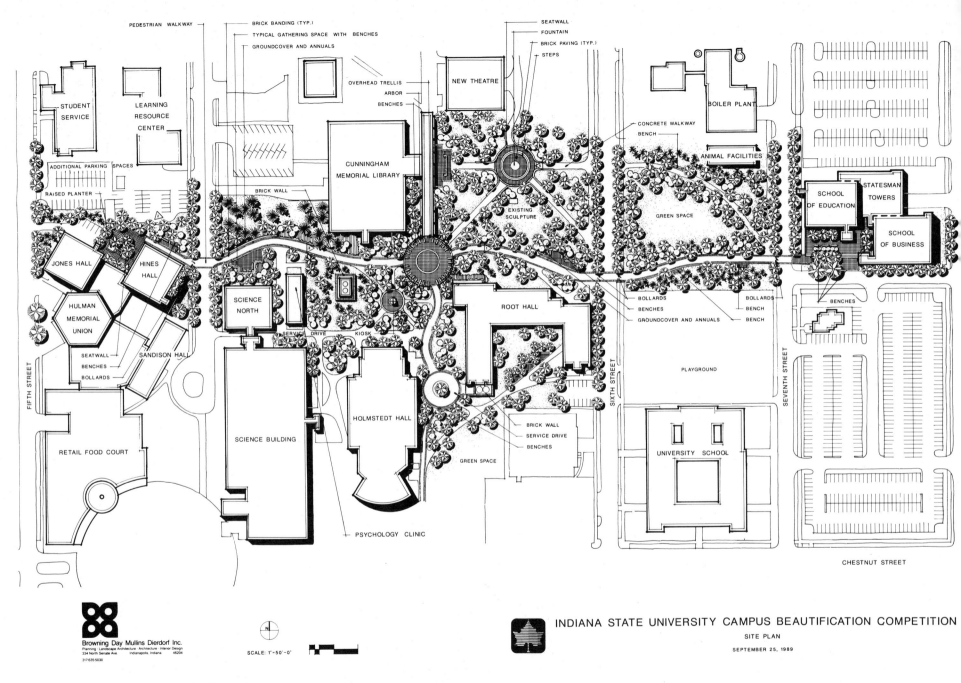

PEDESTRIAN WALKWAY

BRICK BANDING (TYP.)

TYPICAL GATHERING SPACE WITH BENCHES

GROUNDCOVER AND ANNUALS

SEATWALL

FOUNTAIN

BRICK PAVING (TYP.)

STEPS

OVERHEAD TRELLIS

ARBOR

BENCHES

STUDENT SERVICE

LEARNING RESOURCE CENTER

NEW THEATRE

BOILER PLANT

ADDITIONAL PARKING SPACES

CONCRETE WALKWAY

BENCH

ANIMAL FACILITIES

RAISED PLANTER

CUNNINGHAM MEMORIAL LIBRARY

SCHOOL OF EDUCATION

STATESMAN TOWERS

BRICK WALL

GREEN SPACE

SCHOOL OF BUSINESS

JONES HALL

HINES HALL

EXISTING SCULPTURE

HULMAN MEMORIAL UNION

ROOT HALL

SCIENCE NORTH

BOLLARDS

BENCHES

GROUNDCOVER AND ANNUALS

BOLLARDS

BENCH

BENCH

BENCHES

SANDISON HALL

SEATWALL

BENCHES

BOLLARDS

SERVICE DRIVE

KIOSK

PLAYGROUND

SCIENCE BUILDING

HOLMSTEDT HALL

BRICK WALL

SERVICE DRIVE

BENCHES

UNIVERSITY SCHOOL

RETAIL FOOD COURT

GREEN SPACE

PSYCHOLOGY CLINIC

FIFTH STREET

SIXTH STREET

SEVENTH STREET

CHESTNUT STREET

Browning Day Mullins Dierdorf Inc.
Planning · Landscape Architecture · Architecture · Interior Design
334 North Senate Ave.   Indianapolis, Indiana   46204
317-635-5030

BROWNING DAY MULLINS DIERDORF INC.

SCALE: 1"=50'-0"

INDIANA STATE UNIVERSITY CAMPUS BEAUTIFICATION COMPETITION

SITE PLAN

SEPTEMBER 25, 1989

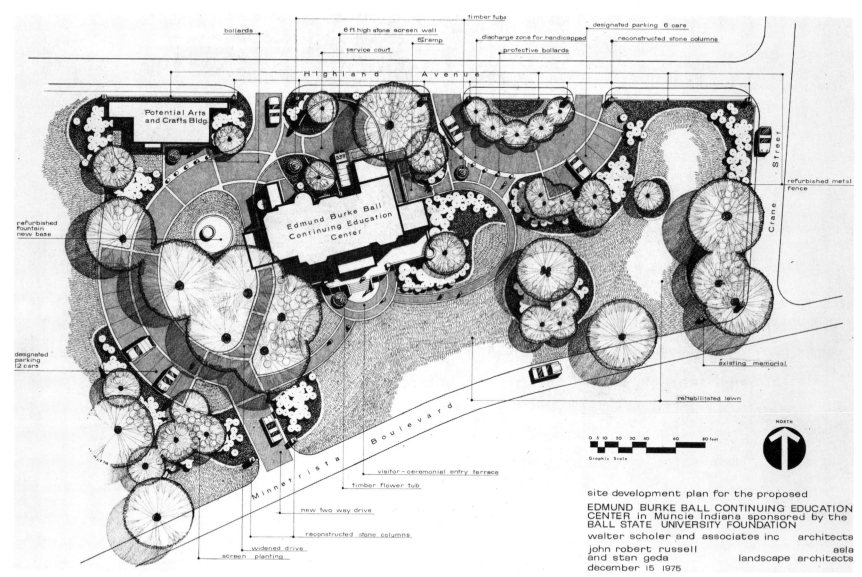

bollards
service court
6 ft. high stone screen wall
5% ramp
timber tubs
discharge zone for handicapped
protective bollards
designated parking 6 cars
reconstructed stone columns

H i g h l a n d   A v e n u e

Potential Arts and Crafts Bldg.

refurbished fountain new base

Edmund Burke Ball Continuing Education Center

C r a n e   Street

refurbished metal fence

designated parking 12 cars

existing memorial

rehabilitated lawn

M i n n e t r i s t a   B o u l e v a r d

visitor - ceremonial entry terrace
timber flower tub

new two way drive

reconstructed stone columns

widened drive
screen planting

0 5 10 20 30 40   60   80 feet
Graphic Scale

NORTH

JOHN ROBERT RUSSELL and STAN GEDA.

site development plan for the proposed
EDMUND BURKE BALL CONTINUING EDUCATION
CENTER in Muncie Indiana sponsored by the
BALL STATE UNIVERSITY FOUNDATION
walter scholer and associates inc   architects
john robert russell   asla
and stan geda   landscape architects
december 15 1975

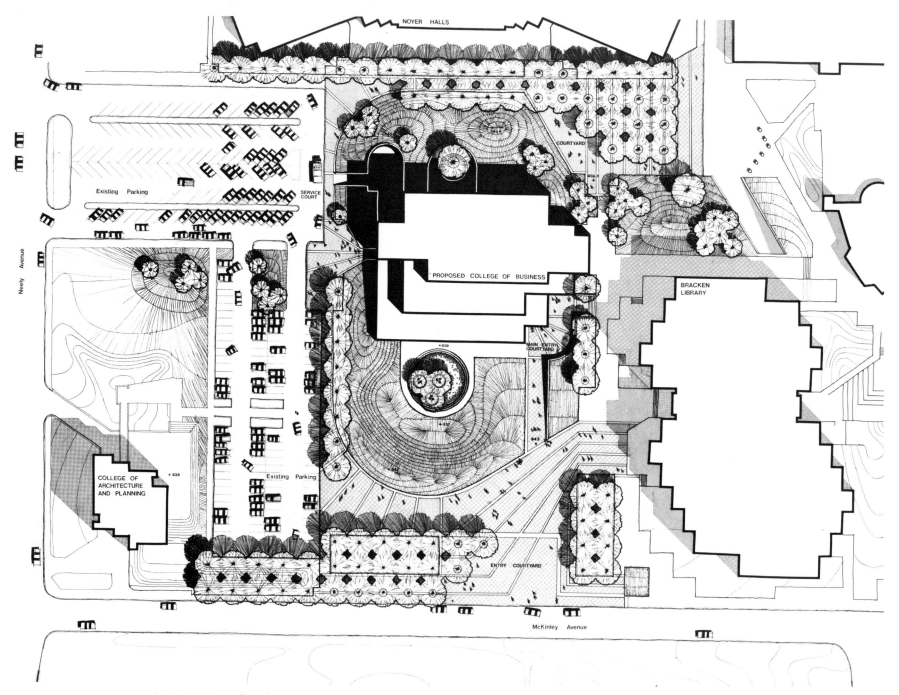

LANDPLUS WEST by Stan Geda. College of Business at Ball State University.

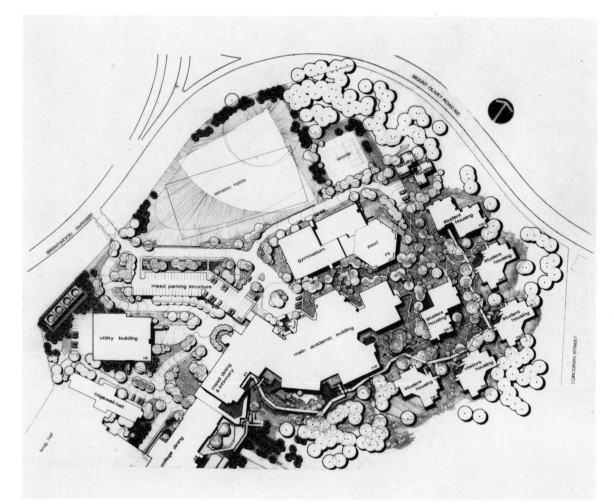

CR3 inc./HUDGINS THOMPSON & BALL. Model Secondary School for the Deaf.

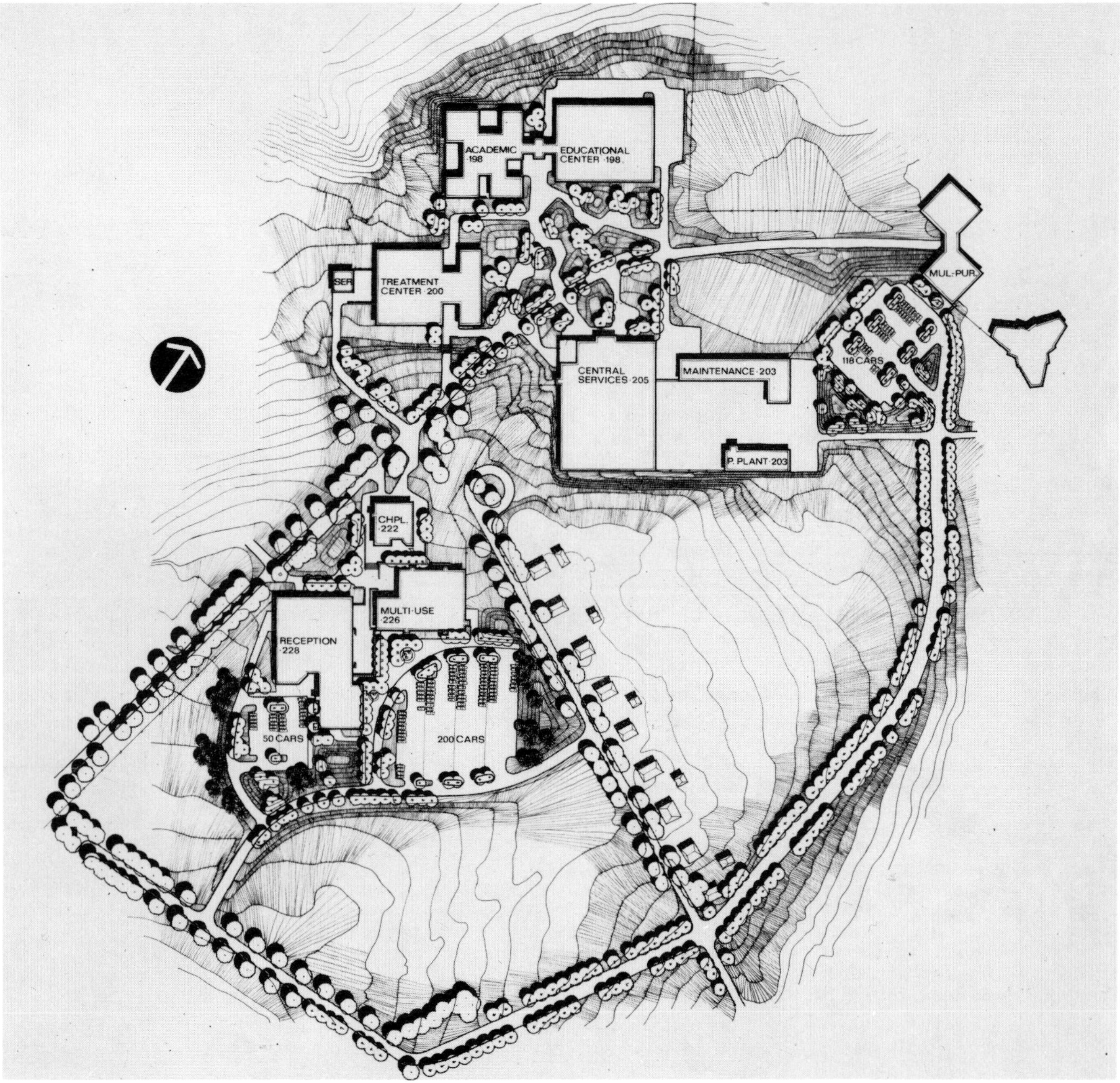
ACADEMIC ·198
EDUCATIONAL CENTER ·198
TREATMENT CENTER ·200
SER
MUL·PUR.
118 CARS
CENTRAL SERVICES·205
MAINTENANCE·203
P. PLANT·203
CHPL. ·222
MULTI·USE ·226
RECEPTION ·228
50 CARS
200 CARS

CR3 inc., by Jeffrey A. Gebrian. Client: Close, Jensen, Miller. Cheshire Corrections Community.

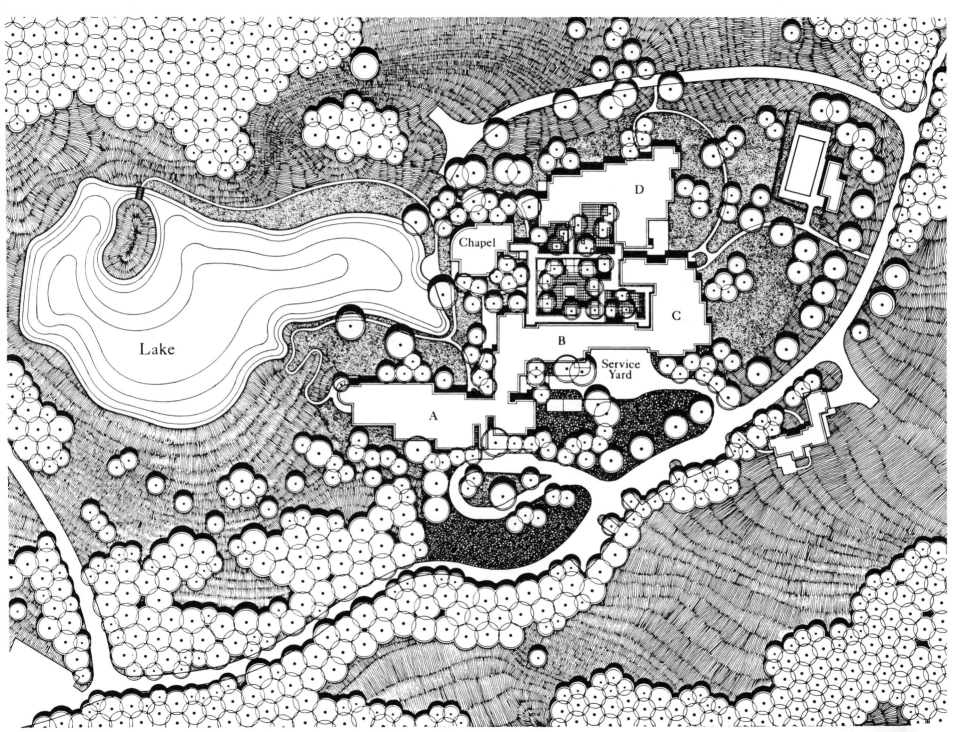

Lake

Chapel

D

B

C

A

Service Yard

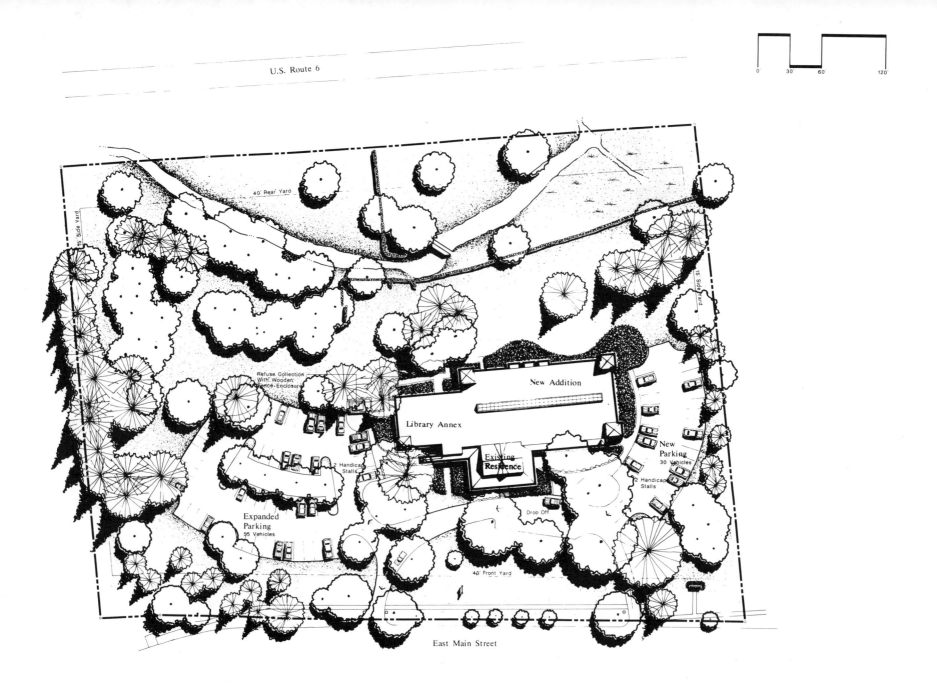

U.S. Route 6

40' Rear Yard

15' Side Yard

15' Side Yard

Refuse Collection
With Wooden
Fence Enclosure

New Addition

Library Annex

New
Parking
30 Vehicles

2 Handicap
Stalls

Existing
Residence

2 Handicap
Stalls

Expanded
Parking
55 Vehicles

Drop Off

40' Front Yard

East Main Street

0   30'   60'   120'

Schematic Site Plan

CR3 inc. Reduced from 18″ x 24″.

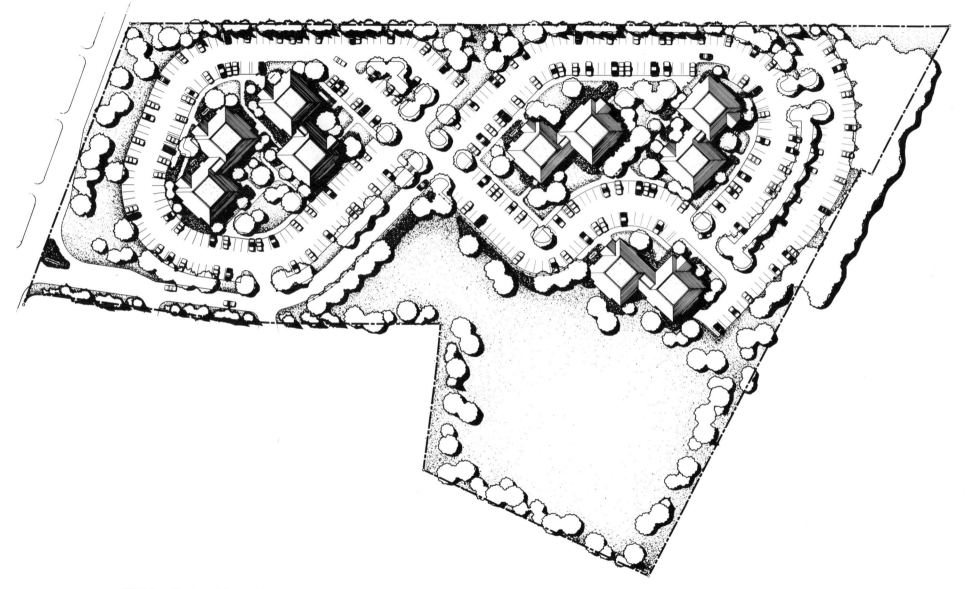

CR3 inc. Reduced from 20″ x 32″.

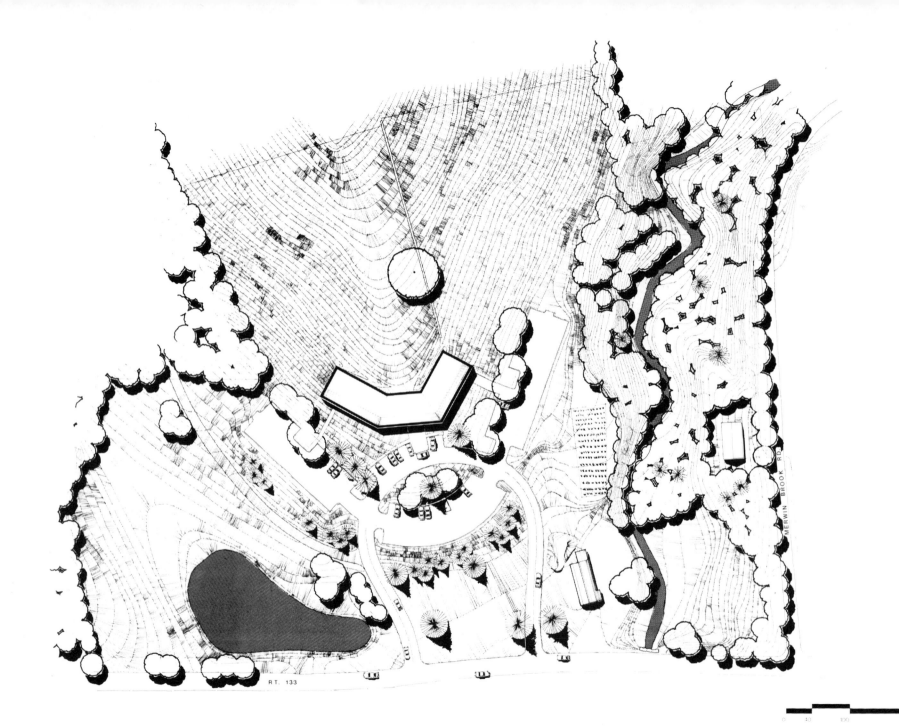

RT. 133

MERWIN BROOK RD.

CR3 inc. Reduced from 27″ x 36″.

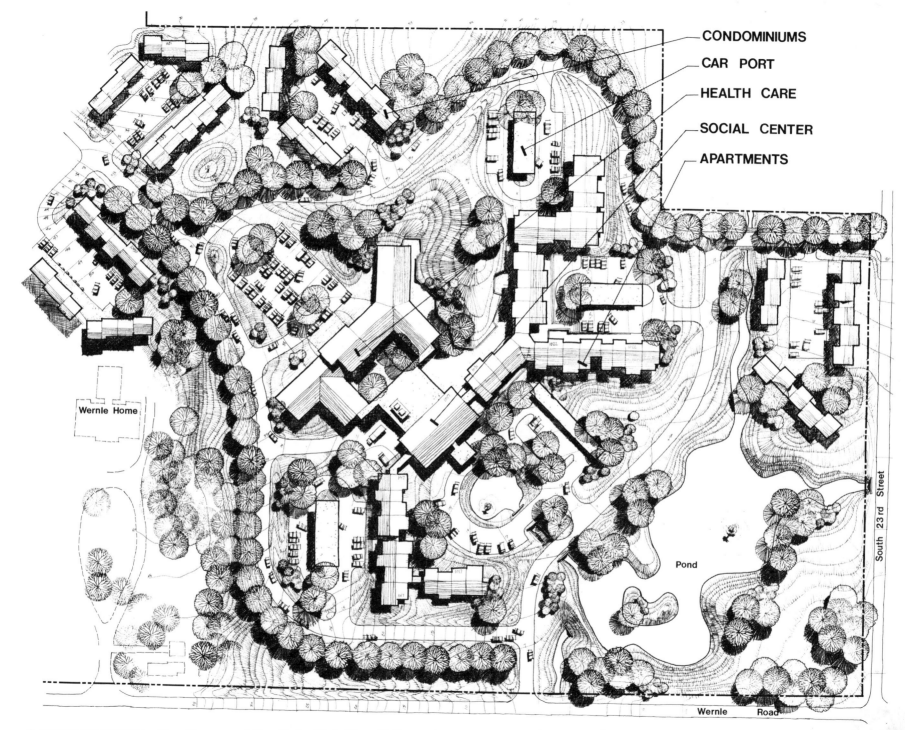

CONDOMINIUMS

CAR PORT

HEALTH CARE

SOCIAL CENTER

APARTMENTS

Wernle Home

Pond

South 23rd Street

Wernle Road

LANDPLUS WEST by Tom Stearns and Stan Geda. Vista Pines Retirement
Community.

117

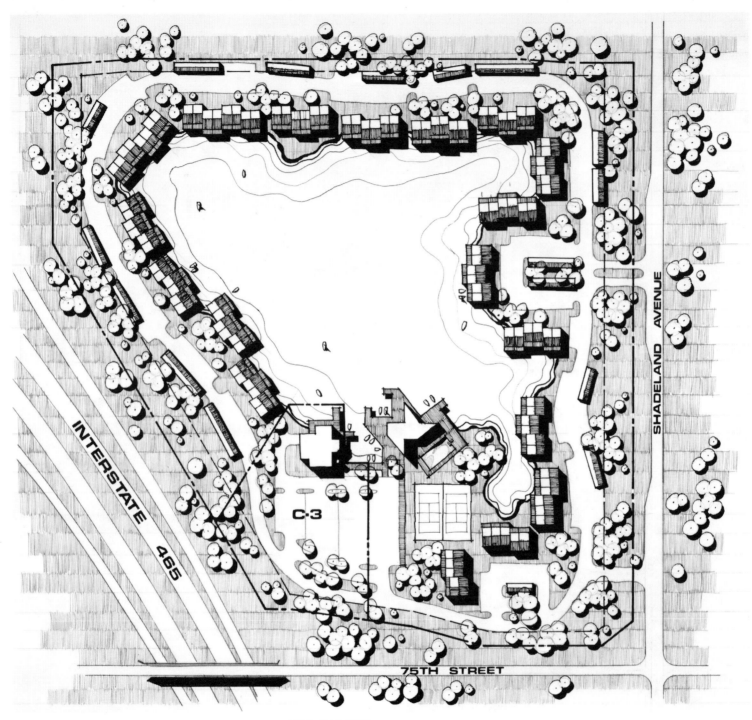

INTERSTATE 465

SHADELAND AVENUE

C-3

75TH STREET

BROWNING DAY MULLINS DIERDORF INC.

118

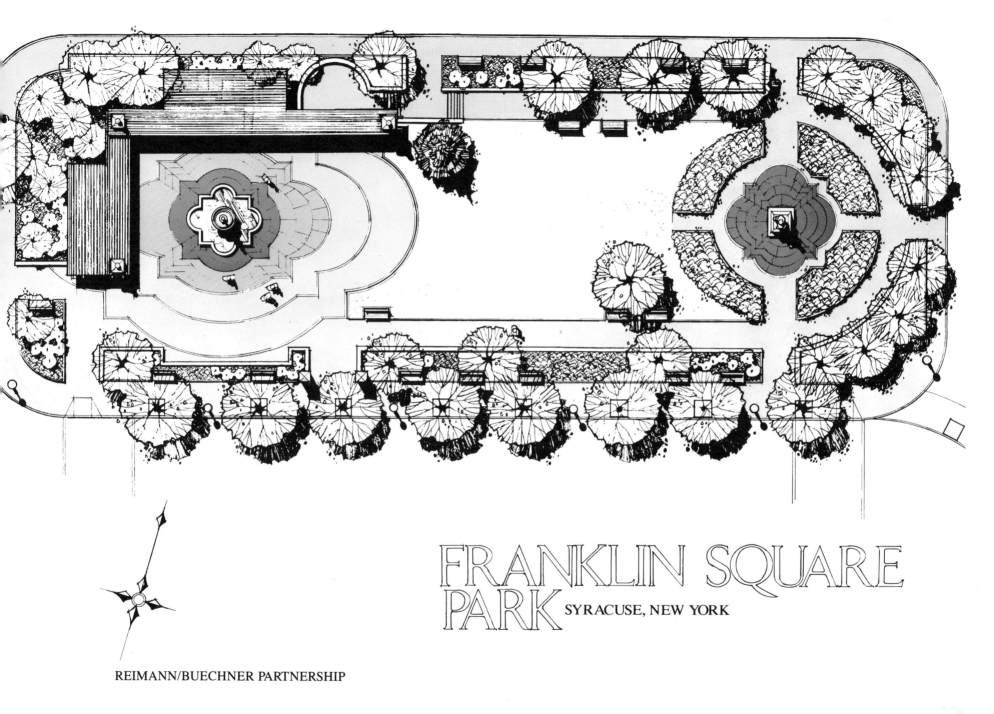

FRANKLIN SQUARE PARK SYRACUSE, NEW YORK

REIMANN/BUECHNER PARTNERSHIP

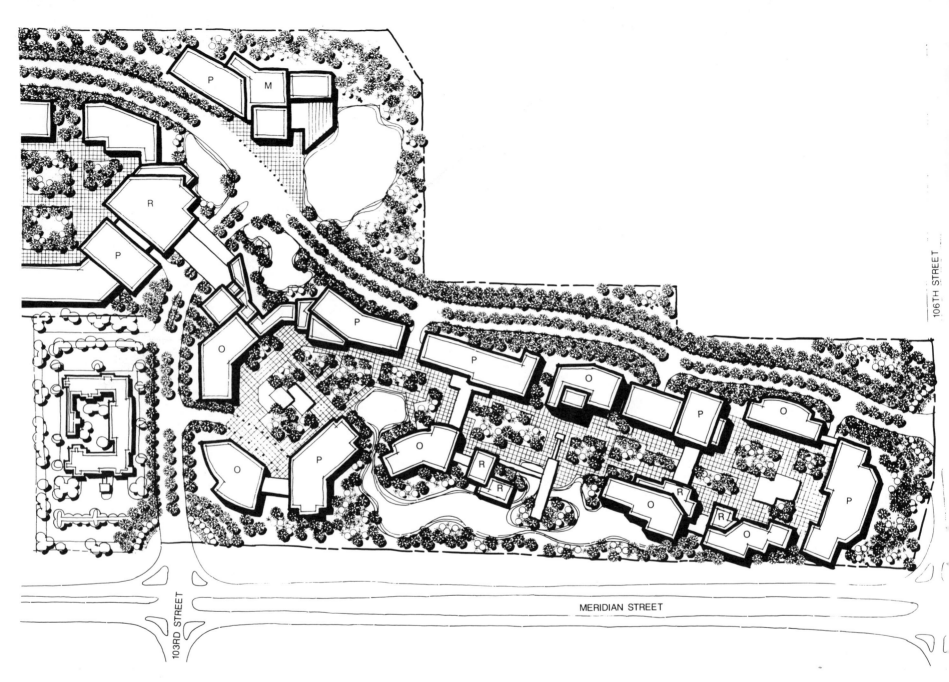

BROWNING DAY MULLINS DIERDORF INC. Meridian at the Interstate, Indianapolis,
reduced from 17″ x 25″.

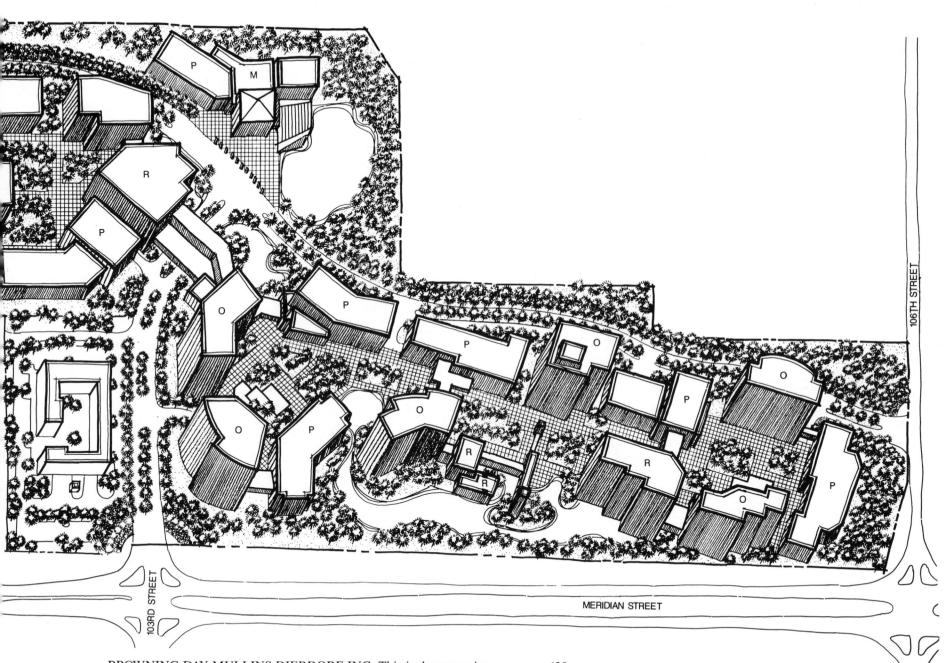

BROWNING DAY MULLINS DIERDORF INC. This is the same site as on page 120, but note the different graphic technique which provides height to the buildings.

BROWNING DAY MULLINS DIERDORF INC. Second Presbyterian Church, reduced from 23″ x 35″.

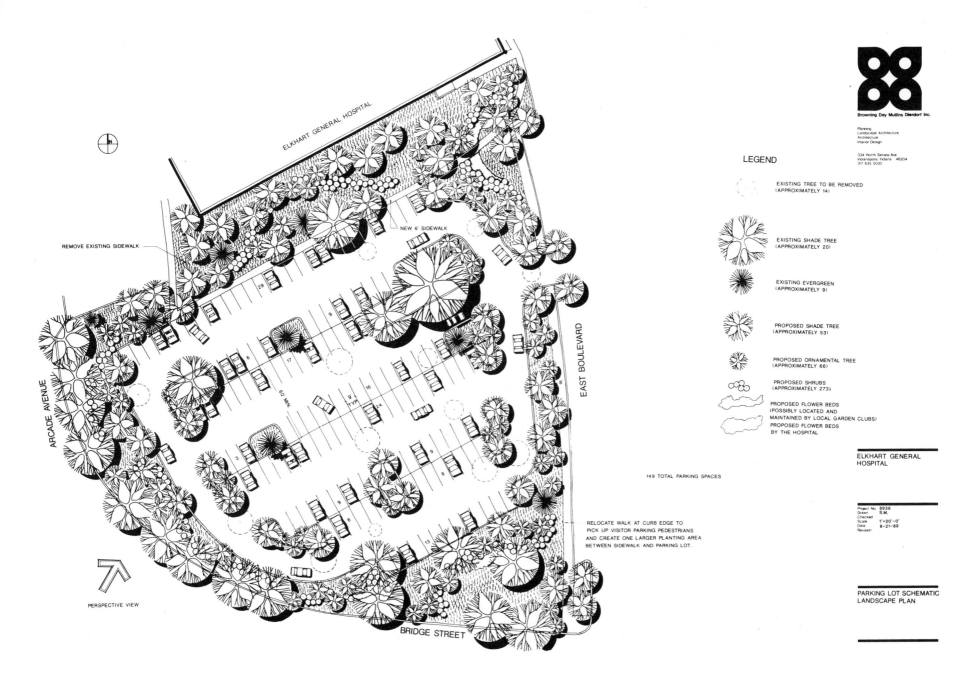

ELKHART GENERAL HOSPITAL

NEW 6' SIDEWALK

REMOVE EXISTING SIDEWALK

ARCADE AVENUE

EAST BOULEVARD

60' MIN.

TYP.

149 TOTAL PARKING SPACES

RELOCATE WALK AT CURB EDGE TO
PICK UP VISITOR PARKING PEDESTRIANS
AND CREATE ONE LARGER PLANTING AREA
BETWEEN SIDEWALK AND PARKING LOT.

PERSPECTIVE VIEW

BRIDGE STREET

Browning Day Mullins Dierdorf Inc.

Planning
Landscape Architecture
Architecture
Interior Design

334 North Senate Ave
Indianapolis Indiana 46204
317 635 5030

LEGEND

EXISTING TREE TO BE REMOVED
(APPROXIMATELY 14)

EXISTING SHADE TREE
(APPROXIMATELY 20)

EXISTING EVERGREEN
(APPROXIMATELY 9)

PROPOSED SHADE TREE
(APPROXIMATELY 53)

PROPOSED ORNAMENTAL TREE
(APPROXIMATELY 66)

PROPOSED SHRUBS
(APPROXIMATELY 273)

PROPOSED FLOWER BEDS
(POSSIBLY LOCATED AND
MAINTAINED BY LOCAL GARDEN CLUBS)
PROPOSED FLOWER BEDS
BY THE HOSPITAL

ELKHART GENERAL
HOSPITAL

Project No 8936
Drawn   S.M.
Checked
Scale   1"=20'-0"
Date   8-21-89
Revision

PARKING LOT SCHEMATIC
LANDSCAPE PLAN

BROWNING DAY MULLINS DIERDORF INC.

123

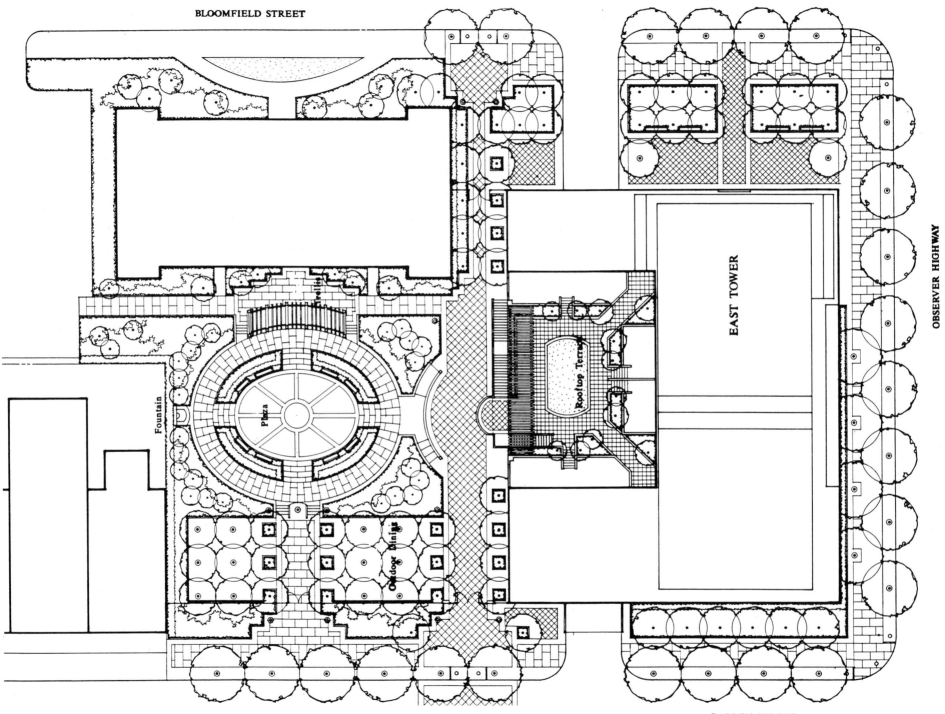

BLOOMFIELD STREET

OBSERVER HIGHWAY

EAST TOWER

Rooftop Terrace

Fountain

Plaza

Outdoor Dining

GARDEN STREET

124   MICELI KULIK WILLIAMS & ASSOCIATES. Observer Park, Hoboken, New Jersey.

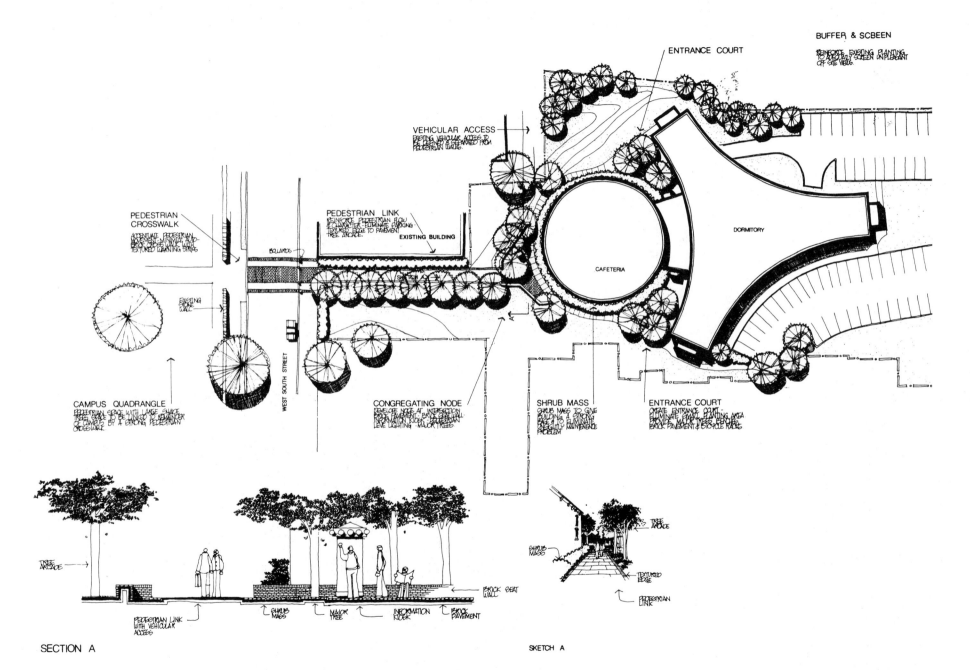

BUFFER & SCREEN
REINFORCE EXISTING PLANTING TO ADEQUATELY SCREEN UNPLEASANT OFF-SITE VIEWS.

ENTRANCE COURT

VEHICULAR ACCESS
EXISTING VEHICULAR ACCESS TO BE DEFINED & SEPARATED FROM PEDESTRIAN WALKS.

PEDESTRIAN CROSSWALK
ACCENTUATE PEDESTRIAN MOVEMENT MINIMIZE AUTO-MOVEMENT IN AREA WITH TEXTURED CROSSING STRIPS.

PEDESTRIAN LINK
REINFORCE PEDESTRIAN FLOW & CHARACTER. ELIMINATE PARKING. TEXTURED EDGE TO PAVEMENT. TREE ARCADE.

EXISTING BUILDING

BOLLARDS

EXISTING STONE WALL

WEST SOUTH STREET

DORMITORY

CAFETERIA

CAMPUS QUADRANGLE
PEDESTRIAN SPACE WITH LARGE SHADE TREES. SPACE TO BE LINKED TO REMAINDER OF CAMPUS BY A STRONG PEDESTRIAN CROSSWALK.

CONGREGATING NODE
DEVELOP NODE AT INTERSECTION. BRICK PAVEMENT. BRICK SEATWALL. INFORMATION KIOSK. PEDESTRIAN LEVEL LIGHTING. MAJOR TREES.

SHRUB MASS
SHRUB MASS TO GIVE BUILDING A STRONG BASE & TO ELIMINATE MAINTENANCE PROBLEM.

ENTRANCE COURT
CREATE ENTRANCE COURT. ELIMINATE SMALL PLANTING AREAS. PROVIDE MAJOR TREES. PROVIDE BRICK PAVEMENT & BICYCLE RACKS.

TREE ARCADE

PEDESTRIAN LINK WITH VEHICULAR ACCESS

SHRUB MASS

MAJOR TREE

INFORMATION KIOSK

BRICK PAVEMENT

BRICK SEAT WALL

SHRUB MASS

TREE ARCADE

TEXTURED EDGE

PEDESTRIAN LINK

SECTION A

SKETCH A

MICELI WEED KULIK. Wilkes College.

125

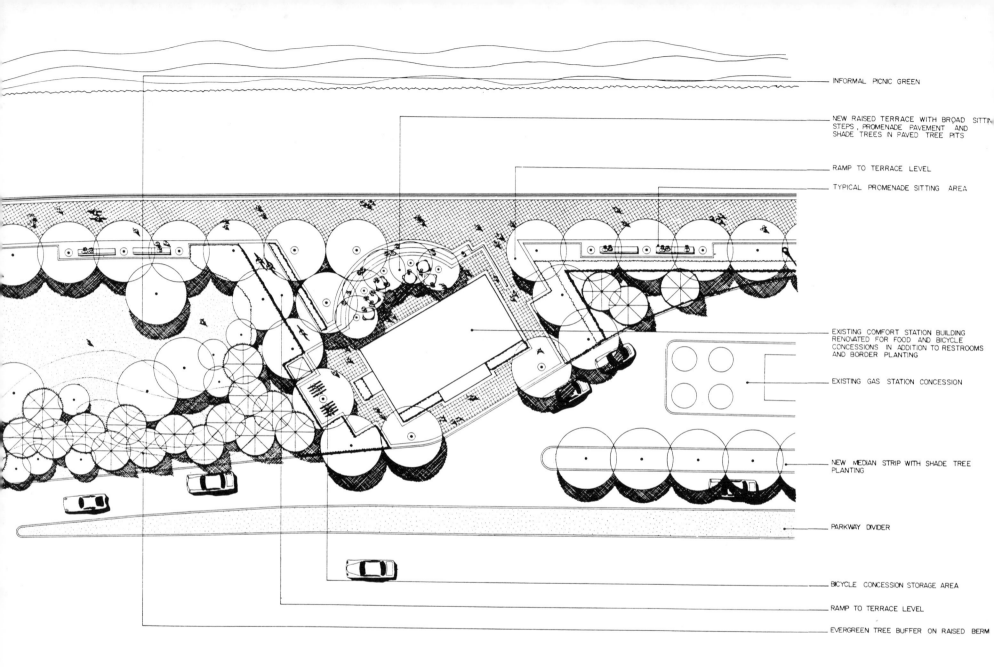

INFORMAL PICNIC GREEN

NEW RAISED TERRACE WITH BROAD SITTIN STEPS, PROMENADE PAVEMENT AND SHADE TREES IN PAVED TREE PITS

RAMP TO TERRACE LEVEL

TYPICAL PROMENADE SITTING AREA

EXISTING COMFORT STATION BUILDING RENOVATED FOR FOOD AND BICYCLE CONCESSIONS IN ADDITION TO RESTROOMS AND BORDER PLANTING

EXISTING GAS STATION CONCESSION

NEW MEDIAN STRIP WITH SHADE TREE PLANTING

PARKWAY DIVIDER

BICYCLE CONCESSION STORAGE AREA

RAMP TO TERRACE LEVEL

EVERGREEN TREE BUFFER ON RAISED BERM

MICELI KULIK WILLIAMS & ASSOCIATES. Flushing Bay Promenade, New York City.

126

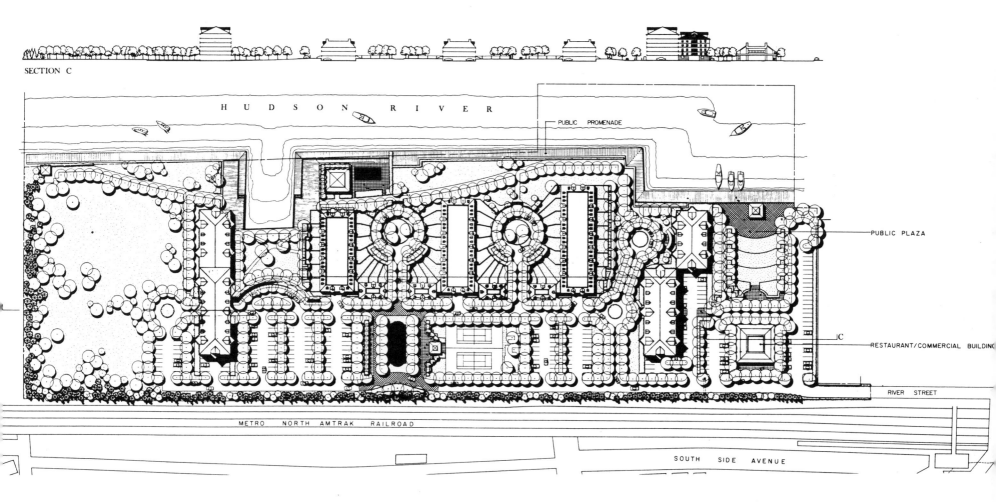

SECTION C

HUDSON RIVER

PUBLIC PROMENADE

PUBLIC PLAZA

RESTAURANT/COMMERCIAL BUILDING

C

RIVER STREET

METRO NORTH AMTRAK RAILROAD

SOUTH SIDE AVENUE

MICELI KULIK WILLIAMS & ASSOCIATES. Harbor-at-Hastings, New York.

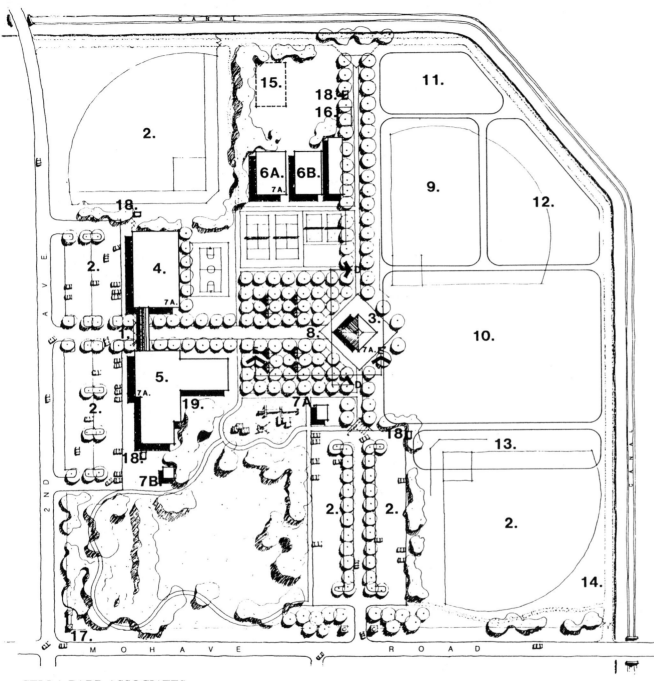

MANATABA · PARK
F A I R · P L A N

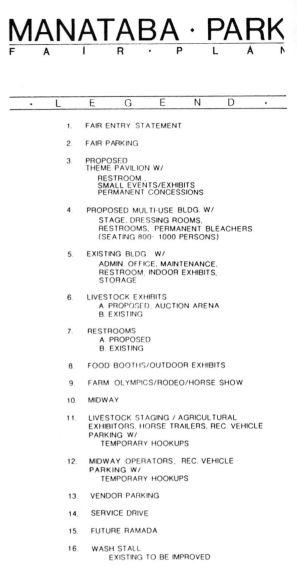

· L E G E N D ·

1.   FAIR ENTRY STATEMENT

2.   FAIR PARKING

3.   PROPOSED
     THEME PAVILION W/
       RESTROOM ,
       SMALL EVENTS/EXHIBITS
       PERMANENT CONCESSIONS

4.   PROPOSED MULTI-USE BLDG. W/
       STAGE, DRESSING ROOMS,
       RESTROOMS, PERMANENT BLEACHERS
       (SEATING 800- 1000 PERSONS)

5.   EXISTING BLDG. W/
       ADMIN. OFFICE, MAINTENANCE,
       RESTROOM, INDOOR EXHIBITS,
       STORAGE

6.   LIVESTOCK EXHIBITS
       A PROPOSED, AUCTION ARENA
       B. EXISTING

7.   RESTROOMS
       A. PROPOSED
       B. EXISTING

8.   FOOD BOOTHS/OUTDOOR EXHIBITS

9.   FARM OLYMPICS/RODEO/HORSE SHOW

10. MIDWAY

11. LIVESTOCK STAGING / AGRICULTURAL
     EXHIBITORS, HORSE TRAILERS, REC. VEHICLE
     PARKING W/
       TEMPORARY HOOKUPS

12. MIDWAY OPERATORS, REC. VEHICLE
     PARKING W/
       TEMPORARY HOOKUPS

13. VENDOR PARKING

14. SERVICE DRIVE

15. FUTURE RAMADA

16. WASH STALL
       EXISTING TO BE IMPROVED

17. MARQUEE

18. TRASH DUMPSTER

19. MAIN ELECTRICAL PANEL

PREPARED FOR
COLORADO RIVER
INDIAN TRIBES

CELLA BARR
ASSOCIATES

12/7/88   41252-01-74

CELLA BARR ASSOCIATES.

128

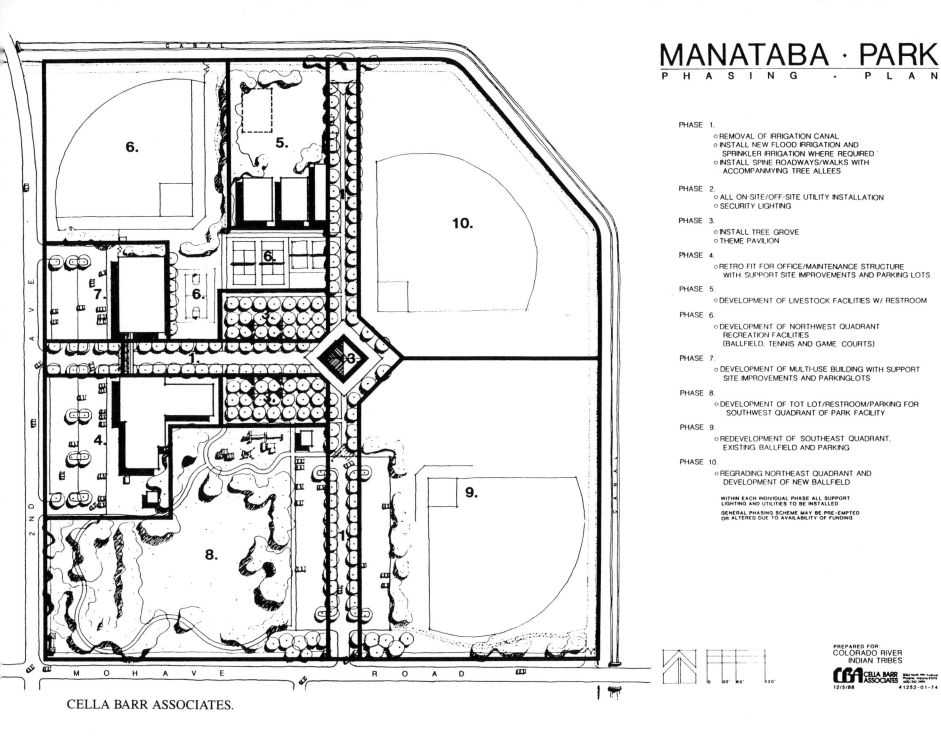

MANATABA · PARK
P H A S I N G · P L A N

PHASE 1.
- o REMOVAL OF IRRIGATION CANAL
- o INSTALL NEW FLOOD IRRIGATION AND
  SPRINKLER IRRIGATION WHERE REQUIRED
- o INSTALL SPINE ROADWAYS/WALKS WITH
  ACCOMPANMYING TREE ALLEES

PHASE 2.
- o ALL ON-SITE/OFF-SITE UTILITY INSTALLATION
- o SECURITY LIGHTING

PHASE 3.
- o INSTALL TREE GROVE
- o THEME PAVILION

PHASE 4.
- o RETRO FIT FOR OFFICE/MAINTENANCE STRUCTURE
  WITH SUPPORT SITE IMPROVEMENTS AND PARKING LOTS

PHASE 5.
- o DEVELOPMENT OF LIVESTOCK FACILITIES W/ RESTROOM

PHASE 6.
- o DEVELOPMENT OF NORTHWEST QUADRANT
  RECREATION FACILITIES
  (BALLFIELD, TENNIS AND GAME COURTS)

PHASE 7.
- o DEVELOPMENT OF MULTI-USE BUILDING WITH SUPPORT
  SITE IMPROVEMENTS AND PARKINGLOTS

PHASE 8.
- o DEVELOPMENT OF TOT LOT/RESTROOM/PARKING FOR
  SOUTHWEST QUADRANT OF PARK FACILITY

PHASE 9.
- o REDEVELOPMENT OF SOUTHEAST QUADRANT.
  EXISTING BALLFIELD AND PARKING

PHASE 10.
- o REGRADING NORTHEAST QUADRANT AND
  DEVELOPMENT OF NEW BALLFIELD

WITHIN EACH INDIVIDUAL PHASE ALL SUPPORT
LIGHTING AND UTILITIES TO BE INSTALLED

GENERAL PHASING SCHEME MAY BE PRE-EMPTED
OR ALTERED DUE TO AVAILABILITY OF FUNDING

PREPARED FOR:
COLORADO RIVER
INDIAN TRIBES

CBA CELLA BARR ASSOCIATES
12/5/88   41252-01-74

CELLA BARR ASSOCIATES.

129

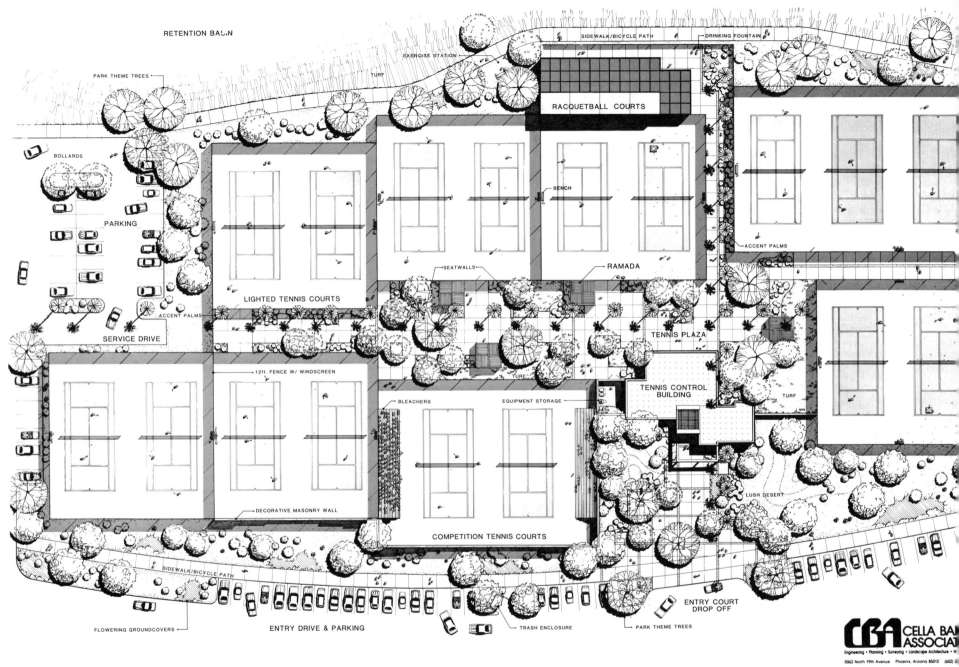

RETENTION BASIN

SIDEWALK/BICYCLE PATH

DRINKING FOUNTAIN

EXERCISE STATION

PARK THEME TREES

TURF

RACQUETBALL COURTS

BOLLARDS

PARKING

ACCENT PALMS

BENCH

ACCENT PALMS

LIGHTED TENNIS COURTS

SERVICE DRIVE

ACCENT PALMS

SEATWALLS

RAMADA

TENNIS PLAZA

12ft. FENCE W/ WINDSCREEN

TURF

TENNIS CONTROL BUILDING

TURF

BLEACHERS

EQUIPMENT STORAGE

DECORATIVE MASONRY WALL

LUSH DESERT

COMPETITION TENNIS COURTS

SIDEWALK/BICYCLE PATH

ENTRY COURT DROP OFF

FLOWERING GROUNDCOVERS

ENTRY DRIVE & PARKING

TRASH ENCLOSURE

PARK THEME TREES

SCOTTSDALE RANCH PARK

TENNIS CONTROL BUILDING & PLAZA AREA

CELLA BARR ASSOCIATES.

130

CBA CELLA BARR ASSOCIAT

Engineering • Planning • Surveying • Landscape Architecture • H

5062 North 19th Avenue   Phoenix, Arizona 85015   (602) 2

CBA JOB NO.: 409

0   20   40   80 feet No

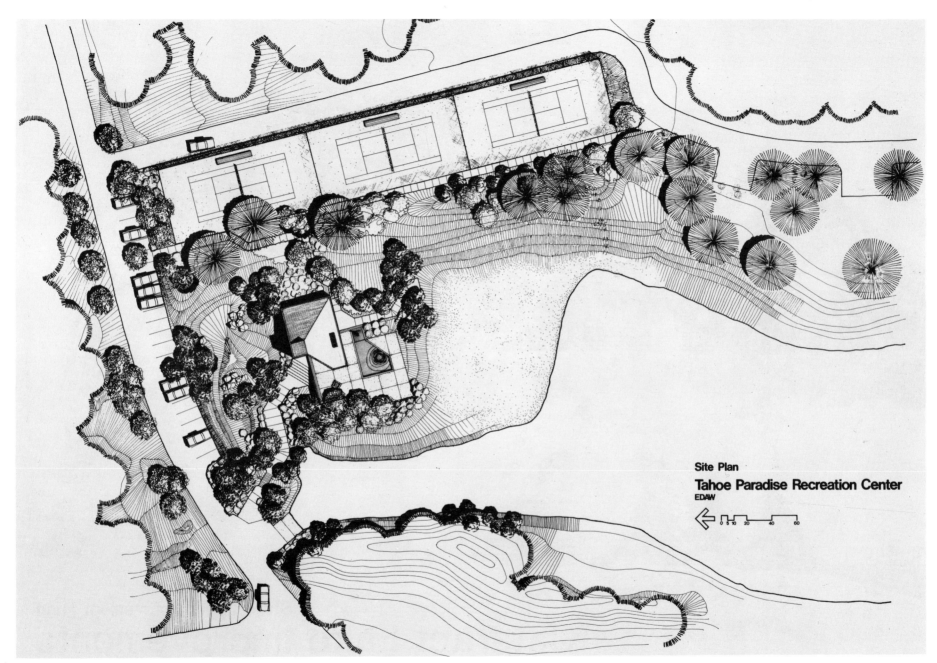

Site Plan
Tahoe Paradise Recreation Center
EDAW

0 5 10   20   40   60

EDAW inc., by Daniel A. Sudquist. Landscape Design Guide for the Citizens of Pueblo.

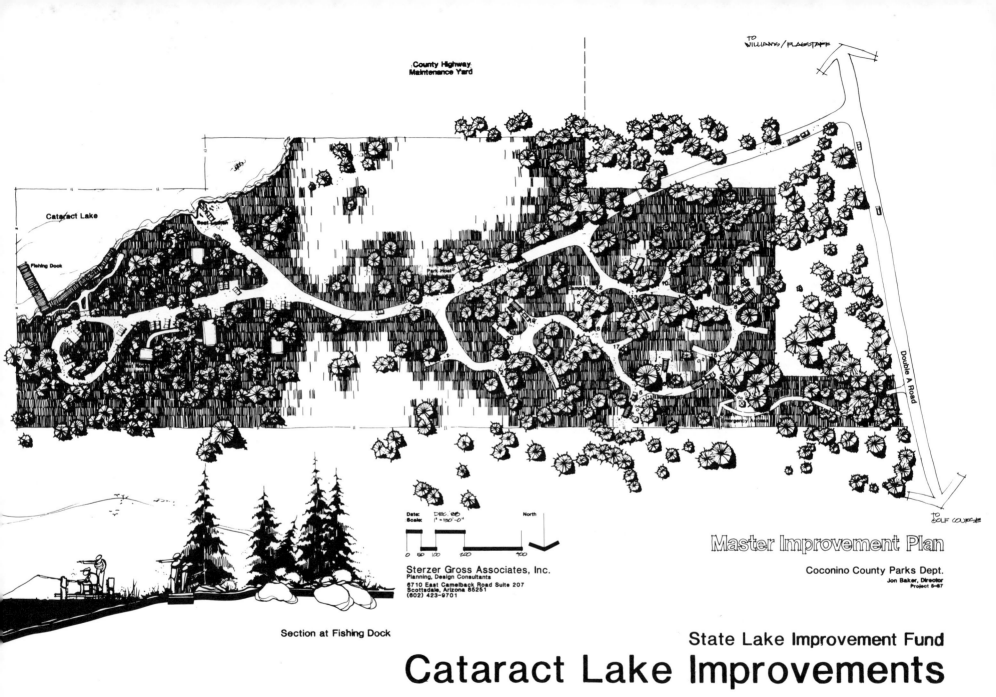

County Highway
Maintenance Yard

TO
WILLIAMS / FLAGSTAFF

Cataract Lake

Fishing Dock

Double A Road

TO
GOLF COURSE

Date: DEC. 88
Scale: 1" = 130'-0"

North

0   50   100   200   400

Sterzer Gross Associates, Inc.
Planning, Design Consultants
6710 East Camelback Road Suite 207
Scottsdale, Arizona 85251
(602) 423-9701

Master Improvement Plan

Coconino County Parks Dept.
Jon Baker, Director
Project 5-87

Section at Fishing Dock

State Lake Improvement Fund

Cataract Lake Improvements

STERZER GROSS ASSOCIATES. Pencil, ink and black tape on mylar, reduced from 24″ x 36″.

Shore Front Park · Pelham Manor, New York

A.E. Bye and Associates · Landscape Architects

A. E. BYE & ASSOCIATES.

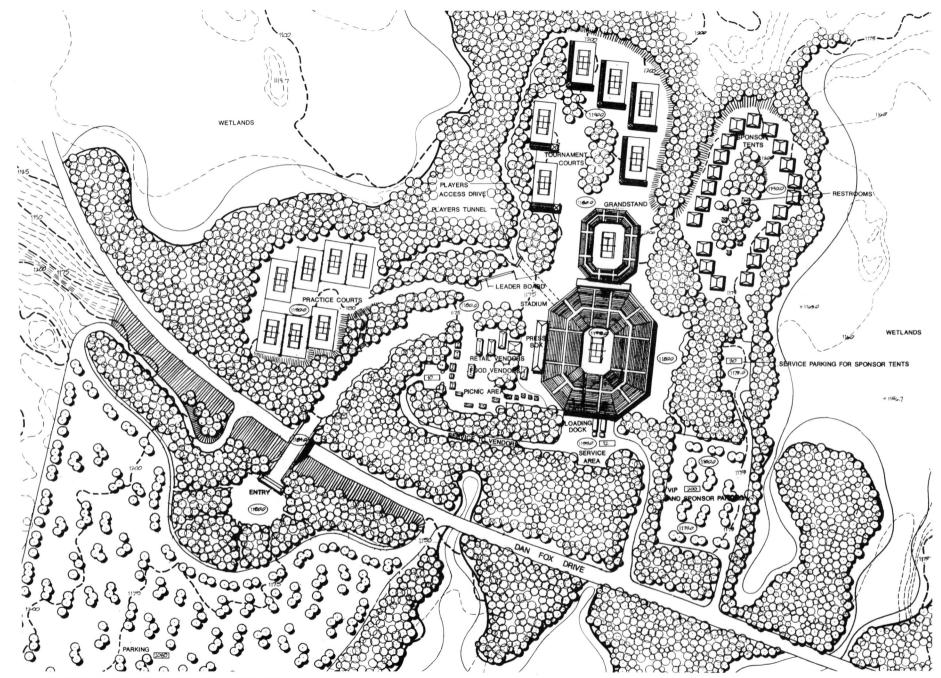

WETLANDS

TOURNAMENT
COURTS

PLAYERS
ACCESS DRIVE

PLAYERS TUNNEL

SPONSOR
TENTS

RESTROOMS

GRANDSTAND

LEADER BOARD

STADIUM

PRACTICE COURTS

WETLANDS

PRESS
BOX

RETAIL VENDORS

FOOD VENDORS

SERVICE PARKING FOR SPONSOR TENTS

PICNIC AREA

SERVICE TO VENDORS

LOADING
DOCK

SERVICE
AREA

ENTRY

VIP
AND SPONSOR PARKING

DAN FOX DRIVE

PARKING

BROWNING DAY MULLINS DIERDORF INC.

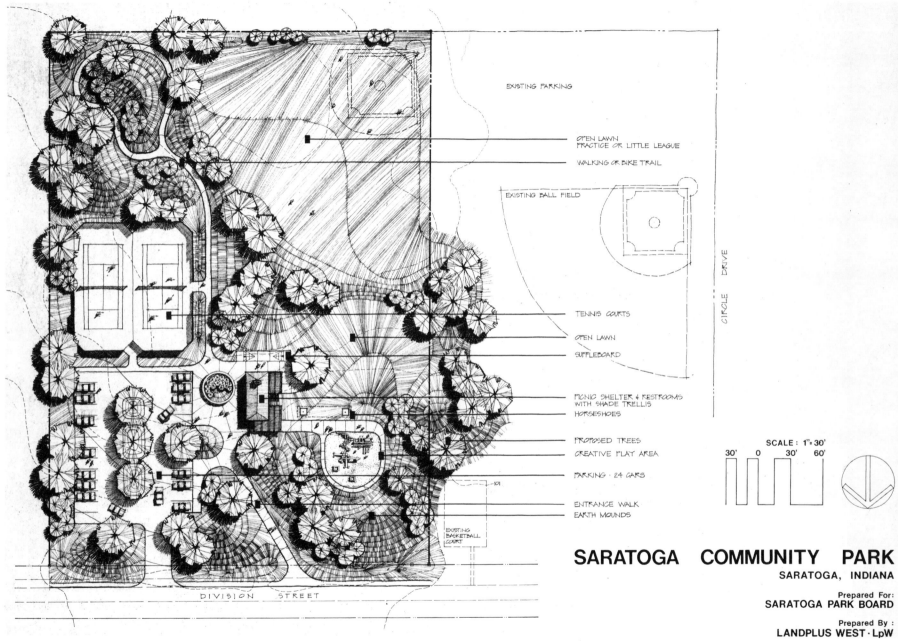

EXISTING PARKING

OPEN LAWN
PRACTICE OR LITTLE LEAGUE

WALKING OR BIKE TRAIL

EXISTING BALL FIELD

CIRCLE DRIVE

TENNIS COURTS

OPEN LAWN

SHUFFLEBOARD

PICNIC SHELTER & RESTROOMS
WITH SHADE TRELLIS

HORSESHOES

PROPOSED TREES

CREATIVE PLAY AREA

PARKING · 24 CARS

ENTRANCE WALK

EARTH MOUNDS

EXISTING
BASKETBALL
COURT

DIVISION STREET

SCALE : 1"=30'
30'   0   30'   60'

SARATOGA COMMUNITY PARK
SARATOGA, INDIANA

Prepared For:
SARATOGA PARK BOARD

Prepared By :
LANDPLUS WEST · LpW

LANDPLUS WEST by Bruce Alexander and Deane Rundell.

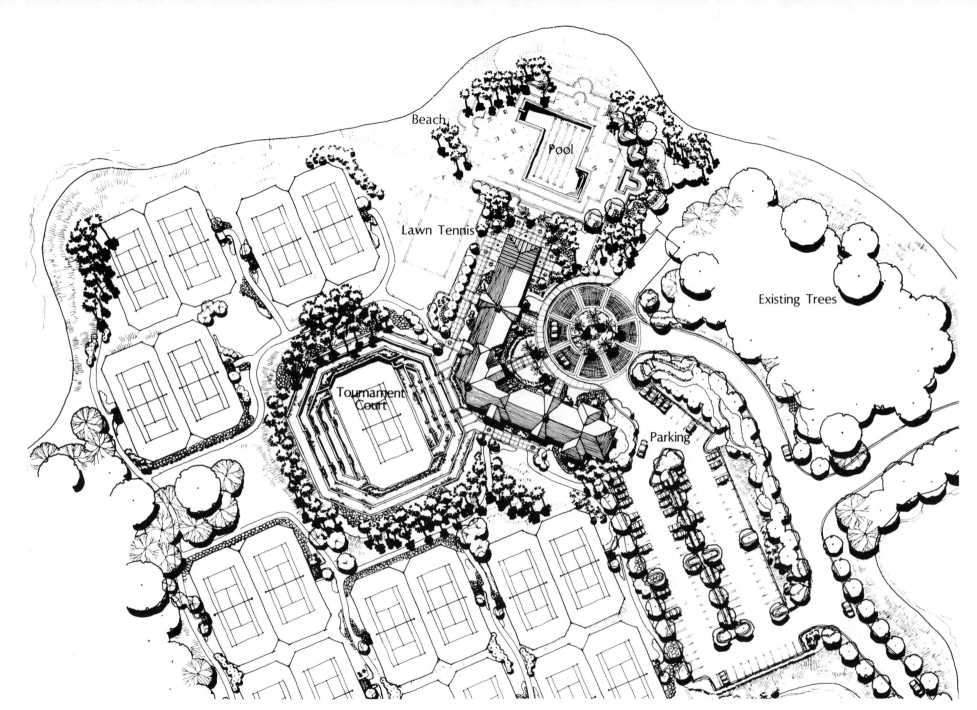

POST BUCKLEY SCHUH & JERNIGAN. The Racquet Club at Heathrow. Ink on mylar, reduced from 18″ x 24″.

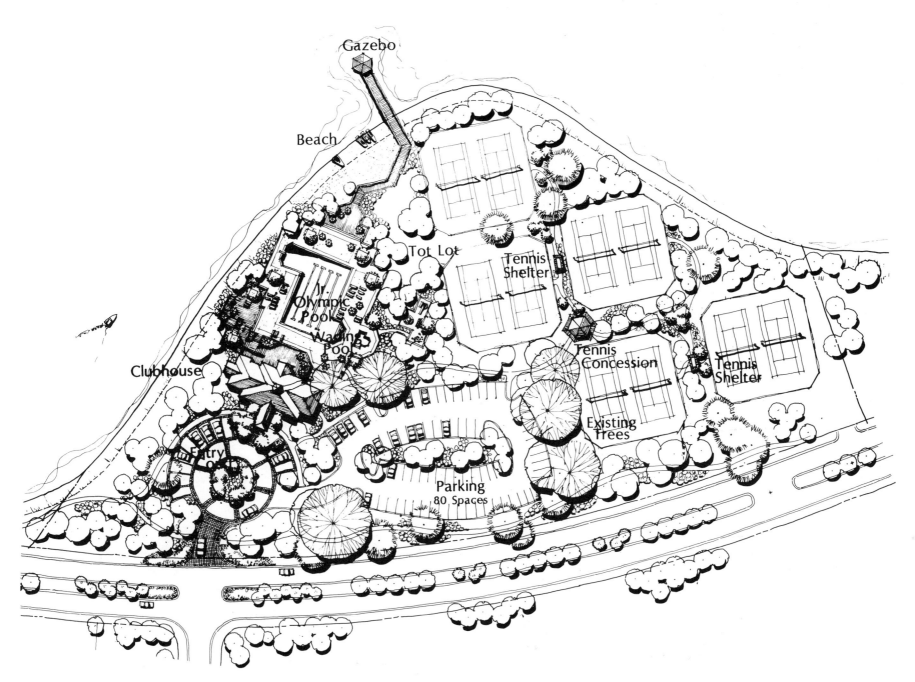

Gazebo

Beach

Tot Lot

Tennis
Shelter

Clubhouse

Olympic
Pool

Wading
Pool

Entry

Tennis
Concession

Tennis
Shelter

Existing
Trees

Parking
80 Spaces

POST BUCKLEY SCHUH & JERNIGAN. Lake Forest Club Site. Ink on mylar reduced
from 15″ x 20″.

POST BUCKLEY SCHUH & JERNIGAN. The Arboretum at DeBary Bajou. Ink on
mylar, reduced from 19″ x 26″.

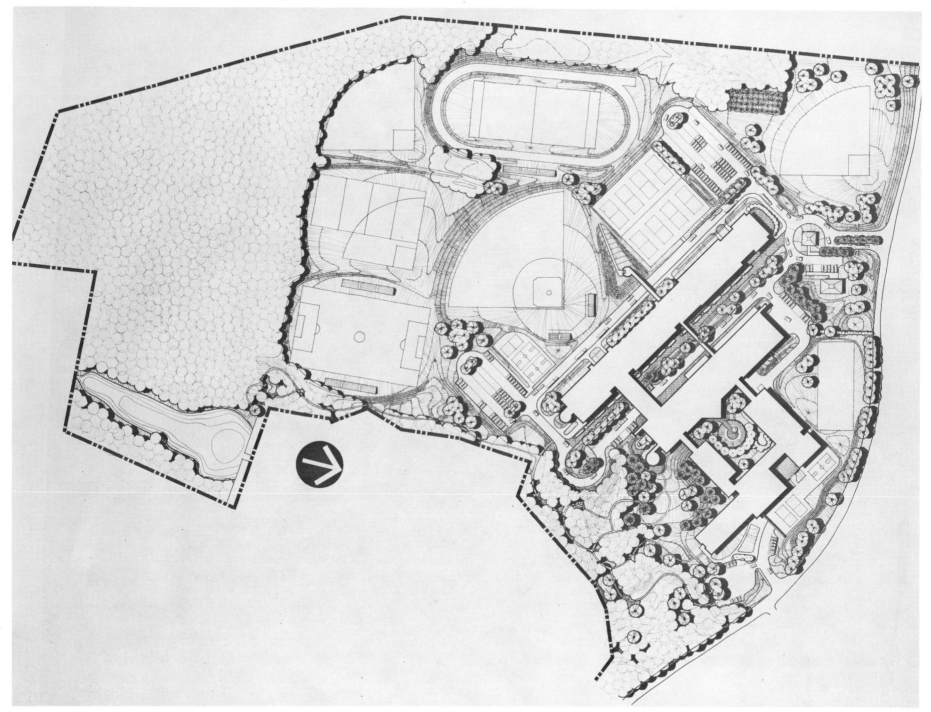

CR3 inc., by Jeffrey A. Gebrian/JETER COOK & JEPSON.

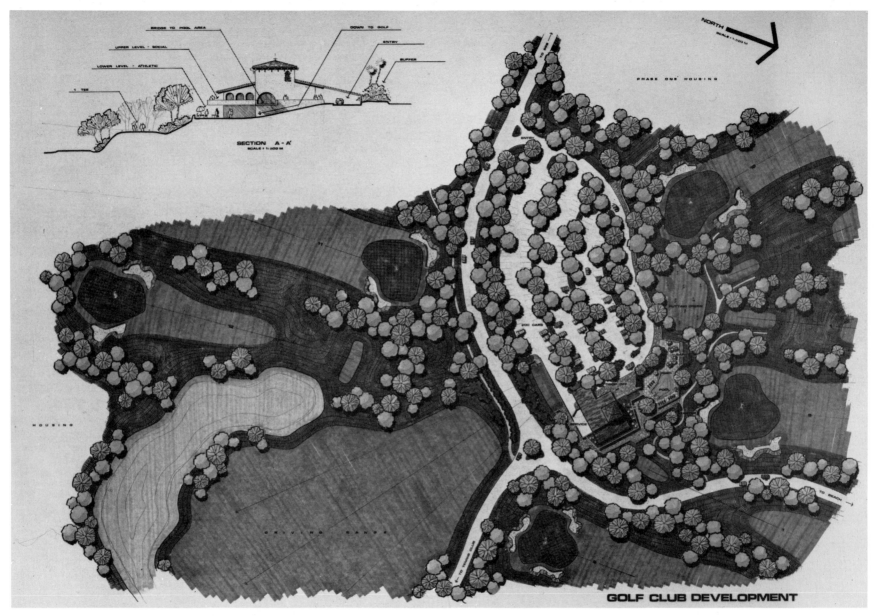

SECTION A-A'
SCALE 1:1:200 M

NORTH
SCALE 1:1:200 M

PHASE ONE HOUSING

GOLF CLUB DEVELOPMENT

EDWARD D. STONE JR. & ASSOCIATES. Palmer Resort.

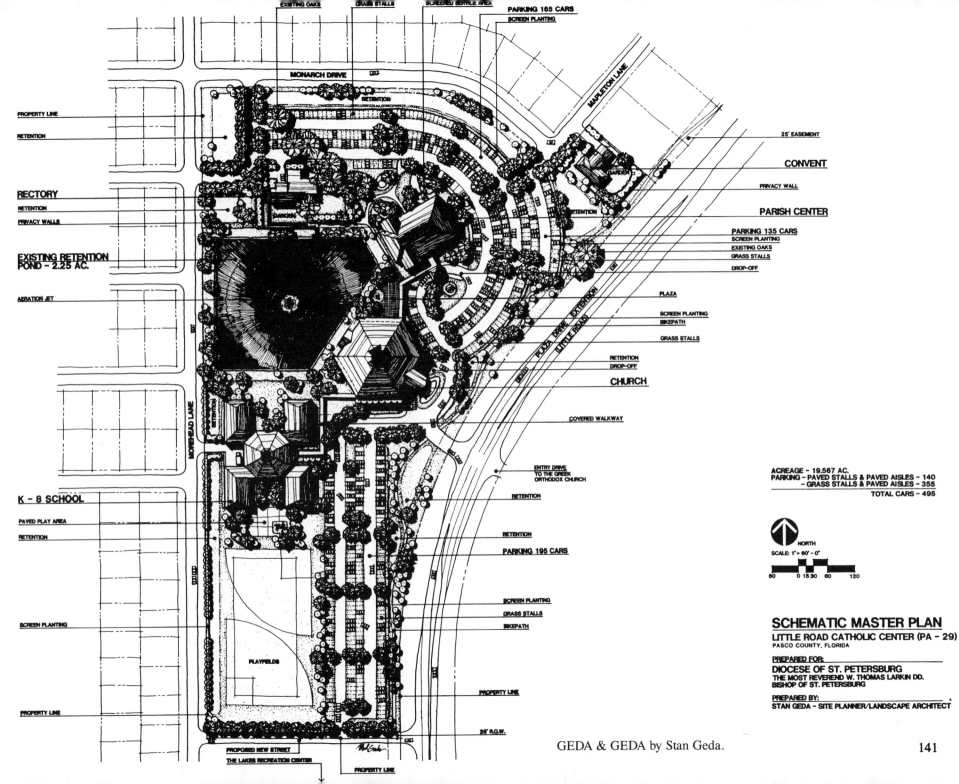

EXISTING OAKS   GRASS STALLS   SCREENED SERVICE AREA   PARKING 165 CARS
SCREEN PLANTING

MONARCH DRIVE

RETENTION

PROPERTY LINE

RETENTION

25' EASEMENT

CONVENT

PRIVACY WALL

GARDEN

RECTORY
RETENTION
PRIVACY WALLS

PARISH CENTER

PARKING 135 CARS
SCREEN PLANTING
EXISTING OAKS
GRASS STALLS
DROP-OFF

EXISTING RETENTION
POND - 2.25 AC.

PLAZA

SCREEN PLANTING
BIKEPATH

AERATION JET

GRASS STALLS

RETENTION
DROP-OFF

CHURCH

COVERED WALKWAY

ENTRY DRIVE
TO THE GREEK
ORTHODOX CHURCH

K - 8 SCHOOL

RETENTION

PAVED PLAY AREA
RETENTION

ACREAGE - 19.567 AC.
PARKING - PAVED STALLS & PAVED AISLES - 140
        - GRASS STALLS & PAVED AISLES - 355
                        TOTAL CARS - 495

RETENTION

PARKING 195 CARS

NORTH

SCALE: 1" = 60' - 0"

60   0 15 30   60   120

SCREEN PLANTING

SCREEN PLANTING
GRASS STALLS
BIKEPATH

SCHEMATIC MASTER PLAN
LITTLE ROAD CATHOLIC CENTER (PA - 29)
PASCO COUNTY, FLORIDA

PREPARED FOR:
DIOCESE OF ST. PETERSBURG
THE MOST REVEREND W. THOMAS LARKIN DD.
BISHOP OF ST. PETERSBURG

PREPARED BY:
STAN GEDA - SITE PLANNER/LANDSCAPE ARCHITECT

PLAYFIELDS

PROPERTY LINE

PROPERTY LINE

PROPERTY LINE

25' R.O.W.

PROPOSED NEW STREET
THE LAKES RECREATION CENTER

PROPERTY LINE

GEDA & GEDA by Stan Geda.

141

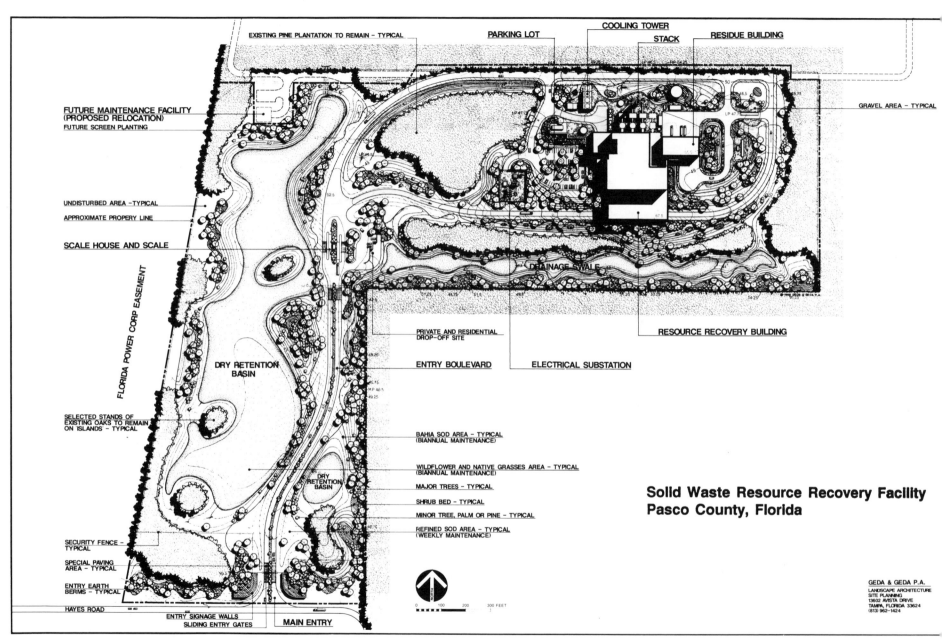

EXISTING PINE PLANTATION TO REMAIN - TYPICAL

PARKING LOT

COOLING TOWER

STACK

RESIDUE BUILDING

GRAVEL AREA - TYPICAL

FUTURE MAINTENANCE FACILITY
(PROPOSED RELOCATION)
FUTURE SCREEN PLANTING

UNDISTURBED AREA - TYPICAL

APPROXIMATE PROPERY LINE

SCALE HOUSE AND SCALE

FLORIDA POWER CORP EASEMENT

DRAINAGE SWALE

DRY RETENTION BASIN

PRIVATE AND RESIDENTIAL
DROP-OFF SITE

RESOURCE RECOVERY BUILDING

ENTRY BOULEVARD

ELECTRICAL SUBSTATION

SELECTED STANDS OF
EXISTING OAKS TO REMAIN
ON ISLANDS - TYPICAL

DRY RETENTION BASIN

BAHIA SOD AREA - TYPICAL
(BIANNUAL MAINTENANCE)

WILDFLOWER AND NATIVE GRASSES AREA - TYPICAL
(BIANNUAL MAINTENANCE)

MAJOR TREES - TYPICAL

SHRUB BED - TYPICAL

MINOR TREE, PALM OR PINE - TYPICAL

REFINED SOD AREA - TYPICAL
(WEEKLY MAINTENANCE)

**Solid Waste Resource Recovery Facility
Pasco County, Florida**

SECURITY FENCE -
TYPICAL

SPECIAL PAVING
AREA - TYPICAL

ENTRY EARTH
BERMS - TYPICAL

HAYES ROAD

ENTRY SIGNAGE WALLS
SLIDING ENTRY GATES

MAIN ENTRY

NORTH

0   100   200   300 FEET

GEDA & GEDA P.A.
LANDSCAPE ARCHITECTURE
SITE PLANNING
13602 AVISTA DRIVE
TAMPA, FLORIDA 33624
(813) 962-1424

GEDA & GEDA by Stan Geda.

142

GEDA & GEDA by Stan Geda.

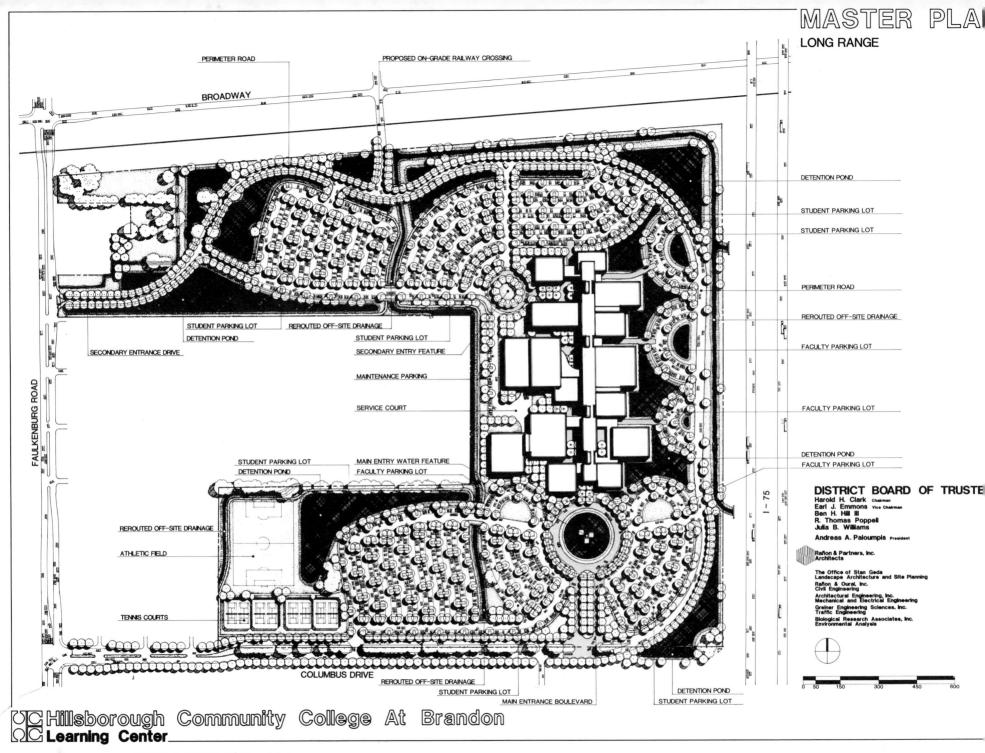

MASTER PLA[N]

LONG RANGE

PERIMETER ROAD

PROPOSED ON-GRADE RAILWAY CROSSING

BROADWAY

DETENTION POND

STUDENT PARKING LOT

STUDENT PARKING LOT

PERIMETER ROAD

STUDENT PARKING LOT

REROUTED OFF-SITE DRAINAGE

REROUTED OFF-SITE DRAINAGE

DETENTION POND

FACULTY PARKING LOT

SECONDARY ENTRANCE DRIVE

STUDENT PARKING LOT

SECONDARY ENTRY FEATURE

MAINTENANCE PARKING

FACULTY PARKING LOT

SERVICE COURT

FAULKENBURG ROAD

STUDENT PARKING LOT

MAIN ENTRY WATER FEATURE

DETENTION POND

DETENTION POND

FACULTY PARKING LOT

FACULTY PARKING LOT

I - 75

REROUTED OFF-SITE DRAINAGE

ATHLETIC FIELD

TENNIS COURTS

COLUMBUS DRIVE

REROUTED OFF-SITE DRAINAGE

STUDENT PARKING LOT

DETENTION POND

MAIN ENTRANCE BOULEVARD

STUDENT PARKING LOT

0 50 150 300 450 600

Hillsborough Community College At Brandon
Learning Center

GEDA & GEDA by Stan Geda

FLUSHING MEADOWS CORONA PARK
SCOPE DEVELOPMENT CONTRACT

A UNISPHERE FOUNTIAN

REHABILITATE POOL JETS, MECHANICAL SYSTEM, AND LIGHTING. RECONSTRUCT PERIMETER COPING TO ALLOW FOR SEATING ALONG INSIDE AND OUTSIDE EDGES. POTENTIAL FOR DEVELOPING NEW LIGHTING DISPLAY AND WATER CHOREOGRAPHY.

B UNISPHERE PLAZA

MAJOR GATHERING SPACE DEFINED BY DISTINCTIVE PAVING AND PERIMETER TREE PLANTING WHICH PROVIDES A SENSE OF SCALE AND RE-INFORCES EDGE OF SPACE. SEATING PROVIDED UNDER TREES. PAVILIONS PROVIDE FOOD CONCESSION SPACE.

C COURT OF NATIONS

COURT CELEBRATES THE NEW YORK CITY BUILDING AS THE FIRST HOME OF THE UNITED NATIONS. PLAZA, PLANTINGS, AND A SMALL AMPHITHEATER FOR FORMAL AND INFORMAL GATHERINGS ARE PROVIDED.

D BOSQUE

FLOWERING TREE ALLÉE BUFFERS PARK FROM ADJACENT PARKING AREAS.

E MULTIPURPOSE GREEN

GREEN SPACE ACCOMMODATES INFORMAL GATHERING AND PLAY AS WELL AS OVERFLOW ACTIVITIES FROM EVENTS STAGED AT THE UNISPHERE PLAZA.

F CROSS AXIS ALLEE

MAJOR PEDESTRIAN LINK TO EDERLE POOL AND MEADOW LAKE. NEW PAVEMENT, SEATING, LIGHTING AND SIGNAGE PROVIDED. EXISTING TREES TO REMAIN AND NEW TREES PLANTED TO RE-INFORCE ALLÉE WHERE APPROPRIATE. WIDTH OF EXISTING PAVING REDUCED.

G PERIMETER LOOP

LINKS ENTRY POINTS FROM GRAND CENTRAL PARKWAY PEDESTRIAN BRIDGES TO MAIN FOUNTAIN AXIS AND CONTAINS SCULPTURE GARDEN ZONE. NEW PAVING, LIGHTING, SEATING, AND SIGNAGE PROVIDED. WIDTH OF EXISTING WALK REDUCED. INTERSECTION WITH CROSS AXIS HIGHLIGHTED BY DECORATIVE PAVING PATTERN.

H INTERNATIONAL SCULPTURE GARDEN

INSTALLATION OF MAJOR SCULPTURAL PIECES BY INTERNATIONAL ARTISTS WITHIN A PASTORAL SETTING. THE LANDSCAPE CONSISTS OF LARGE, UNDULATING MEADOWS AND WOODLAND EDGES THAT CONTAIN MEANDERING PATHS, DETAILED SITTING AND GARDEN SPACES, WILDFLOWER BORDERS, FLOWERING TREE AND SHRUB UNDERSTORY, ETC. A VARIETY OF SPATIAL SEQUENCES, VIEWS, AND VISTAS ARE ALSO PROVIDED.

I PASSERELLE ALLEE

MAJOR PEDESTRIAN LINK BETWEEN TENNIS CENTER AND PASSERELLE BUILDING AND THE UNISPHERE PLAZA. EXISTING ALLÉE RE-INFORCED BY NEW TREE PLANTINGS WHERE APPROPRIATE. NEW LIGHTING, PAVING, AND SEATING PROVIDED.

J REFLECTING POOL

POOL, COPING, AND MECHANICAL SYSTEM COMPLETELY RENOVATED. NEW PAVEMENT PLACED ALONG EDGE TO ALLOW GREATER ACCESSIBILITY AND INTERACTION WITH WATER DISPLAY.

K COURT OF THE ASTRONAUTS

SHRUBS REMOVED TO PROVIDE GREATER VISIBILITY TO ROCKET THROUGH SCULPTURE AND STAIRS ADDED TO FACILITATE BETTER CIRCULATION PATTERN. TREES AND TRELLISED COLONNADE DEFINE EDGE OF SPACE AND SCULPTURE GARDEN ENTRANCE. COURT ALSO PROVIDES POTENTIAL FOR ASTRONAUT MEMORIAL.

L FOUNTAIN OF THE FAIRS

POOL, JET, AND MECHANICAL SYSTEM COMPLETELY RENOVATED. DECORATIVE PAVEMENT PLACED ALONG EDGE TO INCREASE ACCESSIBILITY AND INTERACTION WITH FOUNTAIN.

M RADIAL ALLEE

WIDTH OF EXISTING PAVEMENT REDUCED TO REFLECT SECONDARY IMPORTANCE OF THIS CIRCULATION ROUTE. NEW PAVEMENT AND LIGHTING PROVIDED.

N NEW YORK CITY BUILDING

NEW MAIN ENTRANCE CREATED TO RELATE MUSEUM AND SKATING RINK TO COURT OF NATIONS AND PROVIDE APPROPRIATE TERMINUS FOR MAJOR AXIS OF PARK.

MICELI KULIK WILLIAMS & ASSOCIATES.

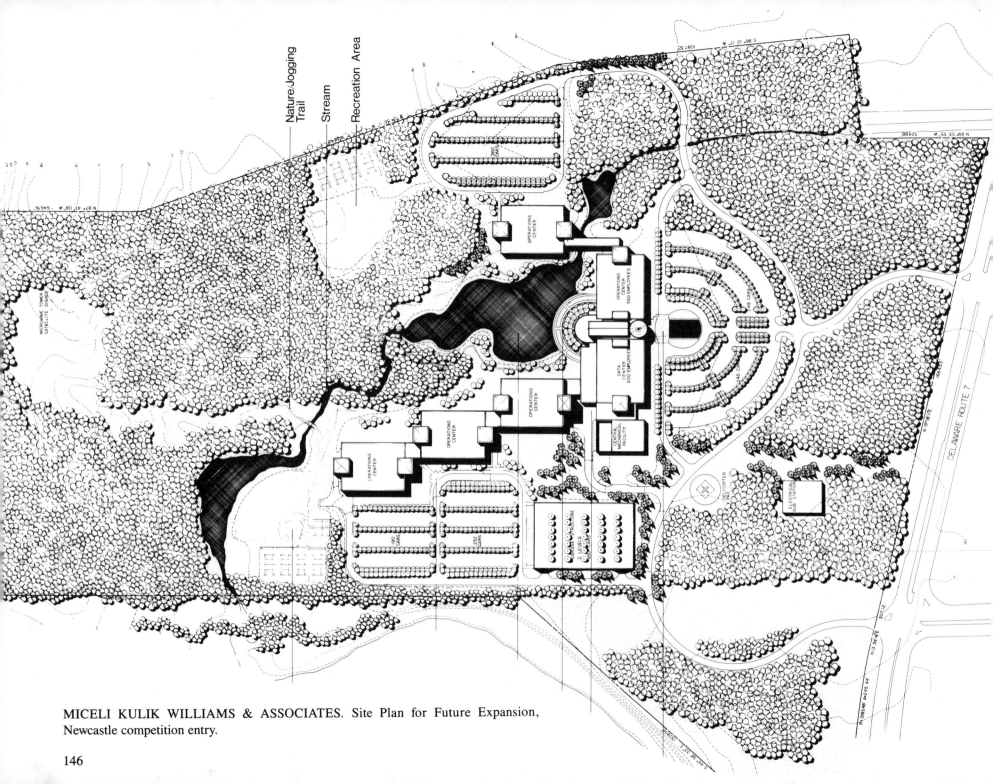

Nature/Jogging Trail

Stream

Recreation Area

MICELI KULIK WILLIAMS & ASSOCIATES. Site Plan for Future Expansion, Newcastle competition entry.

146

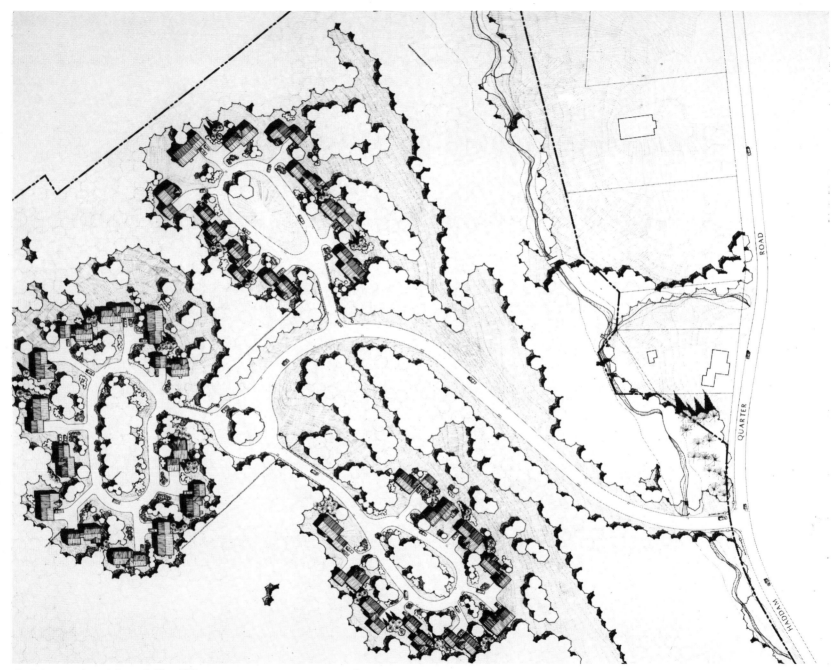

CR3 inc. Reduced from 26″ x 31″.

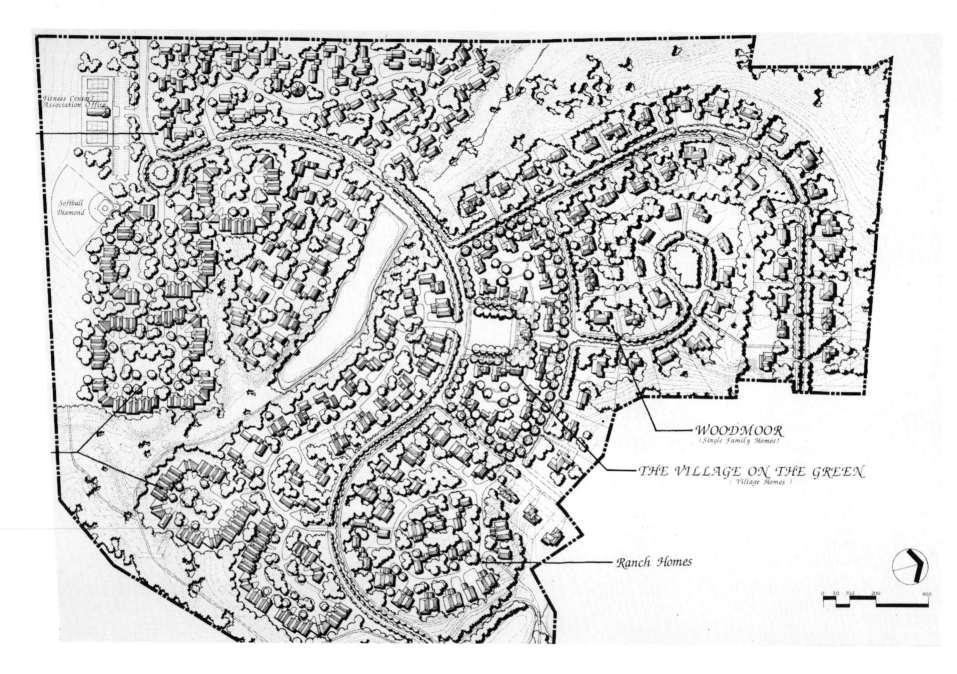

Fitness Center
Association Office

Softball
Diamond

WOODMOOR
(Single Family Homes)

THE VILLAGE ON THE GREEN
(Village Homes)

Ranch Homes

0 50 100 200 400

CR3 inc. Reduced from 24″ x 33″.

148

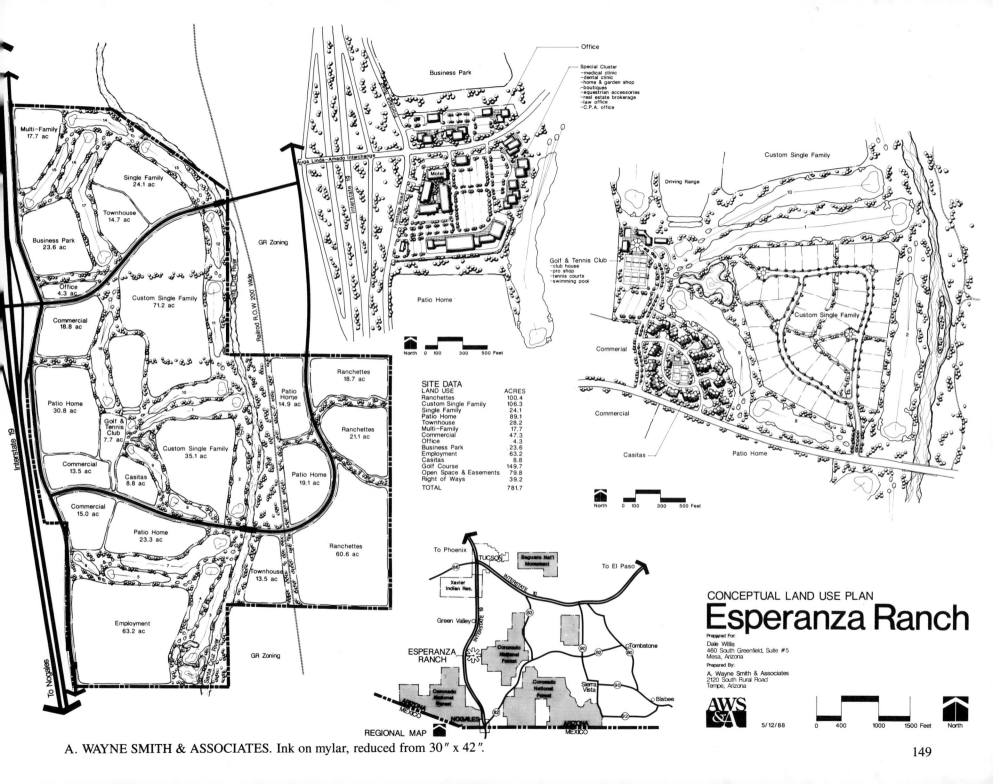

Office

Business Park

Special Cluster
-medical clinic
-dental clinic
-home & garden shop
-boutiques
-equestrian accessories
-real estate brokerage
-law office
-C.P.A. office

Multi-Family
17.7 ac

Single Family
24.1 ac

Townhouse
14.7 ac

Business Park
23.6 ac

Office
4.3 ac

Commercial
18.8 ac

Custom Single Family
71.2 ac

Custom Single Family

Driving Range

GR Zoning

Railroad R.O.W. 200' Wide

Santa Cruz River

Auga Linda–Amado Interchange

Interstate 19

Motel

Frontage Road

Patio Home

Golf & Tennis Club
-club house
-pro shop
-tennis courts
-swimming pool

Custom Single Family

Patio Home
14.9 ac

Ranchettes
18.7 ac

Patio Home
30.8 ac

Golf & Tennis Club
7.7 ac

Custom Single Family
35.1 ac

Commercial
13.5 ac

Casitas
8.8 ac

Commercial
15.0 ac

Patio Home
23.3 ac

Patio Home
19.1 ac

Ranchettes
21.1 ac

Ranchettes
60.6 ac

Townhouse
13.5 ac

Commerial

Commercial

Casitas

Patio Home

Employment
63.2 ac

Interstate 19

To Nogales

North 0 100 300 500 Feet

GR Zoning

SITE DATA

LAND USE	ACRES
Ranchettes	100.4
Custom Single Family	106.3
Single Family	24.1
Patio Home	89.1
Townhouse	28.2
Multi–Family	17.7
Commercial	47.3
Office	4.3
Business Park	.23.6
Employment	63.2
Casitas	8.8
Golf Course	149.7
Open Space & Easements	79.8
Right of Ways	39.2
TOTAL	781.7

North 0 100 300 500 Feet

REGIONAL MAP

To Phoenix

TUCSON

Saguaro Nat'l Monument

To El Paso

Xavier Indian Res.

Green Valley

Interstate 10

Interstate 19

ESPERANZA RANCH

Coronado National Forest

Coronado National Forest

Coronado National Forest

Tombstone

Sierra Vista

Bisbee

ARIZONA
MEXICO

NOGALES

ARIZONA
MEXICO

North

CONCEPTUAL LAND USE PLAN
Esperanza Ranch

Prepared For:
Dale Willis
460 South Greenfield, Suite #5
Mesa, Arizona

Prepared By:
A. Wayne Smith & Associates
2120 South Rural Road
Tempe, Arizona

AWS & A

5/12/88

0 400 1000 1500 Feet North

A. WAYNE SMITH & ASSOCIATES. Ink on mylar, reduced from 30″ x 42″.

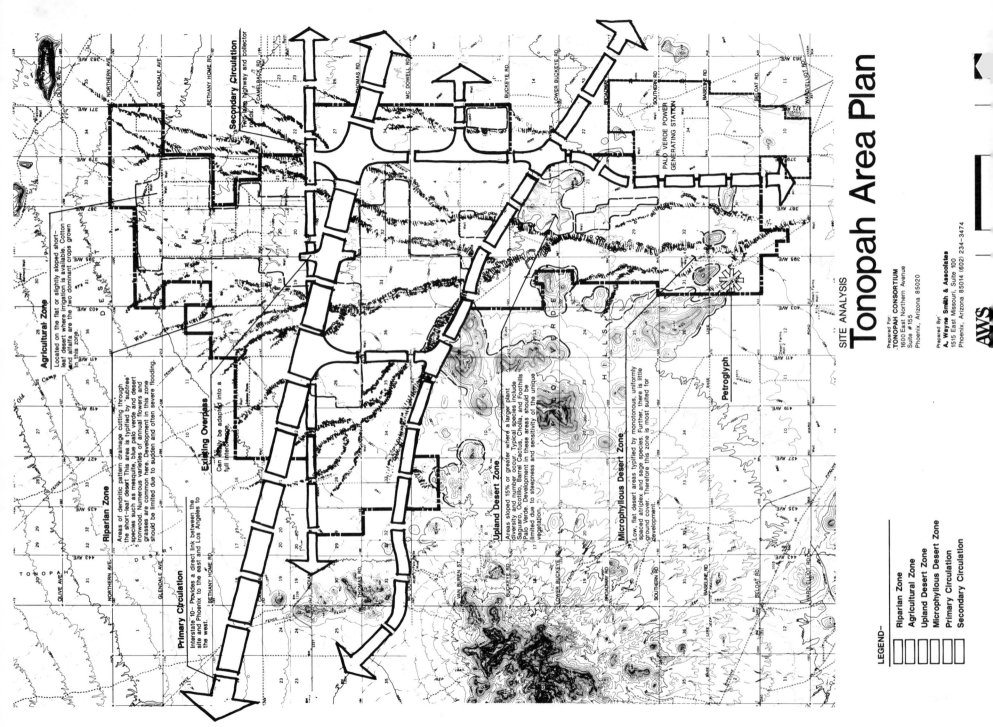

A. WAYNE SMITH & ASSOCIATES. Ink on mylar, reduced from 30″ x 42″.

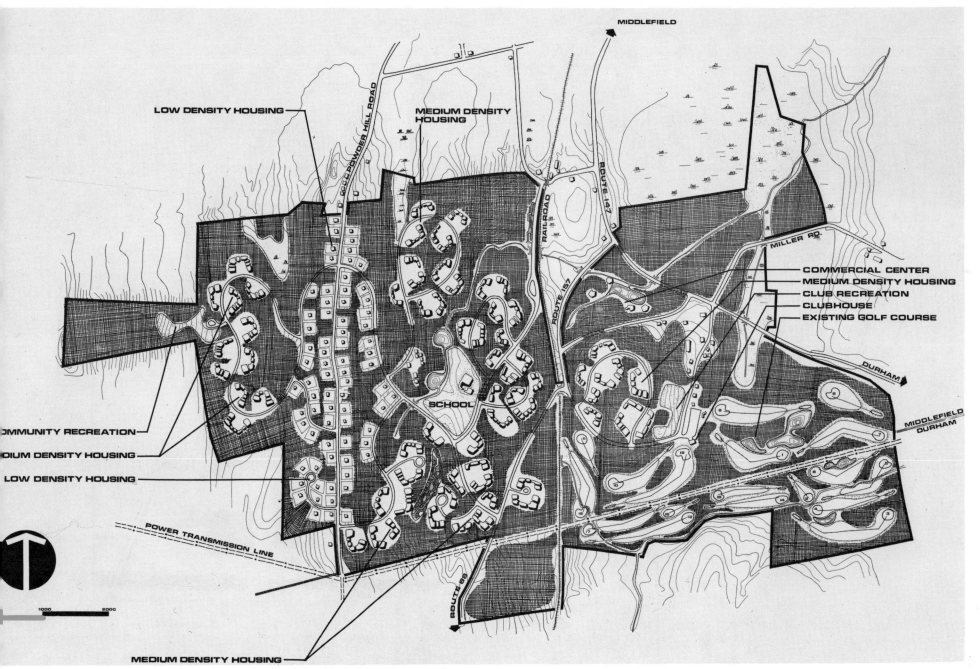

LOW DENSITY HOUSING

MEDIUM DENSITY HOUSING

MIDDLEFIELD

POWDER HILL ROAD

RAILROAD

ROUTE 147

ROUTE 157

MILLER RD.

COMMERCIAL CENTER
MEDIUM DENSITY HOUSING
CLUB RECREATION
CLUBHOUSE
EXISTING GOLF COURSE

DURHAM

MIDDLEFIELD
DURHAM

SCHOOL

COMMUNITY RECREATION

MEDIUM DENSITY HOUSING

LOW DENSITY HOUSING

POWER TRANSMISSION LINE

1000   2000

ROUTE 66

MEDIUM DENSITY HOUSING

CR3 inc., by Jeffrey A. Gebrian/WILLIAM McHUGH. Lyman Farms.

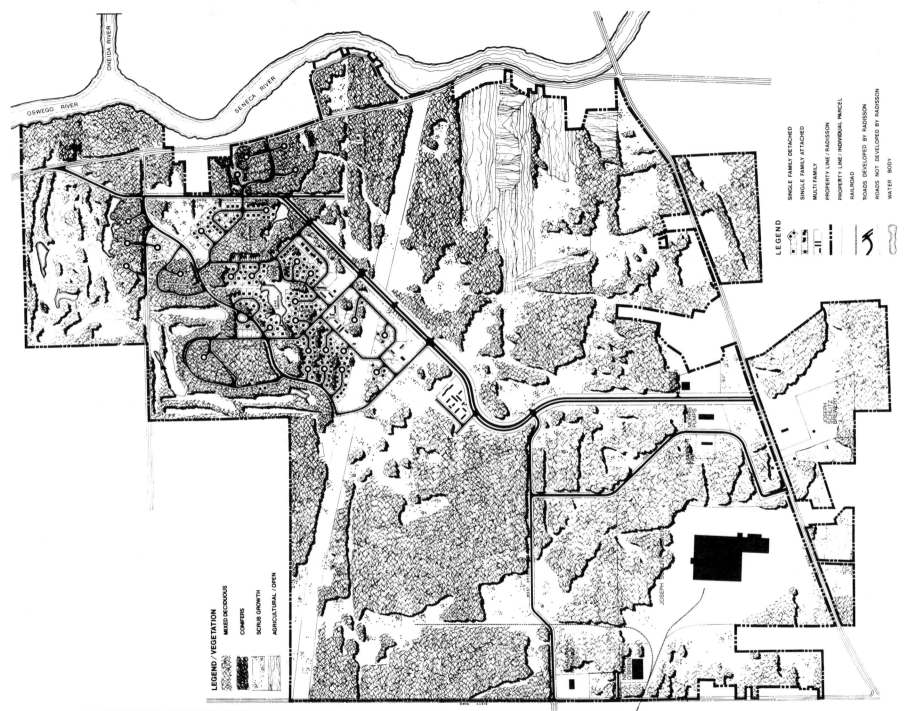

ONEIDA RIVER

OSWEGO RIVER

SENECA RIVER

LEGEND

SINGLE FAMILY DETACHED
SINGLE FAMILY ATTACHED
MULTI FAMILY
PROPERTY LINE / RADISSON
PROPERTY LINE / INDIVIDUAL PARCEL
RAILROAD
ROADS DEVELOPED BY RADISSON
ROADS NOT DEVELOPED BY RADISSON
WATER BODY

LEGEND / VEGETATION

MIXED DECIDUOUS
CONIFERS
SCRUB GROWTH
AGRICULTURAL / OPEN

MORRIS PUMPS

JOSEPH SCHLITZ BREWERY

REIMANN/BUECHNER PARTNERSHIP.

NW 1/4 SECTION 16 SECTION 17, SECTION 18, SECTION 19, and SECTION 20

LAND USE DATA

	LAND USE	ACRES	AVERAGE DENSITY	UNITS
MF	Multi Family	127	18.0 du/ac	2286
TH	Townhouse	203	13.0 du/ac	2639
PH	Patio Home	275	5.5 du/ac	1512
SF	Single Family	437	3.5 du/ac	1529
CSF	Custom Single Family	66	2.5 du/ac	164
	Residential Sub-Total	1108	4.9 du/ac	8130
	Employment	431		
C-2	Commercial	97		
	Office	106		
	Special Use	84		
	Lake/Park	256.5		
	Golf Course	231		
	Country Club	7		
	Compadres Stadium	20		
	School	45		
	Rec. Center	2		
	Road Ways	221		
	Fire Station	1		
	Water Storage	4		
	Water Treatment	80		
	Existing Basha's Facility	25		
	SRP	1.5		
	Total Planing Area	2720		

Used to Calculate Density

All areas are approximate and all sections assumed to contain 640.0 acres

.... Phase 1 Boundary

A NEW TOWN
Ocotillo
MASTER PLAN

Five Hundred Scale

2.20.88

prepared for **OCOTILLO WEST**
1500 East Bethany Home Road Suite 200 Phoenix , Arizona
(602) 264-1300

by **A. Wayne Smith & Associates**
2120 South Rural Road   Tempe , Arizona
(602) 968-8501

A. WAYNE SMITH & ASSOCIATES. Marker on presentation blackline, reduced from 30″ x 42″.

153

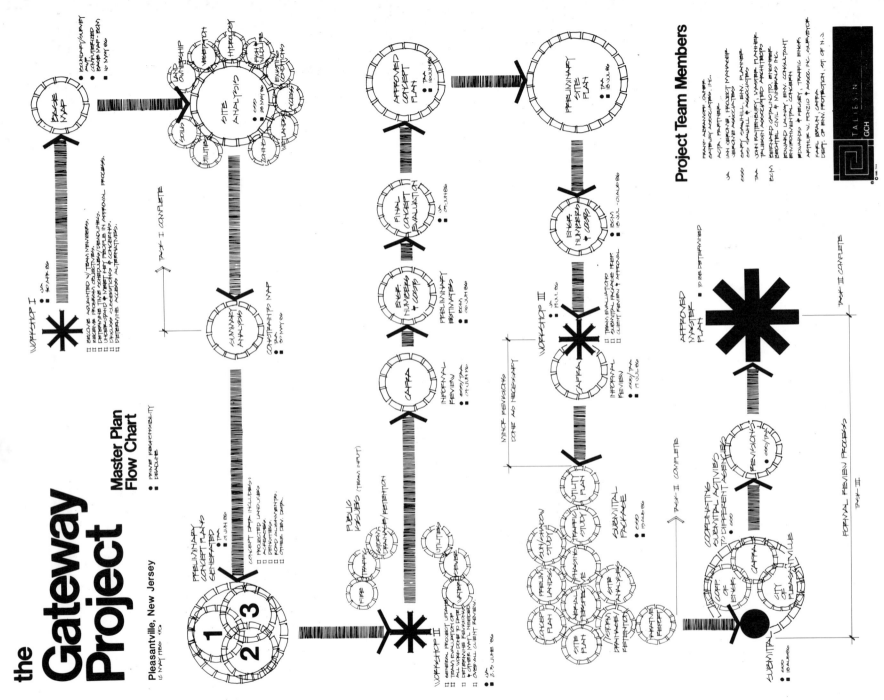

TALIESIN/JOHN STERZER. Ink on mylar, reduced from 24″ x 36″.

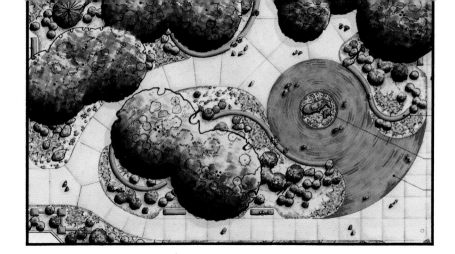

COLOR GRAPHICS

When maximum visual appeal for a plan graphic is desired, color is added to the rendering. As illustrated in the following examples, color can be presented at each level of the design process.

6

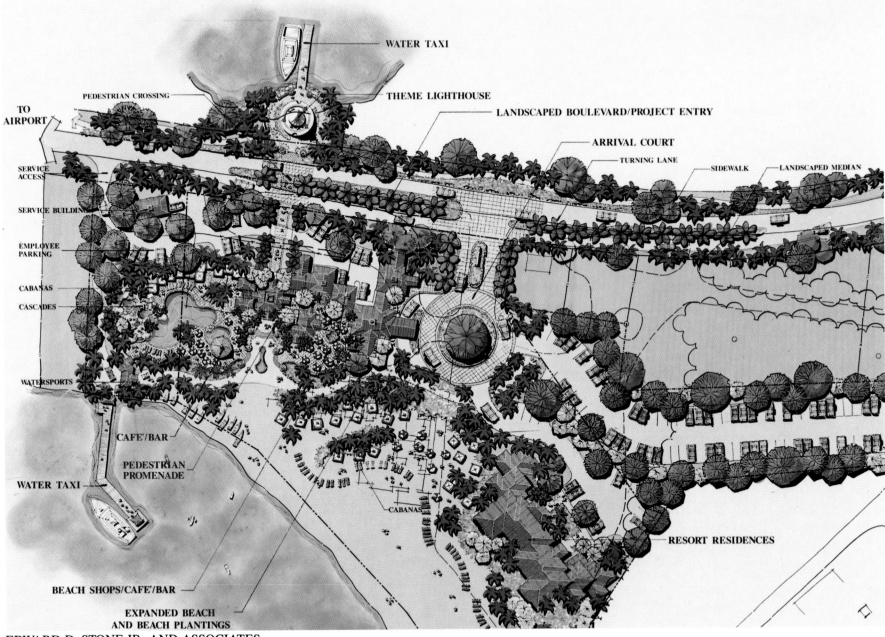

WATER TAXI

PEDESTRIAN CROSSING

THEME LIGHTHOUSE

LANDSCAPED BOULEVARD/PROJECT ENTRY

TO AIRPORT

ARRIVAL COURT

TURNING LANE

SIDEWALK

LANDSCAPED MEDIAN

SERVICE ACCESS

SERVICE BUILDING

EMPLOYEE PARKING

CABANAS

CASCADES

WATERSPORTS

CAFE'/BAR

PEDESTRIAN PROMENADE

WATER TAXI

CABANAS

RESORT RESIDENCES

BEACH SHOPS/CAFE'/BAR

EXPANDED BEACH AND BEACH PLANTINGS

EDWARD D. STONE JR. AND ASSOCIATES.

156

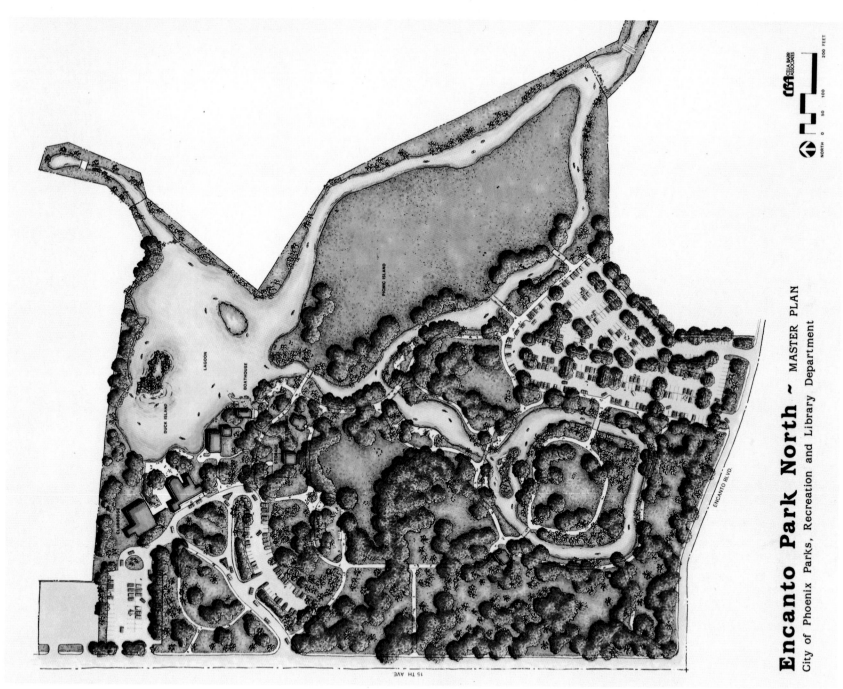

Encanto Park North ~ MASTER PLAN
City of Phoenix Parks, Recreation and Library Department

CELLA BARR ASSOCIATES.

157

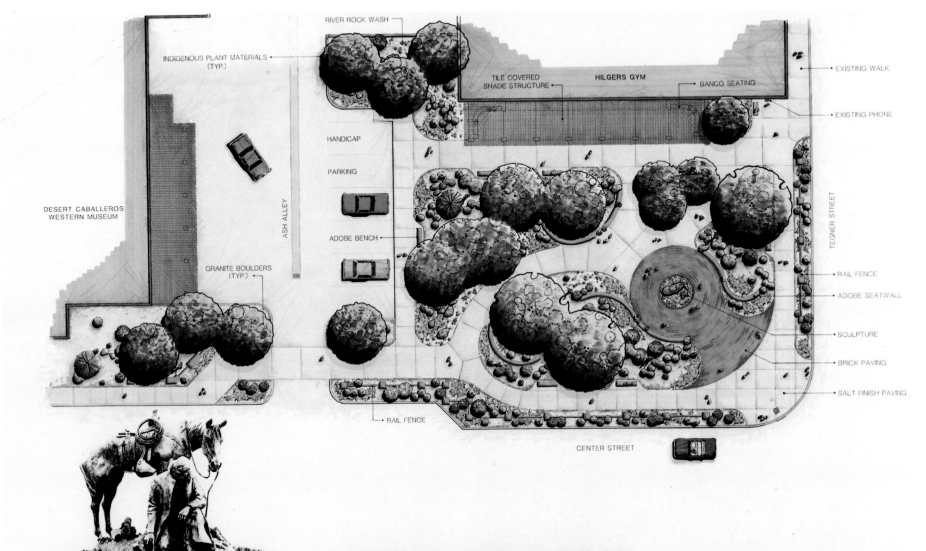

INDIGENOUS PLANT MATERIALS (TYP.)

RIVER ROCK WASH

TILE COVERED SHADE STRUCTURE

HILGERS GYM

BANCO SEATING

EXISTING WALK

EXISTING PHONE

HANDICAP

PARKING

DESERT CABALLEROS WESTERN MUSEUM

ASH ALLEY

ADOBE BENCH

GRANITE BOULDERS (TYP.)

TEGNER STREET

RAIL FENCE

ADOBE SEATWALL

SCULPTURE

BRICK PAVING

SALT FINISH PAVING

RAIL FENCE

CENTER STREET

Sculpture Title: "THANKS FOR THE RAIN"
Artist: JOE BEELER

DESERT CABALLEROS
MUSEUM PARK

SCALE: 1/8"=1'-0"

0   8   24   NORTH

CBA CELLA BARR ASSOCIATES

CELLA BARR ASSOCIATES.

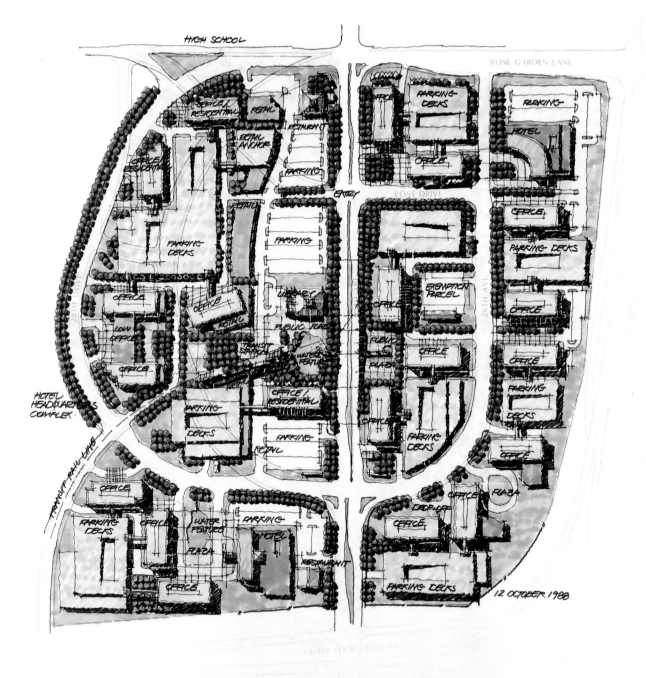

Labels visible within the drawing:

HIGH SCHOOL

ROSE GARDEN LANE

OFFICE/RESIDENTIAL   RETAIL   OFFICE   PARKING DECKS   PARKING

RESTAURANT   HOTEL

RETAIL ANCHOR   OFFICE

OFFICE/RESIDENTIAL   PARKING

OFFICE

RETAIL   ENTRY   ROSS DRIVE

PARKING DECKS   PARKING   PARKING DECKS

OFFICE   OFFICE   OFFICE   EXEMPTION PARCEL   OFFICE

LOW OFFICE   RETAIL   LIBRARY   PUBLIC PLAZA   OFFICE   OFFICE

28TH DRIVE   26TH AVE

OFFICE   TRANSIT STATION   RETAIL   FLEXI PLAZA   OFFICE   PARKING

HOTEL HEADQUARTERS COMPLEX   WATER FEATURE   OFFICE   PARKING DECKS   DECKS

TRANSIT RAIL LINE   OFFICE/RESIDENTIAL   OFFICE   OFFICE

PARKING DECKS   PARKING   OFFICE

RETAIL   PARKING DECKS

OFFICE   OFFICE   PLAZA   OFFICE

PARKING DECKS   OFFICE   WATER FEATURE   PARKING   DROP OFF   OFFICE

PLAZA   HOTEL   RESTAURANT

OFFICE   PARKING DECKS   12 OCTOBER 1988

OUTER LOOP FREEWAY

RTKL ASSOCIATES INC., Architect and Planner. Valley Park Associates, Owner.
Northridge at Deer Valley Village, Phoenix.

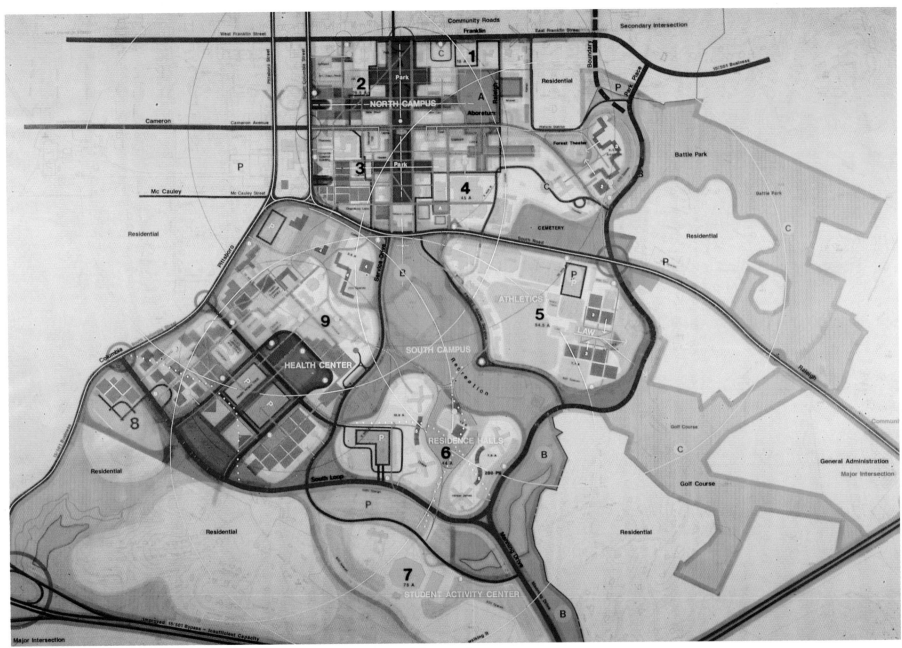

JOHNSON JOHNSON & ROY. J. C. Penney Corporate Headquarters. Ink on mylar;
rendered with pastel, markers and "zip-a-tone" on a blackline print.

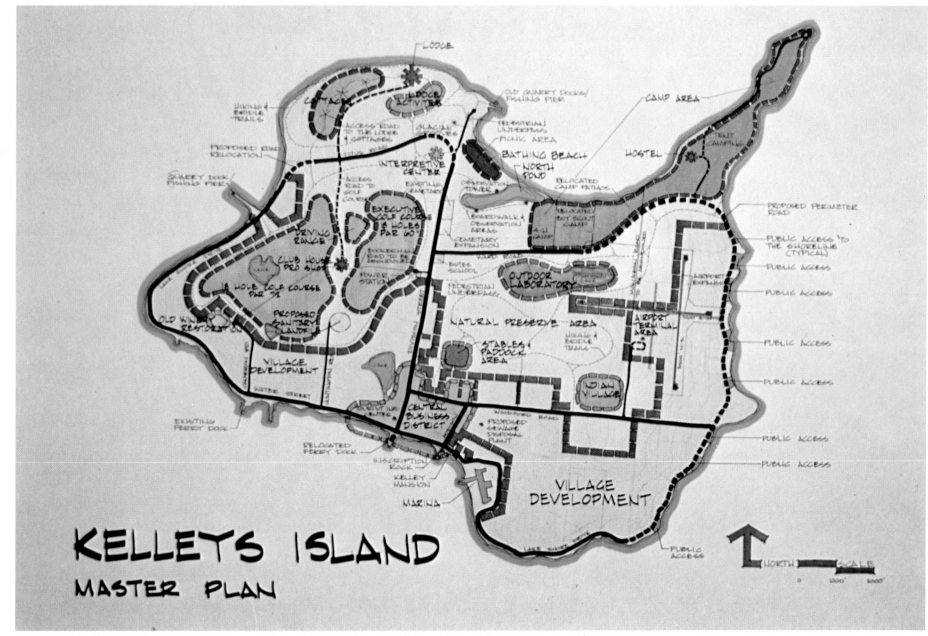

KELLEYS ISLAND

MASTER PLAN

WILLIAM A. BEHNKE ASSOCIATES, by W. Lee Behnke and Russell L. Butier II. Felt
markers on print.

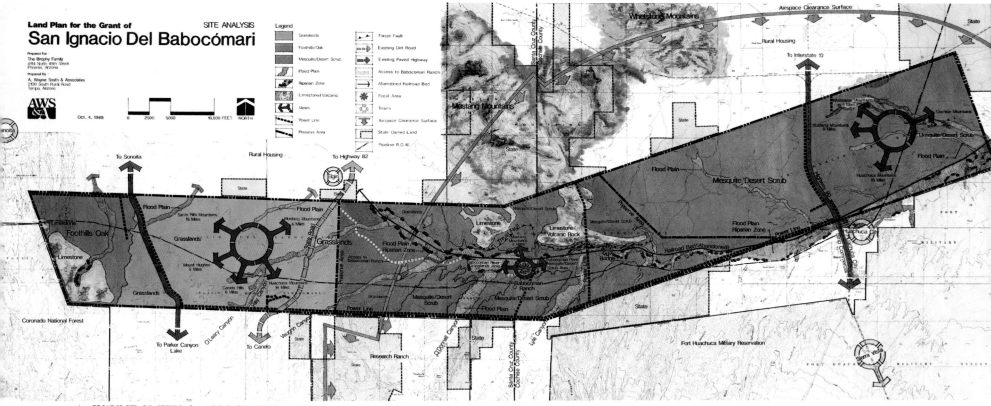

A. WAYNE SMITH & ASSOCIATES. Marker on presentation blackline.

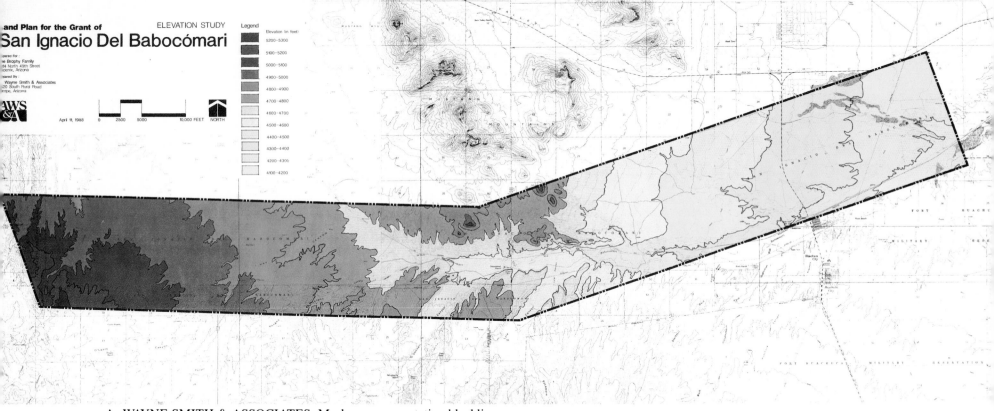

Land Plan for the Grant of

San Ignacio Del Babocómari

ELEVATION STUDY

Prepared For:
The Brophy Family
44 North 49th Street
Phoenix, Arizona

Prepared By:
A. Wayne Smith & Associates
620 South Rural Road
Tempe, Arizona

April 11, 1988

0   2500   5000   10,000 FEET

NORTH

Legend

Elevation (in feet)

	5200-5300
	5100-5200
	5000-5100
	4900-5000
	4800-4900
	4700-4800
	4600-4700
	4500-4600
	4400-4500
	4300-4400
	4200-4300
	4100-4200

A. WAYNE SMITH & ASSOCIATES. Marker on presentation blackline.

165

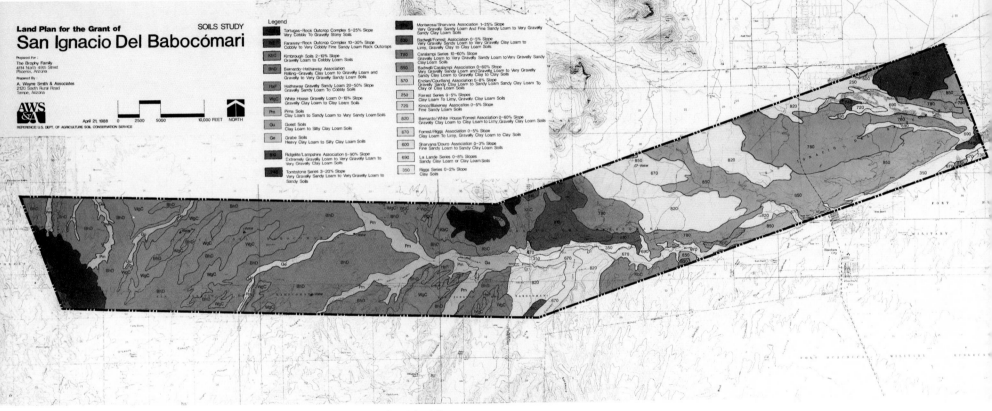

Land Plan for the Grant of
San Ignacio Del Babocómari

SOILS STUDY

Prepared For :
The Brophy Family
4114 North 49th Street
Phoenix, Arizona

Prepared By :
A. Wayne Smith & Associates
2120 South Rural Road
Tempe, Arizona

April 21, 1988   0   2500 5000   10,000 FEET   NORTH

REFERENCE U.S. DEPT. OF AGRICULTURE SOIL CONSERVATION SERVICE

Legend

Tortugas-Rock Outcrop Complex 5-25% Slope
Very Cobbly To Gravelly Stony Soils

Faraway-Rock Outcrop Complex 10-30% Slope
Cobbly to Very Cobbly Fine Sandy Loam Rock Outcrops

KhC — Kimbrough Soils 2-10% Slope
Gravelly Loam to Cobbly Loam Soils

BhD — Bernardo-Hathaway Association
Rolling-Gravelly Clay Loam to Gravelly Loam and
Gravelly to Very Gravelly Sandy Loam Soils

HaF — Hathaway Gravelly Sandy Loam 20-50% Slope
Gravelly Sandy Loam To Cobbly Soils

WgC — White House Gravelly Loam 0-10% Slope
Gravelly Clay Loam to Clay Loam Soils

Pm — Pima Soils
Clay Loam to Sandy Loam to Very Sandy Loam Soils

Gu — Guest Soils
Clay Loam to Silty Clay Loam Soils

Ge — Grabe Soils
Heavy Clay Loam to Silty Clay Loam Soils

BhD — Ridgelite/Lampshire Association 5-90% Slope
Extremely Gravelly Loam to Very Gravelly Loam to
Very Gravelly Clay Loam Soils

T?4B — Tombstone Series 3-20% Slope
Very Gravelly Sandy Loam to Very Gravelly Loam to
Sandy Soils

Monterosa/Sharvana Association 1-25% Slope
Very Gravelly Sandy Loam And Fine Sandy Loam to Very Gravelly
Sandy Clay Loam Soils

830 — Badwell/Forrest Association 0-5% Slope
Very Gravelly Sandy Loam to Very Gravelly Clay Loam to
Limy, Gravelly Clay to Clay Loam Soils

780 — Caralampi Series 10-60% Slope
Gravelly Loam to Very Gravelly Sandy Loam to Very Gravelly Sandy
Clay Loam Soils

850 — Badwell/Caralampi Association 0-60% Slope
Very Gravelly Sandy Loam and Gravelly Loam to Very Gravelly
Sandy Clay Loam to Gravelly Clay to Clay Soils

570 — Ensian/Courtland Association 0-8% Slope
Gravelly Sandy Clay Loam to Sandy Loam Sandy Clay Loam To
Clay of Clay Loam Soils

250 — Forrest Series 0-5% Slopes
Clay Loam To Limy, Gravelly Clay Loam Soils

720 — Kinco/Blakeney Association 0-5% Slope
Fine Sandy Loam Soils

820 — Bernardo/White House/Forrest Association 0-60% Slope
Gravelly Clay Loam to Clay Loam to Limy, Gravelly Clay Loam Soils

670 — Forrest/Riggs Association 0-5% Slope
Clay Loam To Limy, Gravelly Clay Loam to Clay Soils

600 — Sharvana/Douro Association 0-3% Slope
Fine Sandy Loam to Sandy Clay Loam Soils

690 — La Lande Series 0-8% Slopes
Sandy Clay Loam or Clay Loam Soils

350 — Riggs Series 0-2% Slope
Clay Soils

A. WAYNE SMITH & ASSOCIATES. Marker on presentation blackline.

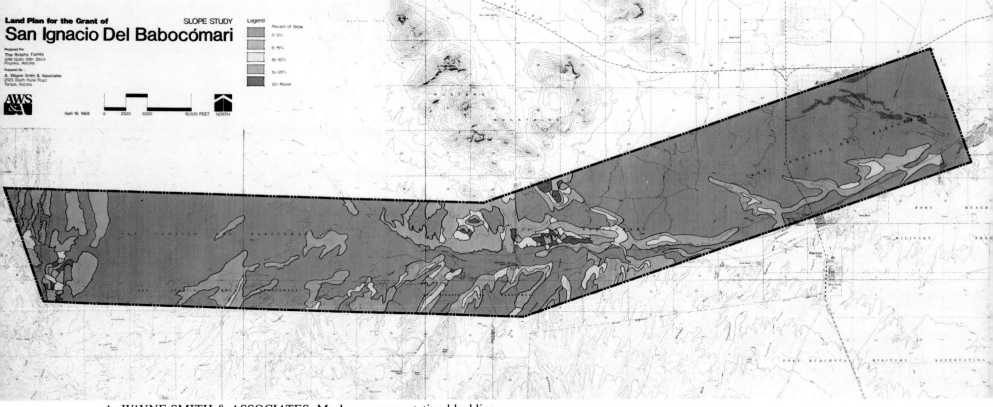

A. WAYNE SMITH & ASSOCIATES. Marker on presentation blackline.

167

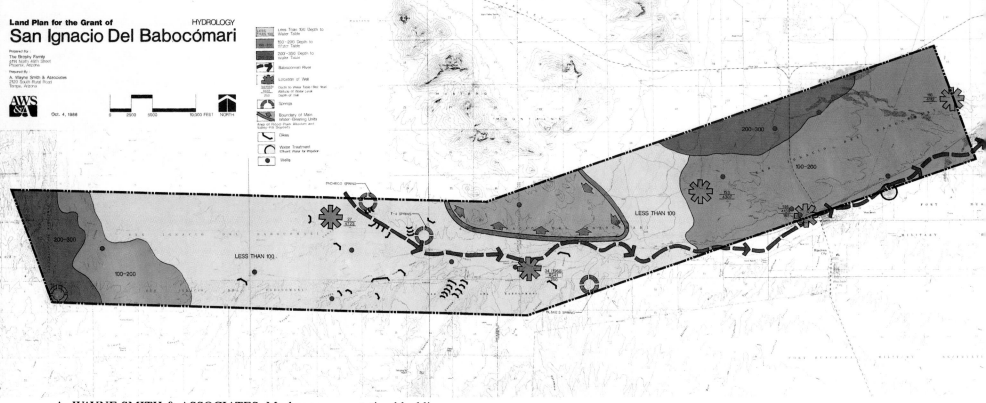

A. WAYNE SMITH & ASSOCIATES. Marker on presentation blackline.

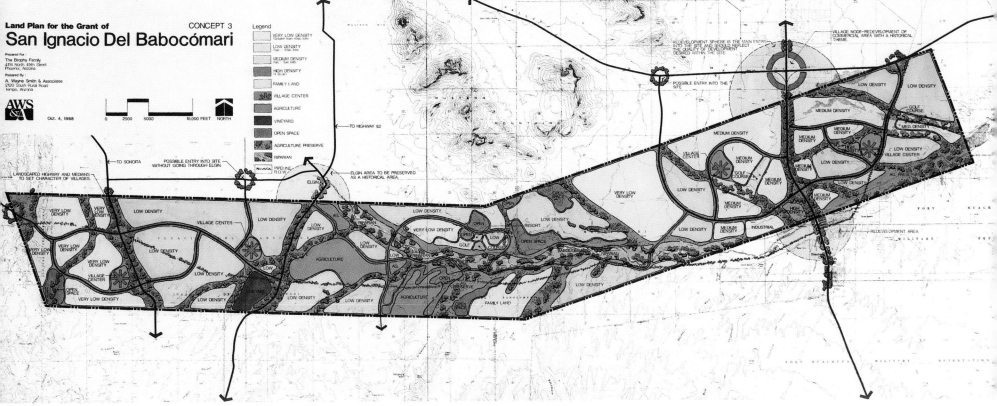

A. WAYNE SMITH & ASSOCIATES. Marker on presentation blackline.

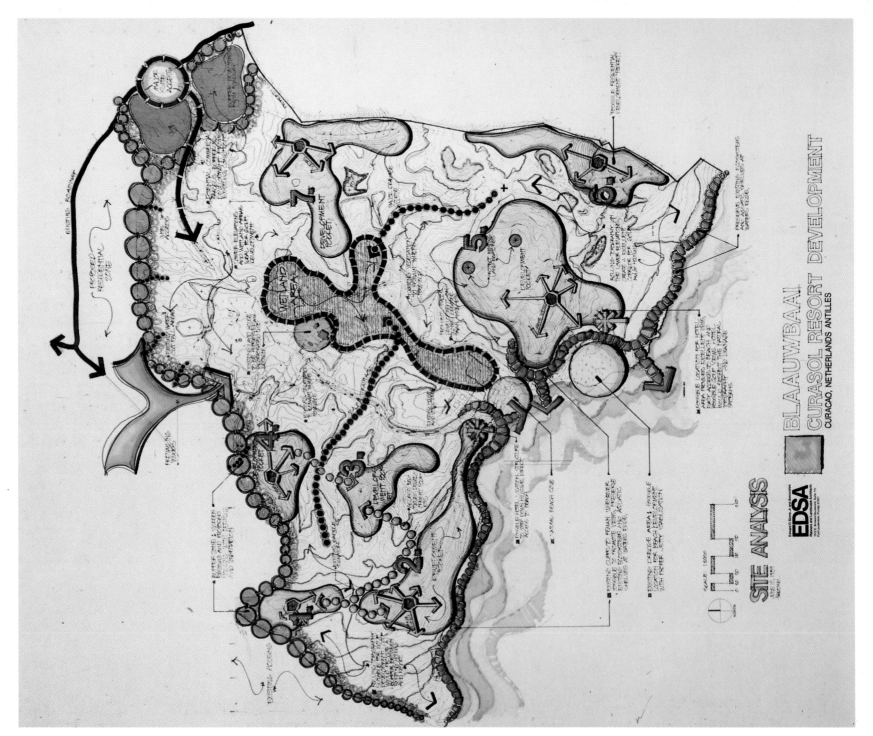

SITE ANALYSIS

BLAAUWBAAI
CURASOL RESORT DEVELOPMENT
CURACAO, NETHERLANDS ANTILLES

EDSA

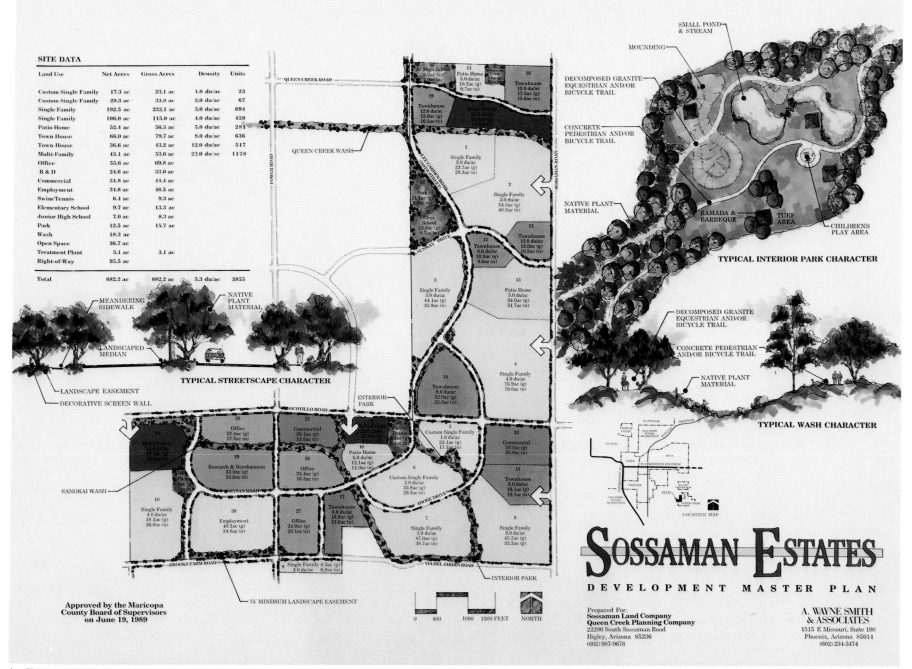

SITE DATA

Land Use	Net Acres	Gross Acres	Density	Units
Custom Single Family	17.3 ac	23.1 ac	1.0 du/ac	23
Custom Single Family	29.3 ac	33.8 ac	2.0 du/ac	67
Single Family	192.5 ac	232.1 ac	3.0 du/ac	694
Single Family	106.0 ac	115.0 ac	4.0 du/ac	459
Patio Home	52.4 ac	56.3 ac	5.0 du/ac	281
Town House	66.0 ac	79.7 ac	8.0 du/ac	636
Town House	36.6 ac	43.2 ac	12.0 du/ac	517
Multi-Family	43.1 ac	53.6 ac	22.0 du/ac	1178
Office	55.6 ac	69.8 ac		
R & D	24.6 ac	33.0 ac		
Commercial	34.8 ac	44.4 ac		
Employment	34.8 ac	48.5 ac		
Swim/Tennis	6.4 ac	9.3 ac		
Elementary School	9.7 ac	13.3 ac		
Junior High School	7.0 ac	8.3 ac		
Park	12.5 ac	15.7 ac		
Wash	18.3 ac			
Open Space	36.7 ac			
Treatment Plant	3.1 ac	3.1 ac		
Right-of-Way	95.5 ac			
Total	882.2 ac	882.2 ac	5.3 du/ac	3855

MEANDERING SIDEWALK

NATIVE PLANT MATERIAL

LANDSCAPED MEDIAN

TYPICAL STREETSCAPE CHARACTER

LANDSCAPE EASEMENT

DECORATIVE SCREEN WALL

SANOKAI WASH

Approved by the Maricopa County Board of Supervisors on June 19, 1989

75' MINIMUM LANDSCAPE EASEMENT

QUEEN CREEK ROAD

QUEEN CREEK WASH

OCOTILLO ROAD

HYSAN ROAD

BROOKS FARM ROAD

VIA DEL JARDIN ROAD

INTERIOR PARK

SMALL POND & STREAM

MOUNDING

DECOMPOSED GRANITE EQUESTRIAN AND/OR BICYCLE TRAIL

CONCRETE PEDESTRIAN AND/OR BICYCLE TRAIL

NATIVE PLANT MATERIAL

RAMADA & BARBEQUE

TURF AREA

CHILDRENS PLAY AREA

TYPICAL INTERIOR PARK CHARACTER

DECOMPOSED GRANITE EQUESTRIAN AND/OR BICYCLE TRAIL

CONCRETE PEDESTRIAN AND/OR BICYCLE TRAIL

NATIVE PLANT MATERIAL

TYPICAL WASH CHARACTER

LOCATION MAP

0   400   1000   1500 FEET   NORTH

SOSSAMAN ESTATES
DEVELOPMENT MASTER PLAN

Prepared For:
Sossaman Land Company
Queen Creek Planning Company
22200 South Sossaman Road
Higley, Arizona 85236
(602) 987-9678

A. WAYNE SMITH & ASSOCIATES
1515 E Missouri, Suite 100
Phoenix, Arizona 85014
(602) 234-3474

A. WAYNE SMITH & ASSOCIATES. Marker on presentation blackline, reduced from 30″ x 42″.

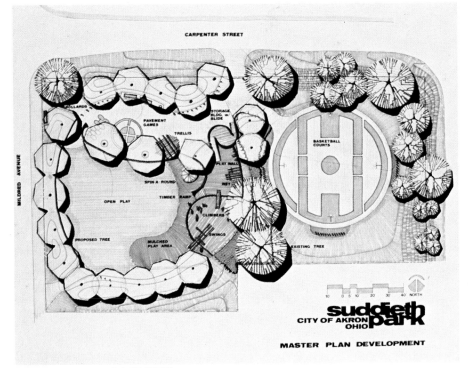

BONNELL & ASSOCIATES.

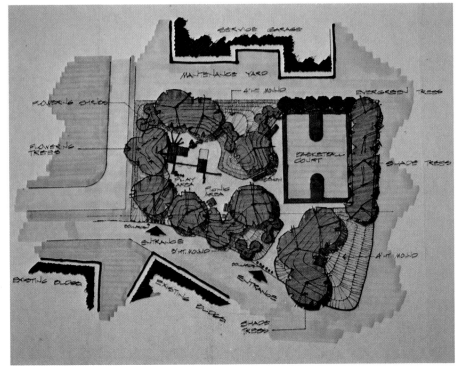

DONALD R. KNOX, INC. by Francis X. Donnelly.

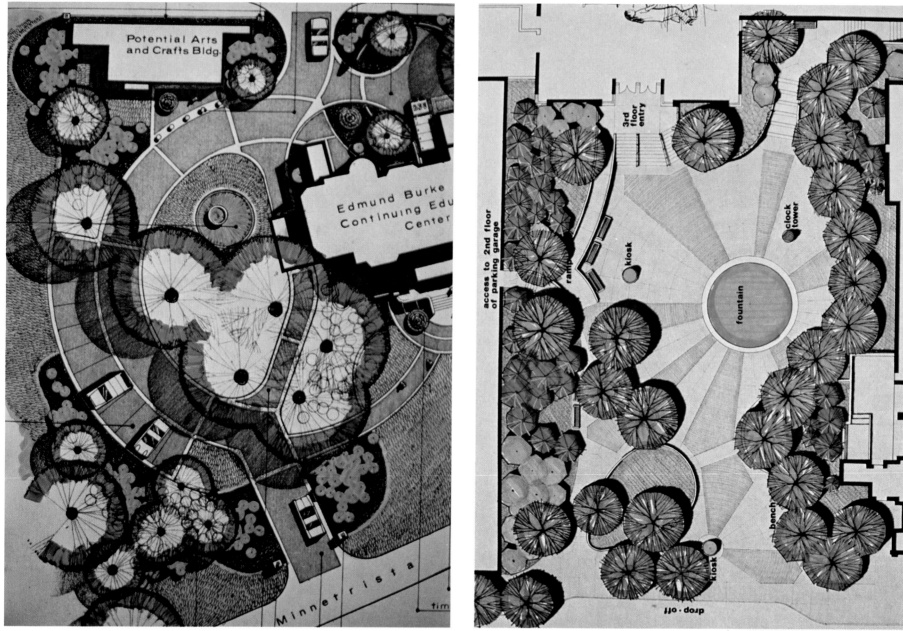

STAN GEDA and JOHN ROBERT RUSSELL. Edmund Burke Ball Continuing
Education Center

BONNELL & ASSOCIATES.

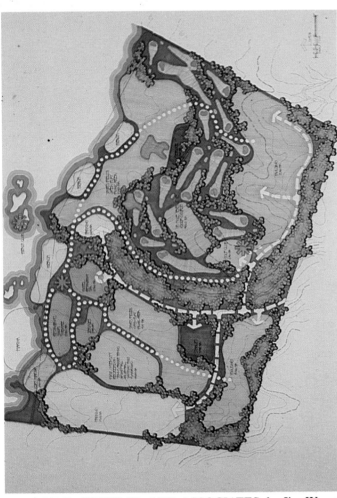

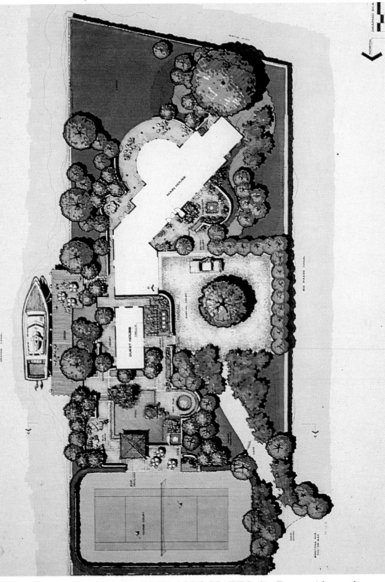

EDWARD D. STONE JR. AND ASSOCIATES, by Jim Weaver.　　　EDWARD D. STONE JR. AND ASSOCIATES, by Bruce Alexander.

SCOTTSDALE RANCH PARK

MASTER PLAN

PREPARED BY:

CBA CELLA BARR ASSOCIATES

PREPARED FOR:

CITY OF SCOTTSDALE ARIZONA

SCOTTSDALE RANCH PARK	30 ACRES
LAGUNA ELEMENTARY SCHOOL	20 ACRES
PROPOSED RECREATION CENTER	6 ACRES
SCOTTSDALE BOYS & GIRLS CLUBS	4 ACRES
SITE TOTAL	60 ACRES

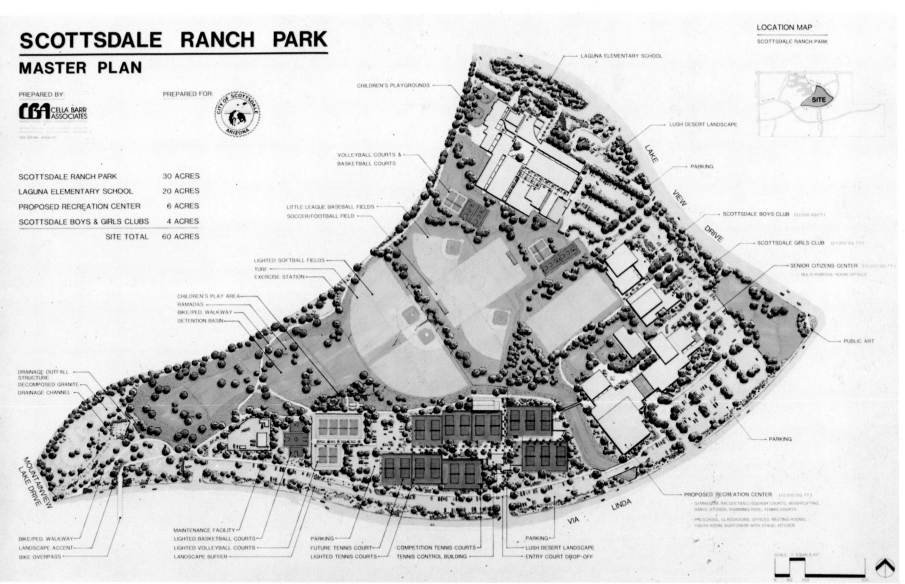

LAGUNA ELEMENTARY SCHOOL

CHILDREN'S PLAYGROUNDS

LUSH DESERT LANDSCAPE

PARKING

VOLLEYBALL COURTS & BASKETBALL COURTS

SCOTTSDALE BOYS CLUB

LITTLE LEAGUE BASEBALL FIELDS

SOCCER/FOOTBALL FIELD

SCOTTSDALE GIRLS CLUB

LIGHTED SOFTBALL FIELDS

TURF

EXERCISE STATION

SENIOR CITIZENS CENTER

MULTI-PURPOSE ROOM, OFFICES

CHILDREN'S PLAY AREA

RAMADAS

BIKE/PED. WALKWAY

DETENTION BASIN

DRAINAGE OUTFALL STRUCTURE

DECOMPOSED GRANITE

DRAINAGE CHANNEL

PUBLIC ART

PARKING

MOUNTAINVIEW LAKE DRIVE

LAKE VIEW DRIVE

VIA LINDA

PROPOSED RECREATION CENTER

GYMNASIUM, RACQUETBALL/SQUASH COURTS, WEIGHTLIFTING, DANCE STUDIOS, SWIMMING POOL, TENNIS COURTS

PRESCHOOL, CLASSROOMS, OFFICES, MEETING ROOMS, YOUTH ROOM, AUDITORIUM WITH STAGE, KITCHEN

BIKE/PED. WALKWAY

LANDSCAPE ACCENT

BIKE OVERPASS

MAINTENANCE FACILITY

LIGHTED BASKETBALL COURTS

LIGHTED VOLLEYBALL COURTS

LANDSCAPE BUFFER

PARKING

FUTURE TENNIS COURT

LIGHTED TENNIS COURTS

COMPETITION TENNIS COURTS

TENNIS CONTROL BUILDING

PARKING

LUSH DESERT LANDSCAPE

ENTRY COURT DROP-OFF

SCALE 1" EQUALS 60'

0   60   120

EDWARD D. STONE JR. AND ASSOCIATES.

183

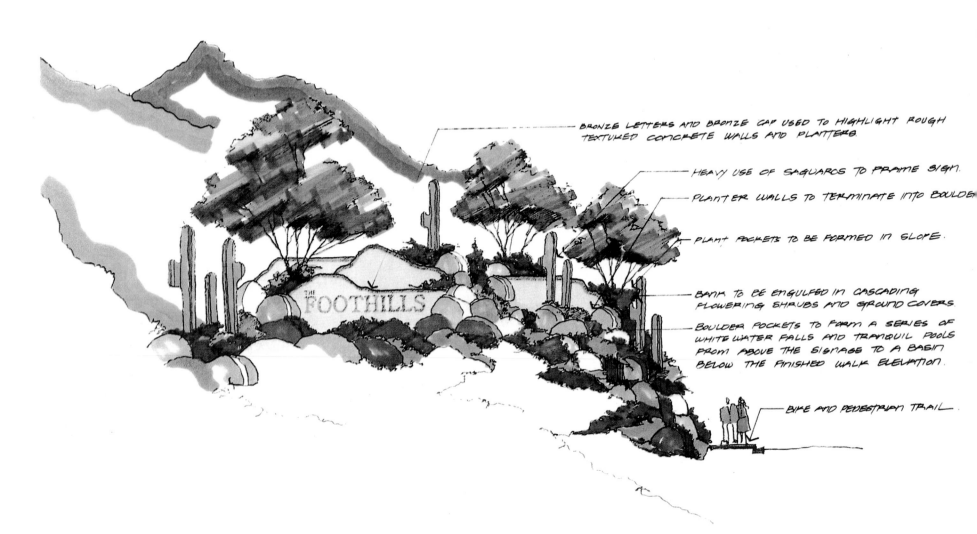

BRONZE LETTERS AND BRONZE CAP USED TO HIGHLIGHT ROUGH TEXTURED CONCRETE WALLS AND PLANTERS.

HEAVY USE OF SAGUAROS TO FRAME SIGN.

PLANTER WALLS TO TERMINATE INTO BOULDER

PLANT POCKETS TO BE FORMED IN SLOPE.

BANK TO BE ENGULFED IN CASCADING FLOWERING SHRUBS AND GROUND COVERS.

BOULDER POCKETS TO FORM A SERIES OF WHITE WATER FALLS AND TRANQUIL POOLS FROM ABOVE THE SIGNAGE TO A BASIN BELOW THE FINISHED WALK ELEVATION.

BIKE AND PEDESTRIAN TRAIL.

THE FOOTHILLS

PRELIMINARY STUDY FOR:
THE FOOTHILLS OVERALL ENTRY MONUMEN
4·6·

AWS & A   A. Wayne Smith & Associa
Planners • Landscape Archite

A. WAYNE SMITH & ASSOCIATES. Original sketch is ink on tissue. Presentation blackline reproduced from tissue original with marker application. Reduced from 24″ x 36″.

A. WAYNE SMITH & ASSOCIATES. Marker on presentation blackline, reduced from 30″ x 42″.

VILLAGE ARCHITECTURAL CHARACTER
A Wayne Smith & Associates Planners Landscape Architects

A. WAYNE SMITH & ASSOCIATES. Marker on presentation blackline, reduced from
30″ x 42″.

SEAVIEW DRIVE   DENSE PLANTING SCREEN PROVIDES
VISUAL BARRIER BETWEEN ROADWAYS

ELEVATIONS & SECTIONS

In most cases, additional sketches and illustrations are required along with plan graphics to fully explain the intent of the design. Examples of perspective sketches, sections and elevations are presented in this chapter.

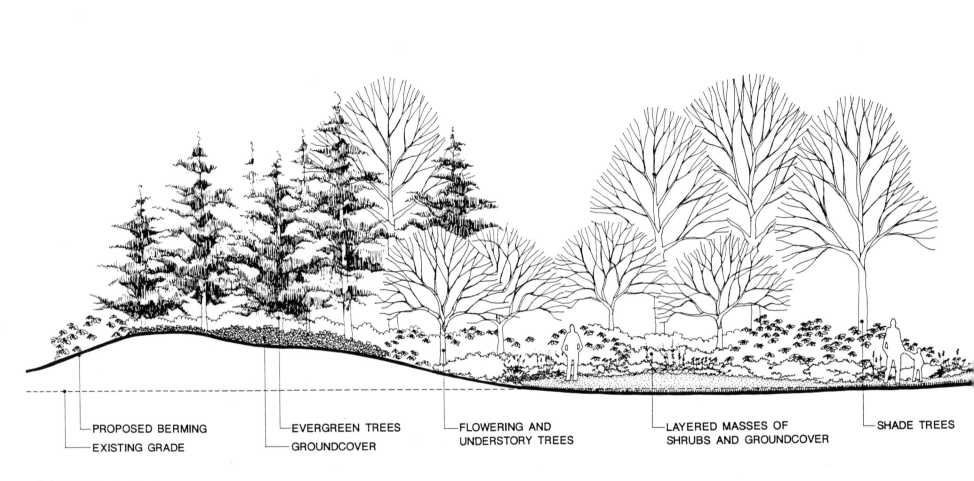

PROPOSED BERMING
EXISTING GRADE

EVERGREEN TREES
GROUNDCOVER

FLOWERING AND
UNDERSTORY TREES

LAYERED MASSES OF
SHRUBS AND GROUNDCOVER

SHADE TREES

GARDEN DETAIL

MICELI KULIK WILLIAMS & ASSOCIATES. Flushing Meadows — Corona Park,
New York.

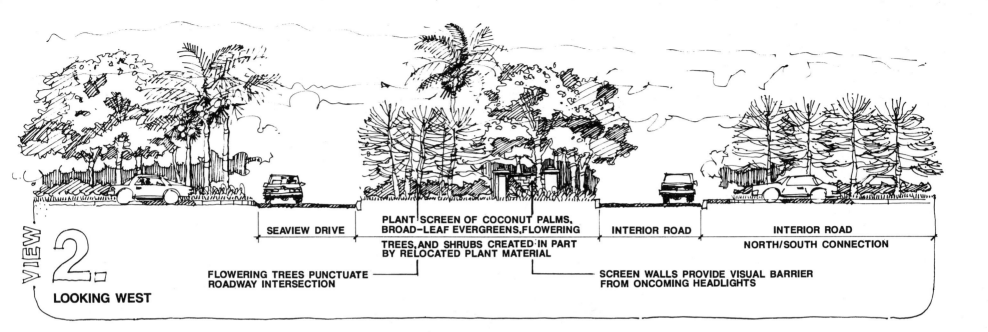

VIEW **2.**
LOOKING WEST

SEAVIEW DRIVE

PLANT SCREEN OF COCONUT PALMS,
BROAD-LEAF EVERGREENS, FLOWERING
TREES, AND SHRUBS CREATED IN PART
BY RELOCATED PLANT MATERIAL

INTERIOR ROAD

INTERIOR ROAD
NORTH/SOUTH CONNECTION

FLOWERING TREES PUNCTUATE
ROADWAY INTERSECTION

SCREEN WALLS PROVIDE VISUAL BARRIER
FROM ONCOMING HEADLIGHTS

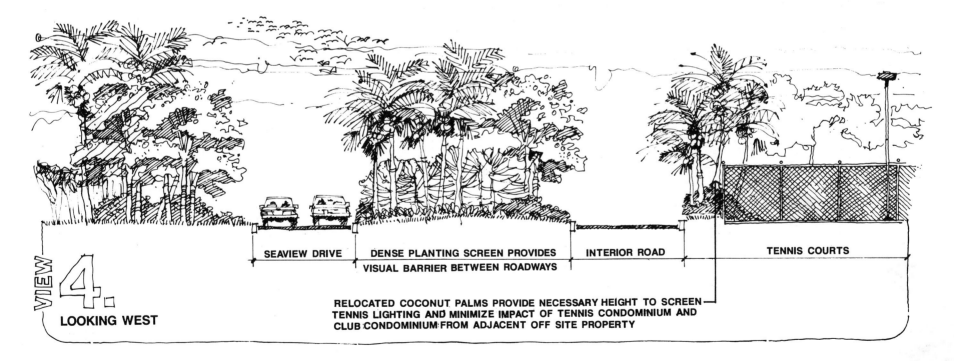

VIEW **4.**
LOOKING WEST

SEAVIEW DRIVE

DENSE PLANTING SCREEN PROVIDES
VISUAL BARRIER BETWEEN ROADWAYS

INTERIOR ROAD

TENNIS COURTS

RELOCATED COCONUT PALMS PROVIDE NECESSARY HEIGHT TO SCREEN
TENNIS LIGHTING AND MINIMIZE IMPACT OF TENNIS CONDOMINIUM AND
CLUB CONDOMINIUM FROM ADJACENT OFF SITE PROPERTY

EDWARD D. STONE JR. AND ASSOCIATES. Key Biscayne Hotel and Villas, reduced
from 18" x 24".

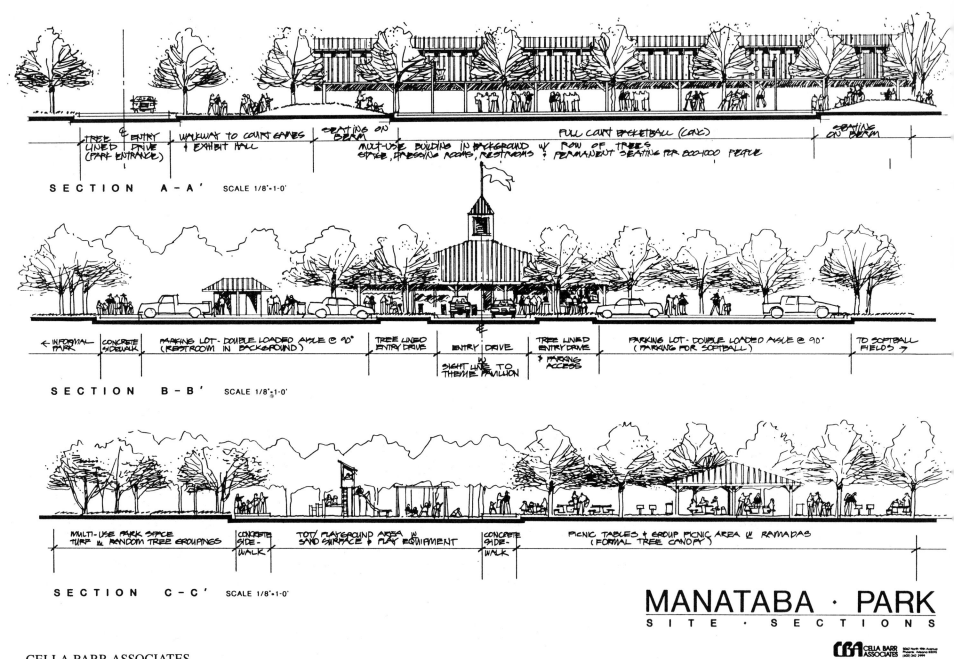

SECTION A - A'   SCALE 1/8"-1-0'

TREE & ENTRY LINED DRIVE (PARK ENTRANCE) | WALKWAY TO COURT GAMES & EXHIBIT HALL | SEATING ON BERM | MULTI-USE BUILDING IN BACKGROUND STAGE, DRESSING ROOMS, RESTROOMS & PERMANENT SEATING FOR 800-1000 PEOPLE | FULL COURT BASKETBALL (CONC) ROW OF TREES | SEATING ON BERM

SECTION B - B'   SCALE 1/8"-1-0'

← INFORMAL PARK | CONCRETE SIDEWALK | PARKING LOT - DOUBLE LOADED AISLE @ 90° (RESTROOM IN BACKGROUND) | TREE LINED ENTRY DRIVE | ENTRY DRIVE SIGHT LINE TO THEME PAVILLION | TREE LINED ENTRY DRIVE & PARKING ACCESS | PARKING LOT - DOUBLE LOADED AISLE @ 90° (PARKING FOR SOFTBALL) | TO SOFTBALL FIELDS →

SECTION C - C'   SCALE 1/8"-1-0'

MULTI-USE PARK SPACE TURF & RANDOM TREE GROUPINGS | CONCRETE SIDE-WALK | TOT/ PLAYGROUND AREA IN SAND SURFACE & PLAY EQUIPMENT | CONCRETE SIDE-WALK | PICNIC TABLES & GROUP PICNIC AREA W/ RAMADAS (FORMAL TREE CANOPY)

MANATABA · PARK
S I T E · S E C T I O N S

CELLA BARR ASSOCIATES.

CBA CELLA BARR ASSOCIATES 3262 North 19th Avenue Phoenix, Arizona 85015 (602) 242-3999 12/7/88   41252-01-74

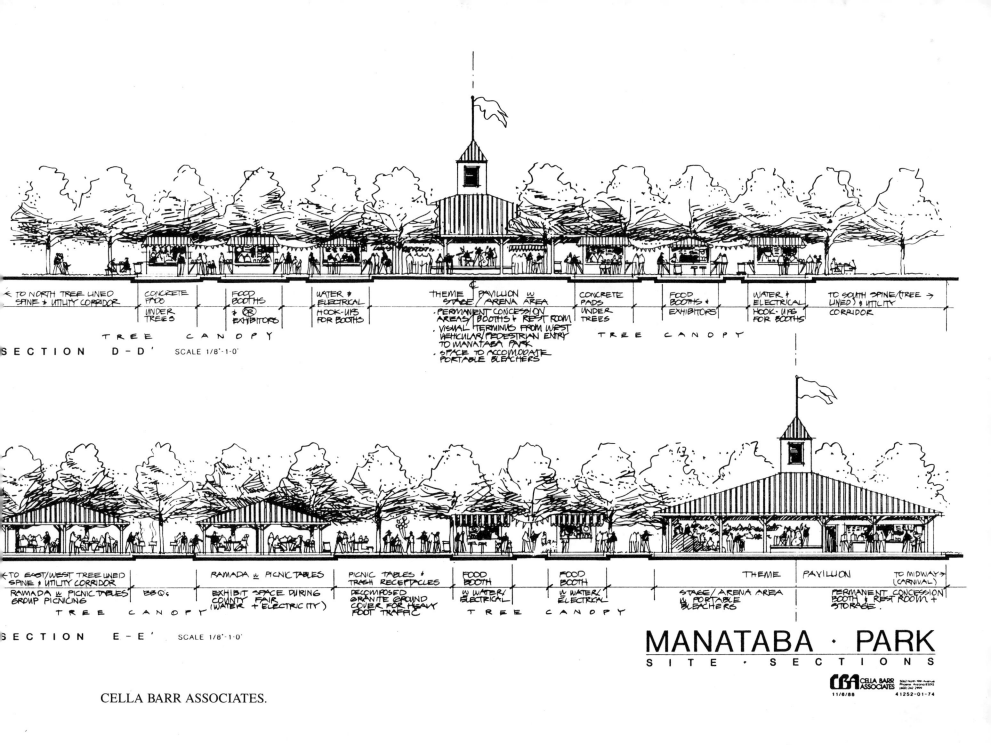

TO NORTH TREE LINED SPINE & UTILITY CORRIDOR | CONCRETE PADS UNDER TREES | FOOD BOOTHS & OR EXHIBITORS | WATER & ELECTRICAL HOOK-UPS FOR BOOTHS | THEME PAVILLION w/ STAGE / ARENA AREA
- PERMANENT CONCESSION AREAS / BOOTHS & REST ROOM
- VISUAL TERMINUS FROM WEST VEHICULAR / PEDESTRIAN ENTRY TO MANATABA PARK
- SPACE TO ACCOMMODATE PORTABLE BLEACHERS | CONCRETE PADS UNDER TREES | FOOD BOOTHS & EXHIBITORS | WATER & ELECTRICAL HOOK-UPS FOR BOOTHS | TO SOUTH SPINE/TREE LINED & UTILITY CORRIDOR

TREE CANOPY   TREE CANOPY

SECTION D-D'   SCALE 1/8"-1'-0"

TO EAST/WEST TREE LINED SPINE & UTILITY CORRIDOR | RAMADA w/ PICNIC TABLES | PICNIC TABLES & TRASH RECEPTACLES | FOOD BOOTH w/ WATER/ ELECTRICAL | FOOD BOOTH w/ WATER/ ELECTRICAL | THEME | PAVILLION | TO MIDWAY (CARNIVAL)

RAMADA w/ PICNIC TABLES GROUP PICNICING | BBQ's | EXHIBIT SPACE DURING COUNTY FAIR (WATER + ELECTRICITY) | DECOMPOSED GRANITE GROUND COVER FOR HEAVY FOOT TRAFFIC | | | STAGE/ARENA AREA w/ PORTABLE BLEACHERS | PERMANENT CONCESSION BOOTH & REST ROOM + STORAGE.

TREE CANOPY   TREE CANOPY

SECTION E-E'   SCALE 1/8"-1'-0"

MANATABA · PARK
S I T E · S E C T I O N S

CELLA BARR ASSOCIATES.

CBA CELLA BARR ASSOCIATES   5062 North 19th Avenue Phoenix, Arizona 85015 (602) 242-2999
11/6/88   41252-01-74

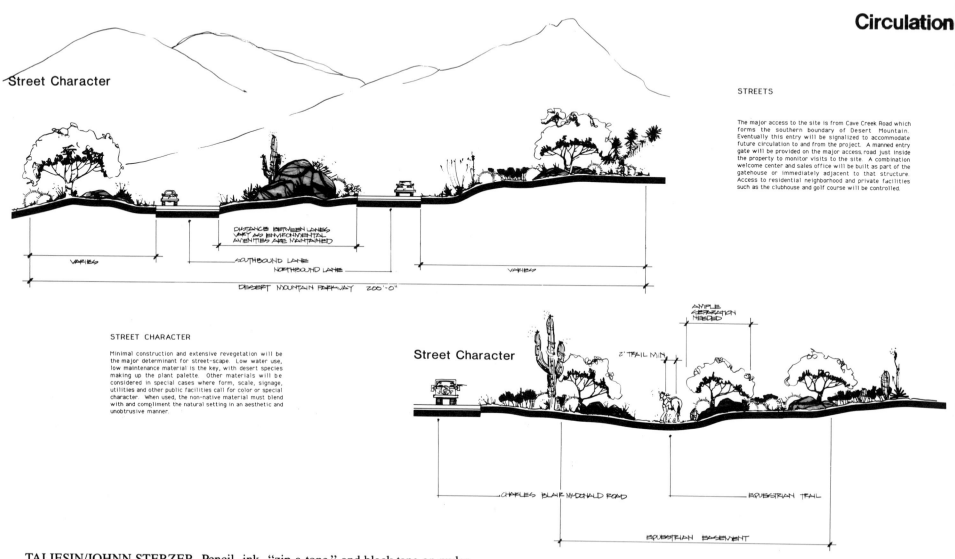

Street Character

STREETS

The major access to the site is from Cave Creek Road which forms the southern boundary of Desert Mountain. Eventually this entry will be signalized to accommodate future circulation to and from the project. A manned entry gate will be provided on the major access road just inside the property to monitor visits to the site. A combination welcome center and sales office will be built as part of the gatehouse or immediately adjacent to that structure. Access to residential neighborhood and private facilities such as the clubhouse and golf course will be controlled.

DISTANCE BETWEEN LANES VARY AS ENVIRONMENTAL AMENITIES ARE MAINTAINED

VARIES

SOUTHBOUND LANE
NORTHBOUND LANE

VARIES

DESERT MOUNTAIN PARKWAY 200'-0"

STREET CHARACTER

Minimal construction and extensive revegetation will be the major determinant for street-scape. Low water use, low maintenance material is the key, with desert species making up the plant palette. Other materials will be considered in special cases where form, scale, signage, utilities and other public facilities call for color or special character. When used, the non-native material must blend with and compliment the natural setting in an aesthetic and unobtrusive manner.

Street Character

AMPLE SEPARATION NEEDED

2' TRAIL MIN

CHARLES BLAIR MCDONALD ROAD

EQUESTRIAN TRAIL

EQUESTRIAN EASEMENT

TALIESIN/JOHN STERZER. Pencil, ink, "zip-a-tone," and black tape on mylar.
Reduced from 24″ x 36″.

192

Golf Course & Fringe Areas

experience which gives an entirely new appreciation of the native desert. The experience of golf course to transitional zone to pure desert becomes an interpretive tool which shows the beauty of the upper Sonoran vegetation in a new light.

GOLF COURSE

Designed in harmony with the desert setting, turf areas are kept to a minimum. The course interlocks as a jigsaw puzzle with "fingers" of desert penetrating the fairways, creating natural hazards. Landscape revegetation or preservation of natural stands will serve to unify the courses as a whole into the surrounding desert. Intensity of vegetation may be increased in selected fringe areas to create a suitable transitional area between the green of the grass and the muted tones of the desert.

Where any area is disturbed due to construction, every effort will be expended to return it to its natural state. Our emphasis is on the integration of development with the natural setting, with the development taking a back seat to the native desert. The goal is to avoid creating a "typical" suburban setting.

Residential uses fronting the golf course take advantage of the panoramic vistas across the turf and landscape to the mountain backdrop. The desert weaves from the open areas, through the residences to the course edges and blends into the playing areas, creating an aisle for man and animals.

There are ample setbacks for easements, walks, pathways and hedges to buffer the residences from the course, yet maintain an aesthetic visual tie. These setbacks also serve as safety margins from the errant shot, as well as allowing the creation of windows both onto and from the course. Indigenous material is left in-site whenever possible and practical.

Through the careful and diligent application of this design philosophy, the golf course does not intrude into the Desert Mountain experience as an expanse of lawn covering the desert floor. Instead, the course becomes a desert apparition, almost a mirage, picking its way through the boulders and down the canyons like a mountain sheep, carefully avoiding any unnecessary obstruction of the desert environs.

Golf Course Vista

The extreme limitation of grassed areas and the enhancement and revegetation of the natural areas and disturbed construction fringes, not only minimizes water use but provides additional wildlife habitat. The tees and greens appear like pools of water with the flow of the minimal fairways connecting them as the course weaves in and out of the native terrain.

CIRCULATION

The integration of landscape, engineering and other design elements along the Desert Mountain roadways is necessary to maintain the open and free feeling of the desert. The feeling is an "attitude" based upon scenic visitors, stands of prime native vegetation and unique natural landforms. Landscaping of medians and buffers will be limited to desert plant material. Existing vegetation will be preserved wherever possible.

Generous buffers along all roadway frontages serve to provide space for trails and pathways as well as to mitigate impacts of traffic and related activity noise. Roadways follow natural terrain whenever possible and always take the least visual cross between points, dodging behind hills and into depression when feasible.

Flexibility in design standards become necessary if Desert Mountain is to protect the fragile native environment. Excessive cuts and fills are avoided and alignments are site walked and field adjusted before final approval. The roadways are designed to take maximum advantage of natural features, vistas and other items and areas of interest to the traveller.

Natural Features In The Golf Course
Use of Natural Features as Golf Course Amenities

GOLF COURSES AND FRINGE AREAS

Introducing a golf course in a desert environment makes it a challenge to produce a harmonious relationship between the two. The lushness of the tees and greens do not easily blend with the austerity of the native desert. The transition between course and desert can be artfully controlled and orchestrated into an aesthetically satisfying juxtaposition.

This is done by drastic reduction of irrigated areas, choice of plant materials that are native/indigenous low water users, utilizing undisturbed areas, natural washed and landforms/boulders as hazard areas, and arranging the playable area to follow the least visible, topographically responsive path among the natural features and vegetation.

The key to the golf courses of Desert Mountain is that they are not the primary amenity visually, following the city light and the mountains, and, as such, are designed specifically to avoid conflict with the primary views. The courses remain an obviously valuable asset to the development in their own right and are carefully snaked through the topography, around hills, down washes, and into valleys. All areas disturbed by golf course construction are completely revegetated with indigenous materials. A carefully developed transitional area is created around each course to blend the "grass to granite" into a smooth flow from lush to desert.

The bright green of the golf course contrasts with the muted tones of the desert to create an "inviting" visual character. This relationship does not appear in conflict at all -- rather it gives the viewer a point of comparison and

Typical Golf Course Treatment

TALIESIN/JOHN STERZER. Pencil, ink, "zip-a-tone," and black tape on mylar. Reduced from 24" x 36".

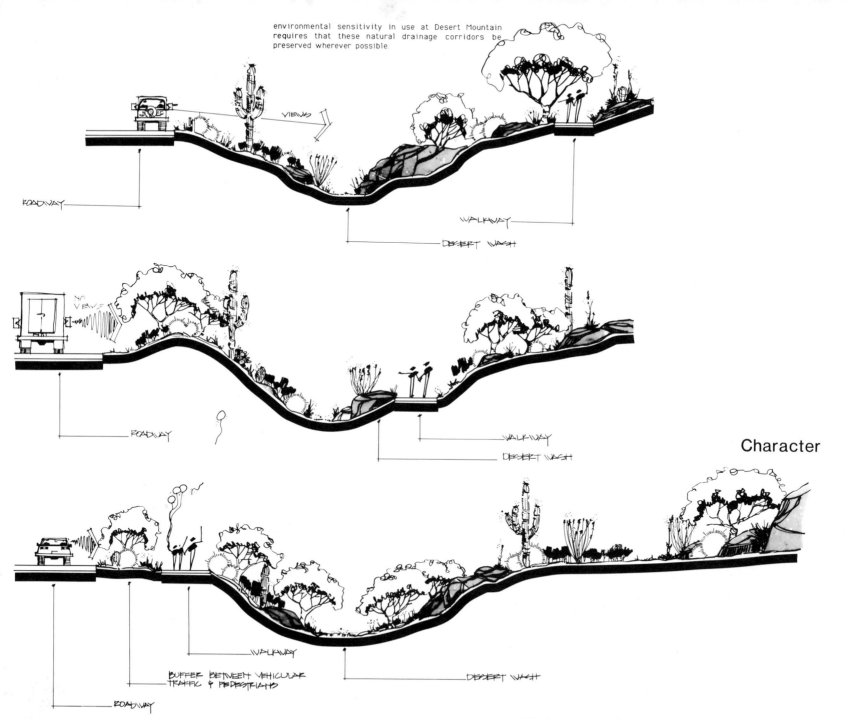

environmental sensitivity in use at Desert Mountain requires that these natural drainage corridors be preserved wherever possible.

VIEWS

ROADWAY

WALKWAY

DESERT WASH

NO VIEWS

ROADWAY

WALKWAY

DESERT WASH

Character

WALKWAY

BUFFER BETWEEN VEHICULAR TRAFFIC & PEDESTRIANS

DESERT WASH

ROADWAY

TALIESIN/JOHN STERZER. Pencil, ink, "zip-a-tone," and black tape on mylar. Reduced from 17″ x 21″.

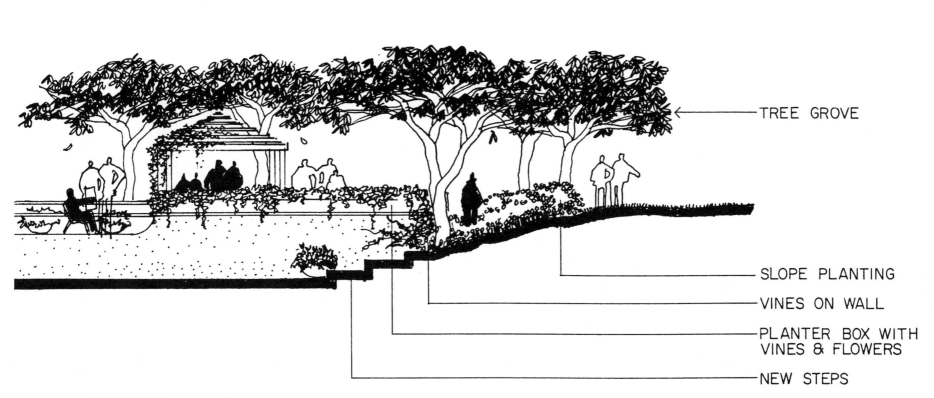

TREE GROVE

SLOPE PLANTING

VINES ON WALL

PLANTER BOX WITH
VINES & FLOWERS

NEW STEPS

SECTION

MICELI KULIK WILLIAMS & ASSOCIATES. Saint George's Club, Bermuda.

195

sum'mer·y, *a.* of, like, or characteristic of summer; summerlike.

sum'ming up, a concise summation; as, the state's attorney began his *summing up.*

sum'mist, *n.* one who makes an abridgment. [Rare.]

sum'mit, *n.* [Fr. *sommet,* dim. of OFr. *som,* a summit, from L. *summum,* the highest part.]

  1. the top or apex; the highest point, part, or elevation; as, the *summit* of a mountain.

  2. the highest state or degree; the acme; as, the general arrived at the *summit* of fame.

  3. (a) the highest level of officialdom; specifically, in connection with diplomatic negotiations, the level restricted to heads of government; as, a meeting at the *summit;* (b) a conference at the summit.

  4. in mathematics, the point at which three or more surfaces of a polyhedron meet.

  Syn.—apex, peak, top, pinnacle, crown.

sum'mit, *a.* of the heads of government; as, a *summit* parley.

sum'mit·less, *a.* having no summit.

graphic

copper cap

rose tan stucco

sommet marker

THE SOMMET

flowering native grandcovers

Native vegetation - specimen cactus always with mesquite or palo verde shrubbery in natural massing, groups of 10-30 plants with sympathetic combinations.

THE SOMMET GRAPHIC

A. WAYNE SMITH & ASSOCIATES. Ink on vellum.

A. Wayne Smith & Associates · Planners · Landscape Arch

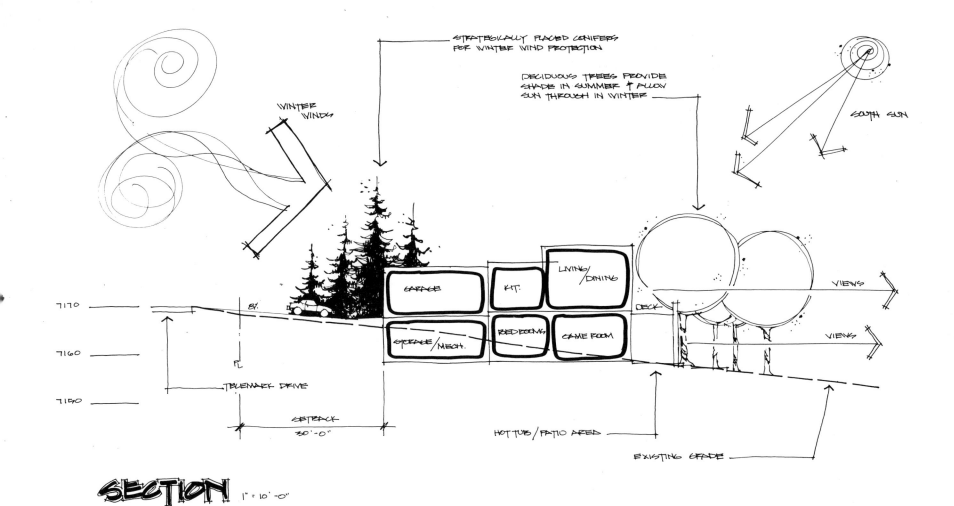

STRATEGICALLY PLACED CONIFERS
FOR WINTER WIND PROTECTION

DECIDUOUS TREES PROVIDE
SHADE IN SUMMER + ALLOW
SUN THROUGH IN WINTER

SOUTH SUN

WINTER
WINDS

GARAGE   KIT.   LIVING/
DINING

DECK   VIEWS

7170

STORAGE/MECH.   BEDROOMS   GAME ROOM

VIEWS

7160

PL

TELEMARK DRIVE

7150

SETBACK
30'-0"

HOT TUB/PATIO AREA

EXISTING GRADE

SECTION 1" = 10'-0"

JOHNN STERZER. Ink of sketching tissue, reduced from 11″ x 18″.

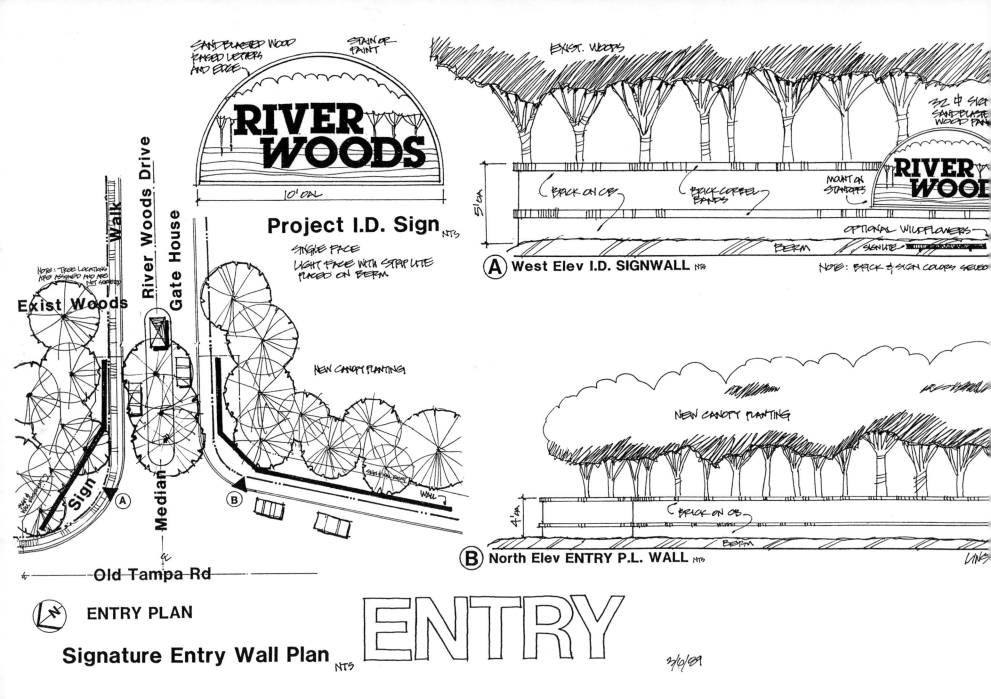

SAND BLASTED WOOD
RAISED LETTERS
AND EDGE

STAIN OR
PAINT

EXIST. WOODS

32 Φ SIGN
SANDBLASTED
WOOD PANEL

RIVER WOODS

10' OAL

Project I.D. Sign NTS

SINGLE FACE

LIGHT FACE WITH STRIP LITE
PLACED ON BERM

BRICK ON CB

BRICK CORBEL
BANDS

MOUNT ON
STANDOFFS

RIVER WOOD

51 OA

OPTIONAL WILDFLOWERS

BERM   SIGN LITE

(A) West Elev I.D. SIGNWALL NTS   NOTE: BRICK & SIGN COLORS SELECTED

Walk

River Woods Drive

Gate House

Exist Woods

NOTE: TREE LOCATIONS
ARE ASSUMED AND ARE
NOT SURVEYED

NEW CANOPY PLANTING

Sign

Median

SIGN WALL BERM

WALL

(A)

(B)

NEW CANOPY PLANTING

BRICK ON CB

4' OA

BERM

(B) North Elev ENTRY P.L. WALL NTS   LINS

Old Tampa Rd

(N) **ENTRY PLAN**

ENTRY

Signature Entry Wall Plan NTS

3/9/89

DAVID LINSTRUM.

Arrival Court

Plan

Scale

0   32   64   128

Low Shrub Mass
Decorative Pavement
Reflecting Pool
Evergreen Hedge
Pedestrian Walk
Tree Alleé

A'

A'

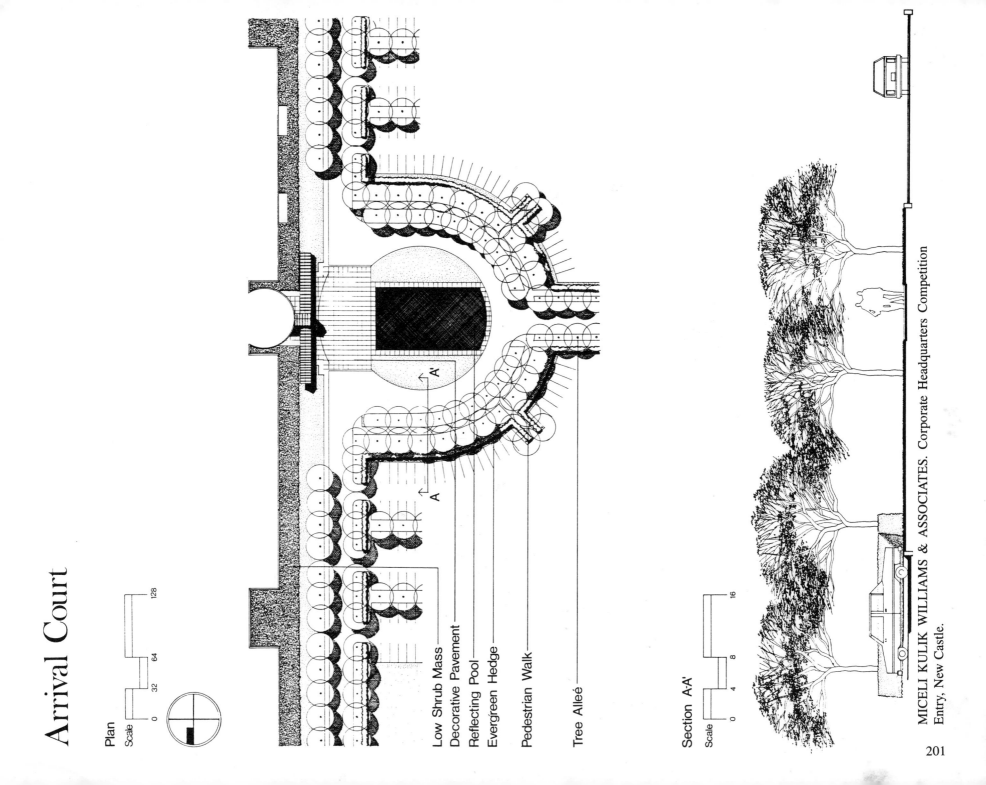

Section A·A'

Scale

0   4   8   16

MICELI KULIK WILLIAMS & ASSOCIATES. Corporate Headquarters Competition Entry, New Castle.

201

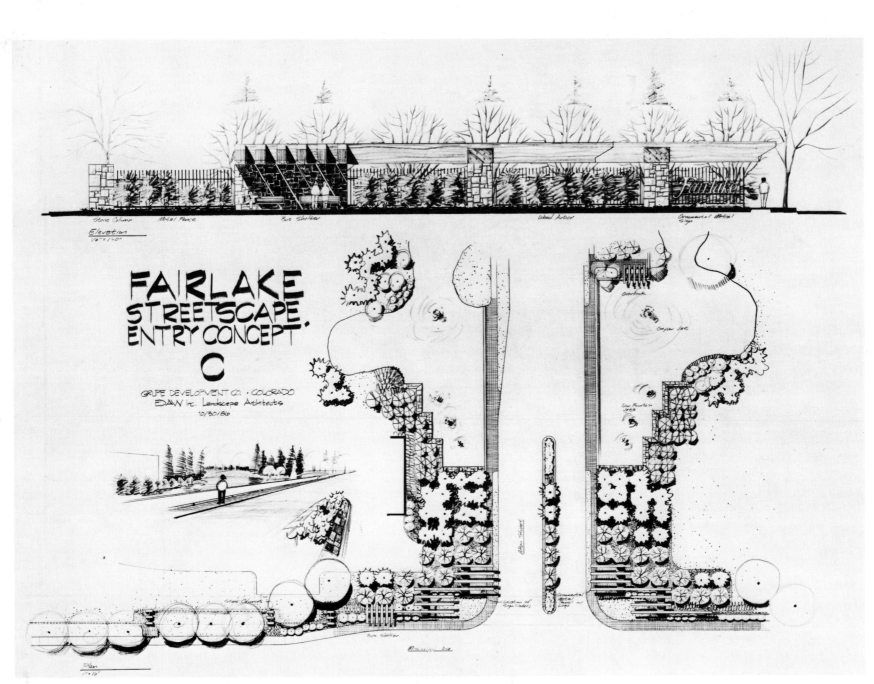

EDAW inc., by Clarke Mapes. Pencil on mylar, reduced from 24″ x 36″.

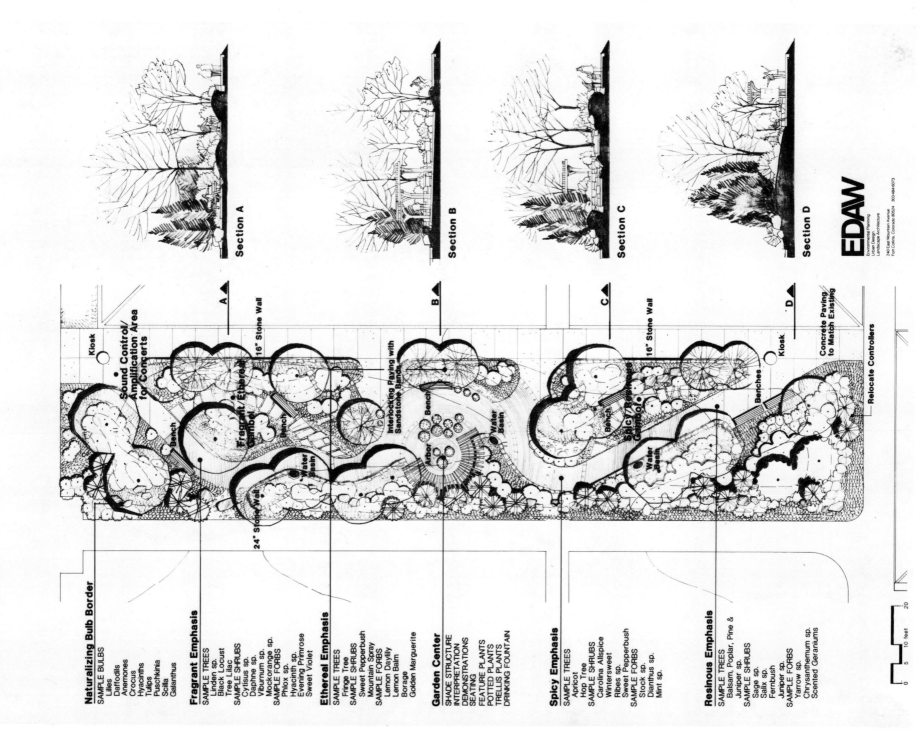

FRAGRANCE GARDEN
Denver Botanic Gardens

Section A

Section B

Section C

Section D

EDAW

Environmental Planning
Urban Design
Landscape Architecture

240 East Mountain Avenue
Fort Collins, Colorado 80524   303-484-6073

Kiosk

Sound Control/
Amplification Area
for Concerts

16" Stone Wall

24" Stone Wall

Fragrant/Ethereal
Combo

Bench

Water
Basin

Interlocking Paving with
Sandstone Bands

Bench

Arbor

Bench

Water
Basin

Spicy/Resinous
Combo

Bench

Benches

16" Stone Wall

Water
Basin

Kiosk

Relocate Controllers

Concrete Paving
to Match Existing

Naturalizing Bulb Border
SAMPLE BULBS
Lilies
Daffodils
Anemones
Crocus
Hyacinths
Tulips
Puschkinia
Scilla
Galanthus

Fragrant Emphasis
SAMPLE TREES
Linden sp.
Black Locust
Tree Lilac
SAMPLE SHRUBS
Cytisus sp.
Daphne sp.
Viburnum sp.
Mockorange sp.
SAMPLE FORBS
Phlox sp.
Hyacinth sp.
Evening Primrose
Sweet Violet

Ethereal Emphasis
SAMPLE TREES
Fringe Tree
SAMPLE SHRUBS
Sweet Pepperbush
Mountain Spray
SAMPLE FORBS
Lemon Daylily
Lemon Balm
Borage
Golden Marguerite

Garden Center
SHADE STRUCTURE
INTERPRETATION
DEMONSTRATIONS
SEATING
FEATURE PLANTS
POTTED PLANTS
TRELLIS PLANTS
DRINKING FOUNTAIN

Spicy Emphasis
SAMPLE TREES
Apricot
Hop Tree
SAMPLE SHRUBS
Carolina Allspice
Wintersweet
Ribes sp.
Sweet Pepperbush
SAMPLE FORBS
Stock sp.
Dianthus sp.
Mint sp.

Resinous Emphasis
SAMPLE TREES
Balsam, Poplar, Pine &
Juniper sp.
SAMPLE SHRUBS
Sage sp.
Salix sp.
Fernbush
Juniper sp.
SAMPLE FORBS
Chrysanthemum sp.
Yarrow sp.
Scented Geraniums

0 5   10 feet 20

EDAW inc., by Herb Schaal. Pencil on mylar, reduced from 24″ x 36″.

REDWOOD BRIDGE ACROSS CREEK PROVIDES ACCESS TO ENTIRE TRAIL SYSTEM

PINES ARE PROPOSED ALONG CREEK TO PROVIDE COLOR IN THE WINTER MONTHS

STREET TREES PROVIDE SHADE AND REINFORCE THE PATTERN ALREADY ESTABLISHED

TYPICAL STREET S

SALADO CREEK CROSSING

BARK MULCH TRAIL TO MEANDER ALONG CREEK EDGE AND FOCUS VIEWS TO SURROUNDING HILLSIDES

PINE TREES SERVE AS AN EVERGREEN BACKDROP PURPLE LEAF PLUMS & RED TWIGGED DOGWOODS PROVIDE SEASONAL INTEREST. LOW EVERGREEN SHRUBS SERVE AS FOUNDATION PLANTING WHILE SPRING BULBS HIGHLIGHT THE MONUMENT

REDWOOD SIGNS THROUGHOUT THE TRAIL SYSTEM TO INFORM THE PEDESTRIAN OF THEIR LOCATION WITHIN THE SYSTEM AND TO SERVE AS AN EDUCATIONAL TOOL TO THE PUBLIC ON THE LOCAL FLORA & FAUNA

3' HIGH BY 20' LONG STONE WALL TO MATCH THAT AT SMOKEY BEAR MUSEUM DIES INTO EARTH BERM. COPPER LETTERS ANNOUNCE THE VILLAGE OF CAPITAN

CAPITAN, NEW MEXICO

ENTRY MONUMENT LOCATION ALONG ROUTE 380 INTO CAPITAN

ENTRY MON

NATURE TRAIL SIGNAGE

CHARACTER SKETCHES

Capitan, New Mexico

A. WAYNE SMITH & ASSOCIATES. Ink on mylar.

204

Prepared For: Village of Capitan
Capitan, New Mexico

Prepared By: Easterling & Associates
5643 Paradise Blvd.
Albuquerque, New Mexico

A. Wayne Smith & Associates
2120 South Rural Road
Tempe, Arizona 85257

AWS&A

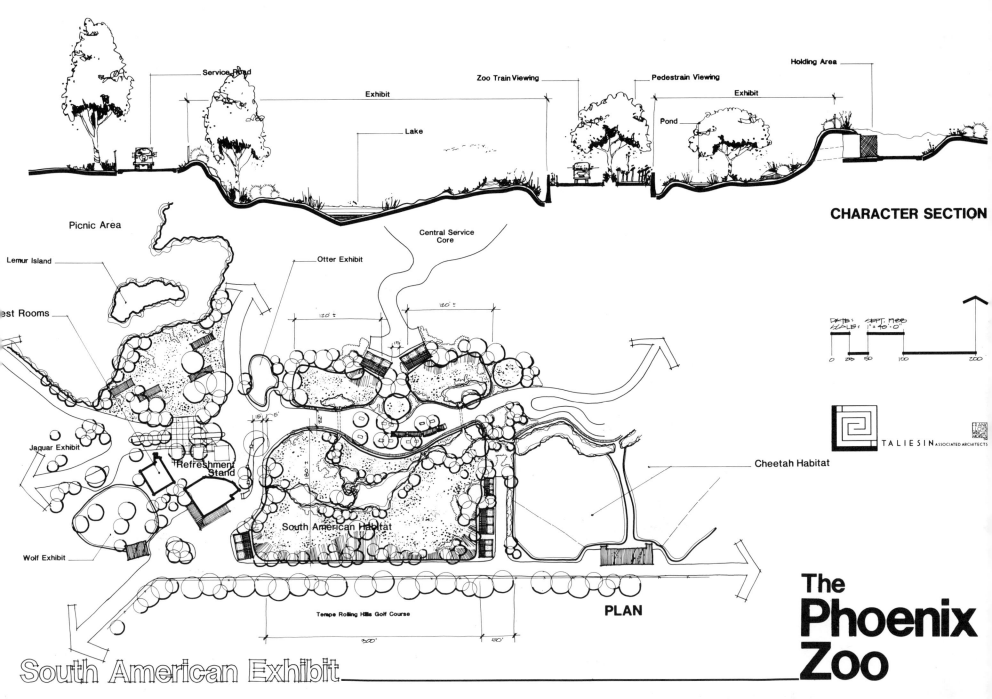

CHARACTER SECTION

Service Road

Picnic Area

Lemur Island

est Rooms

Jaguar Exhibit

Wolf Exhibit

Exhibit

Lake

Zoo Train Viewing

Pedestrain Viewing

Holding Area

Exhibit

Pond

Otter Exhibit

Central Service Core

Refreshment Stand

South American Habitat

Tempe Rolling Hills Golf Course

Cheetah Habitat

PLAN

TALIESIN ASSOCIATED ARCHITECTS

South American Exhibit

The Phoenix Zoo

TALIESIN/ALLEN GROSS/JOHN STERZER. Ink, pencil and black tape on mylar.
Reduced from 24″ x 36″.

CLUSTER # 3

PAVING TREATMENT

ENTRY SIGN

CLUSTER # I

EXISTING EUCALYPTUS

EXISTING EUCALYPTUS

COLUMN DETAIL W/LIGHT ELEMENT IN

GRAPHIC ELEMENT

LOW PLANTER

BRANDON
HOMES

PRELIMINARY ENTRY DESIGN FOR PARCEL 10 A - GAINEY RANCH BRANDON HOMES

A. Wayne Smith & Associates · Planners · Landscape Architects

A. WAYNE SMITH & ASSOCIATES. Pencil and ink on vellum.

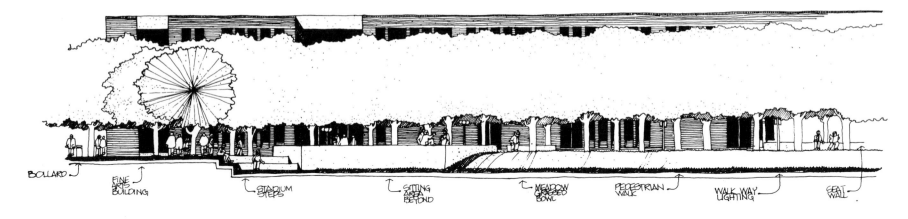

SECTION A·A

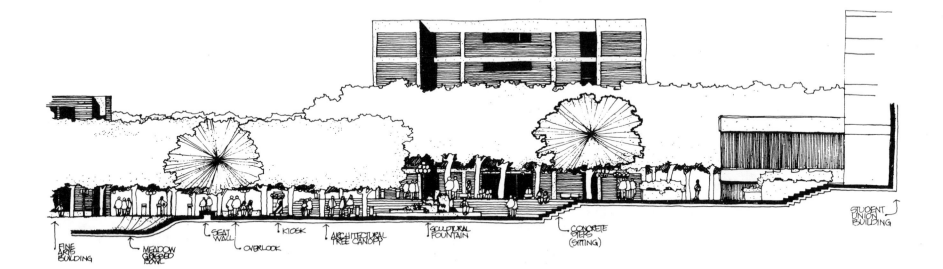

SECTION B·B

MICELI WEED KULIK. Student Center Mall.

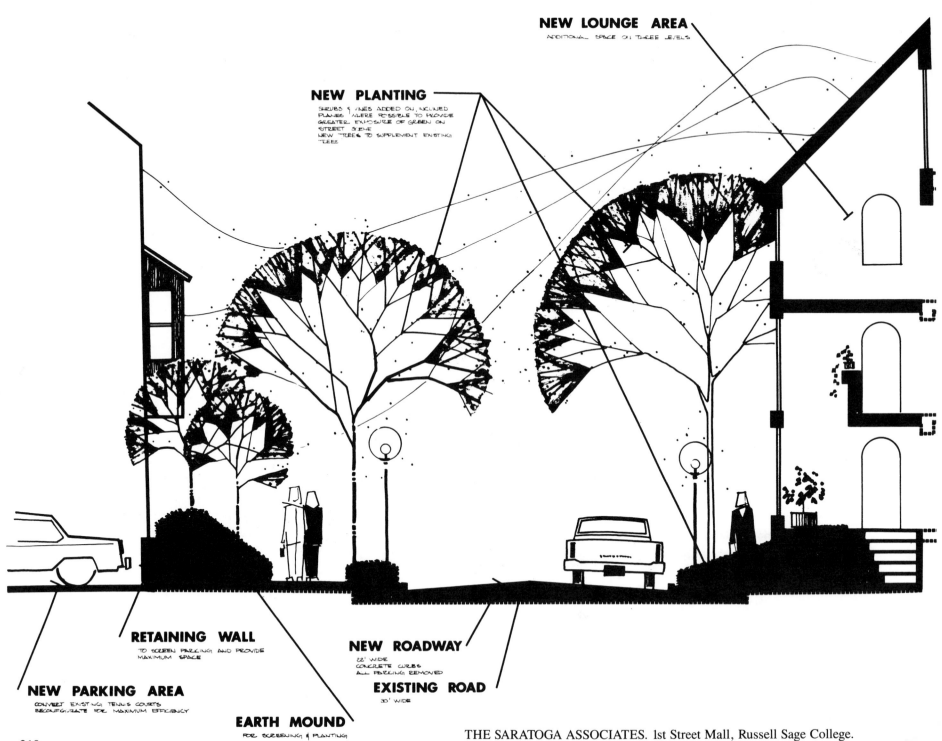

NEW LOUNGE AREA
ADDITIONAL SPACE ON THREE LEVELS

NEW PLANTING
SHRUBS & VINES ADDED ON INCLINED
PLANES WHERE POSSIBLE TO PROVIDE
GREATER EXPOSURE OF GREEN ON
STREET SCENE
NEW TREES TO SUPPLEMENT EXISTING
TREES

RETAINING WALL
TO SCREEN PARKING AND PROVIDE
MAXIMUM SPACE

NEW ROADWAY
22' WIDE
CONCRETE CURBS
ALL PARKING REMOVED

EXISTING ROAD
30' WIDE

NEW PARKING AREA
CONVERT EXISTING TENNIS COURTS
RECONFIGURATE FOR MAXIMUM EFFICIENCY

EARTH MOUND
FOR SCREENING & PLANTING

THE SARATOGA ASSOCIATES. 1st Street Mall, Russell Sage College.

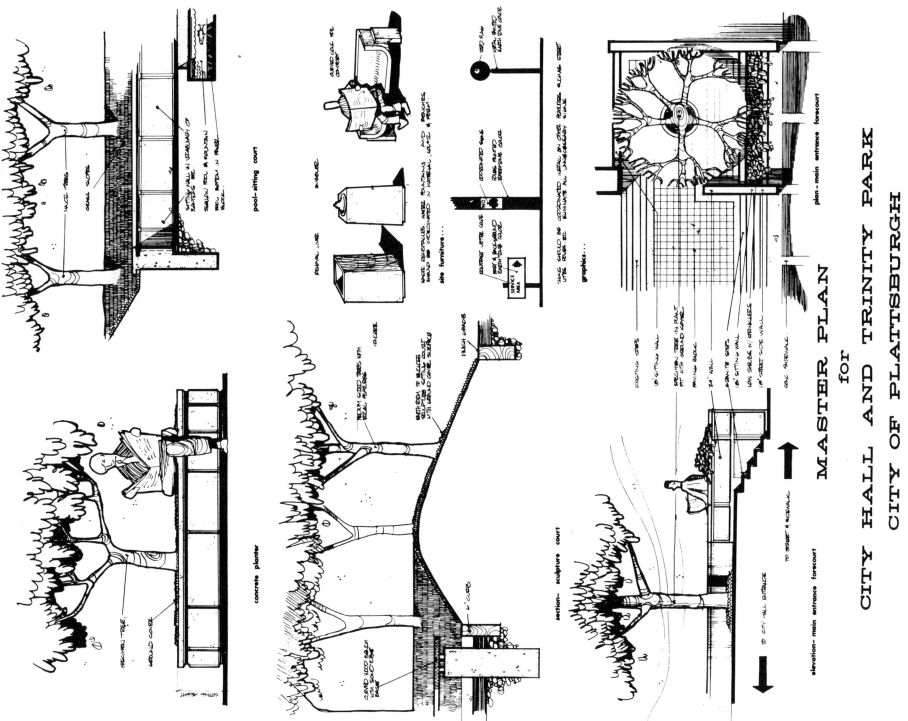

pool-sitting court

site furniture . . .

graphics . . .

plan - main entrance forecourt

concrete planter

section - sculpture court

elevation - main entrance forecourt

THE SARATOGA ASSOCIATES.

MASTER PLAN
for
CITY HALL AND TRINITY PARK
CITY OF PLATTSBURGH

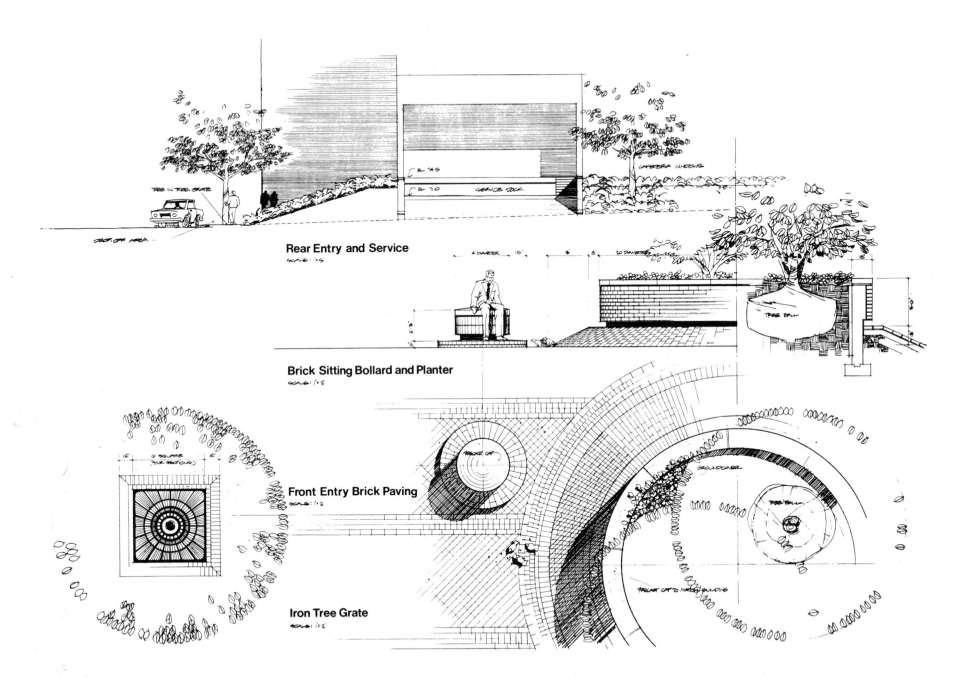

Rear Entry and Service
SCALE: 1"=5'

Brick Sitting Bollard and Planter
SCALE: 1"=2'

Front Entry Brick Paving
SCALE: 1"=2'

Iron Tree Grate
SCALE: 1"=2'

JOHNSON AND DEE.

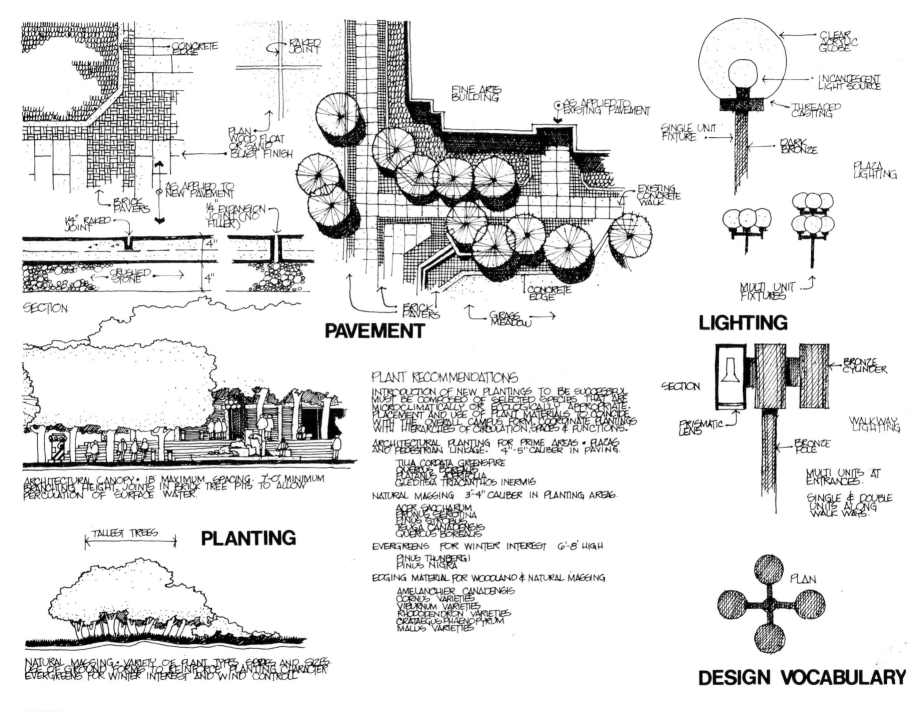

PAVEMENT

LIGHTING

PLANTING

DESIGN VOCABULARY

PLANT RECOMMENDATIONS

INTRODUCTION OF NEW PLANTINGS TO BE SUCCESSFUL MUST BE COMPOSED OF SELECTED SPECIES THAT ARE MICROCLIMATICALLY OR ECOLOGICALLY APPROPRIATE. PLACEMENT AND USE OF PLANT MATERIALS TO COINCIDE WITH THE OVERALL CAMPUS FORM. COORDINATE PLANTINGS WITH HIERARCHIES OF CIRCULATION, SPACES & FUNCTIONS.

ARCHITECTURAL PLANTING FOR PRIME AREAS • PLAZAS AND PEDESTRIAN LINKAGE. 4"-5" CALIBER IN PAVING.

TILIA CORDATA GREENSPIRE
QUERCUS BOREALIS
PLATANUS ACERFOLIA
GLEDITSIA TRIACANTHOS INERMIS

NATURAL MASSING 3"-4" CALIBER IN PLANTING AREAS.

ACER SACCHARUM
PRUNUS SEROTINA
PINUS STROBUS
TSUGA CANADENSIS
QUERCUS BOREALIS

EVERGREENS FOR WINTER INTEREST 6'-8' HIGH
PINUS THUNBERGI
PINUS NIGRA

EDGING MATERIAL FOR WOODLAND & NATURAL MASSING

AMELANCHIER CANADENSIS
CORNUS VARIETIES
VIBURNUM VARIETIES
RHODODENDRON VARIETIES
CRATAEGUS PHAENOPYRUM
MALUS VARIETIES

MICELI WEED KULIK. Student Center Mall.

INDEX